RODALE'S

GARDEN INSECT, DISEASE & WEED

Identification Guide

RODALE'S

GARDEN INSECT, DISEASE & WEED
Identification Guide

Miranda Smith and Anna Carr

Illustrations by Robin Brickman

RODALE PRESS, EMMAUS, PENNSYLVANIA

Portions of this book previously appeared in *Rodale's Color Handbook of Garden Insects* (1979) by Anna Carr.

Printed in the United States of America

Book Design by Glen Burris

Library of Congress Cataloging-in-Publication Data

Smith, Miranda, 1944–
    Rodale's garden insect, disease & weed identification guide / Miranda Smith and Anna Carr ; illustrations by Robin Brickman.
        p.   cm.
    Bibliography: p.
    Includes index.
    ISBN 0–87857–758–0
    ISBN 0–87857–759–9 (pbk.)
    1. Garden pests—Identification. 2. Plant diseases. 3. Weeds—Identification. I. Carr, Anna, 1955–   . II. Brickman, Robin. III. Rodale Press. IV. Title. V. Title: Rodale's garden insect, disease, and weed identification guide. VI. Title: Garden insect, disease, and weed identification guide.
SB603.5.S65   1988
635'.049—dc19   88–4969
                                                CIP

Distributed in the book trade by St. Martin's Press

4 6 8 10 9 7 5 3   hardcover
4 6 8 10 9 7 5 3   paperback

Contents

Contents

Introduction

If you were to spend an afternoon sifting through the soil and examining the plants in one square yard of your garden, chances are you'd find a surprising variety of the wild plants we call weeds and well over 2,000 insects, ranging from microscopic springtails to large beetles and butterflies. Very few of these would pose any threat to the health and productivity of your garden. The fact is, most insects, some diseases, and many weeds are directly beneficial to man, and all are useful and necessary to the economy of nature. Insects and diseases aid in the decomposition of organic matter and, with weeds, in the formation of soil. Insects are responsible for the pollination of almost every fruit, flower, and vegetable crop. They also keep weeds in check, and provide us with silk, shellac, beeswax, honey, and other valuable products. If nothing else, insects and weeds serve as food for birds, reptiles, small mammals, and other insects.

Then what about the insects we call pests and the unwanted plants we call weeds? From a strictly ecological perspective, there are no such things. Webworms, bean beetles, goldenrod, and purslane are as necessary to the natural balance of things as bees, earthworms, carrots, and roses. All living things have a special niche in the food chain.

As gardeners and farmers, we tend to forget this natural relationship among living things. We select the plants we want to grow, we determine how long they are going to live and what they will produce, and we nurture them to the exclusion of all other plants and animals. Native wildflowers that spring up in the garden become weedy competition to our crops, and insects that feed on the plants or injure them in any way are our enemies. Diseases that threaten crops' productivity or ornamental plants' health or appearance are intolerable. Sprayers and dusters in hand, we set about planning their demise.

Introduction

It would be ridiculous to suggest that gardeners and farmers let weeds flourish or ignore the insects and diseases destroying their crops. When Nature takes over, she rarely has man's immediate needs in mind. But, more often than not, we indiscriminately kill all the insects and pull all the weeds we find in the garden, whether or not they are actually damaging or choking out our plants. In our obsession with destroying all possible competitors, we forget that most of the insects present are actually *helping* us produce food, that some plant-eating species are necessary to complete the food chain, and that many weeds are as lovely as any cultivated flower. Whether toxic chemical pesticides, fungicides, and herbicides, or natural poisons such as rotenone and pyrethrum are used, the results are much the same: Pest species are eliminated and the insects, birds, and mammals that feed on them are also killed or leave the garden for greener pastures. The natural balance of predators, plant-eaters, and pollinators is disrupted.

We hope that this book will make you aware of the value of *all* garden insects and weeds, and will inform you of their life cycles, their growth habits, and the roles they play in the garden's ecology. We also hope that it will teach you to recognize common disease symptoms, learn which are really harmful, and determine how to prevent or control them. Carry *Rodale's Garden Insect, Disease, and Weed Identification Guide* into the garden with you. Learn the name of that insect or disease on your squash plant and, before you take steps to destroy it, decide whether or not it is really a problem. And is that yellow-flowered plant near the tomatoes really a harmful weed, or is it a nitrogen-producing legume that's enriching your soil? You might be doing yourself a favor by leaving the controls at home.

Insects

An Overview

What Is an Insect?

With over four million of them on each acre of the earth, it is surprising that few of us actually know what insects really are. For some reason, we want to place every little creature in this tremendous class—particularly if it is a pesky, creepy-crawly one. Spiders, centipedes, mites, millipedes, scorpions, ticks, and harvestmen are continually mistaken for insects, when they are actually no more closely related to insects than lobsters or mollusks are. What then *is* an insect?

Basically, insects are small, backboneless animals (invertebrates). They share certain physical characteristics that, together, distinguish them from all other animals.

Three body segments. Insects are usually elongate in form, with three distinct sections of the body: *head, thorax,* and *abdomen.* The main sensing organs—eyes, antennae, and mouthparts—are on the head. The thorax bears wings and legs, and the abdomen has most of the digestive and reproductive organs as well as breathing holes (called spiracles).

Outer skeleton. The body parts are sometimes difficult to detect, since the insect's entire body is covered with a coat of armor. Instead of a backbone and skeleton as we know it, an insect possesses a hard, jointed frame on the outside of its body. This *exoskeleton* is made of chemical substances and proteins secreted by the insect's body. It is braced and ridged at various points to provide support as well as protection. Insoluble in water, alcohol, and most acids and enzymes, it provides a barrier to the world. It also makes the insect's body a rather clumsy package at times. Movement is difficult, and growth can occur only when the exoskeleton is split during molts.

Six jointed legs. All insects have three pairs of legs attached to the thorax. Three pairs give the animal greater balance and mobility than any other number. In walking,

STRUCTURE OF A TYPICAL INSECT

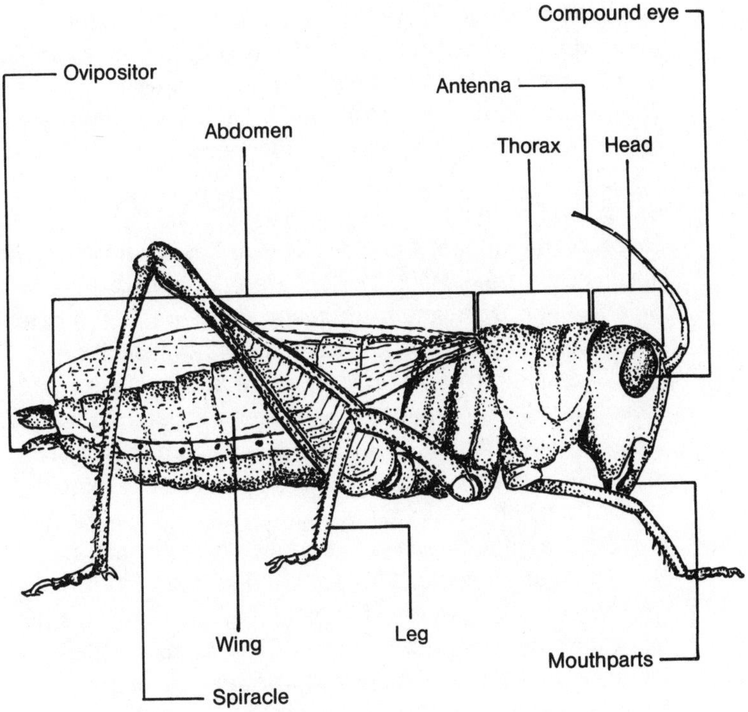

Compound eye

Ovipositor

Antenna

Abdomen

Thorax   Head

Wing   Leg

Mouthparts

Spiracle

the insect moves the middle leg on one side of the body together with the front and hind legs on the opposite side. This leaves three legs forming a stable tripod on the ground.

In addition to six legs, caterpillars have up to five pairs of plump, fleshy false legs that enable them to move more easily. These *prolegs* are hooked so that the larva can hang effortlessly from the host plant. Sawflies also have prolegs.

Two or four wings. Although many insects are wingless at some point in their lives, most adults possess one or

INSECTS
An Overview

two pairs of wings. The wings are actually part of the
body wall. They begin as soft saclike outgrowths, and
later flatten and dry into solid membranous structures.
They are supported by a framework of tubes and connected to the thorax by a series of muscles.

Using the Entries
To follow the entries, it helps to have a basic knowledge of
how insects are classified within the Animal Kingdom.
Scientists group animals into major divisions on the basis
of structure. The largest divisions are *phyla,* which are
subdivided into *classes.* Insects make up the class
Insecta or Hexapoda (meaning six-legged) of the phylum
Arthropoda (meaning joint-legged). Any animal with six
jointed legs is an insect. Mites and spiders have jointed
legs, but they have eight, not six, of them. Hence, they
belong to a different class in the phylum Arthropoda.
      The class Insecta is further divided into 26 *orders.*
Orders are large groups of insects that share similar wing
structures. Members of the order Coleoptera (beetles), for
instance, are distinguished by a front pair of leathery or
brittle wings that meet in a straight line down the center of
the back. Insects belonging to the order Hemiptera (true
bugs) possess front wings that are partly thickened and
partly membranous. The order name appears beneath
each chapter head in this section. To find the chapter you
want when identifying an insect, check the descriptions in
the charts, Key to Common Garden Insects (larval stage
and nymph and adult stages), on pages 18, 19, 20
and 21.
      Each order contains one or more *families.* The family
name always ends in "-idae" and refers to some particular feature its members share. Beetles belonging to the
family Buprestidae are hard-bodied, brightly colored,
metallic insects. In the larval stage, they have a flatheaded appearance, and are known as the flatheaded

wood borers. Members may look exactly alike, or they may resemble one another only slightly, but all have a flat head.

The most fundamental levels of classification, and the ones that are most used to identify insects, are the *genus* and *species.* The genus name refers to a small group of closely related members of a family. It is always capitalized. The species name is seldom capitalized. It refers to a single insect that can be distinguished from others in the genus by a particular feature or habit. Thus, both the asparagus beetle and the spotted asparagus beetle belong to the genus *Crioceris* but, since their markings and habits are slightly different, they are distinguished by separate species names: *asparagi* and *duodecimpunctata.* These, together with the genus name, are the insects' formal names. In this section, they appear just below the common name at the top of each insect entry.

How Insects Live and Grow
Since their bodies are encased in rigid shells, insects cannot grow gradually as we do. Instead, they grow in stages. They feed until their coat becomes too tight, then they stop eating and rest while it splits open. Meanwhile, a new shell has formed beneath the original one so, when the insect crawls out of its old armor, it is already protected. This is called *molting.* After molting, it feeds voraciously until it outgrows its new shell, then molts again. In this way, it gradually increases in size. The form of the insect between each molt is called an *instar.* Most insects pass through 3 to 6 instars. However, depending upon temperature and food supply, there may be up to 30 instars before insects reach maturity.

Insects are not born with all their adult features. They acquire these during certain moltings, and pass through a series of "form changes." This process is known as *metamorphosis.* True bugs, grasshoppers, crickets, mantids,

INSECTS
An Overview

INCOMPLETE METAMORPHOSIS

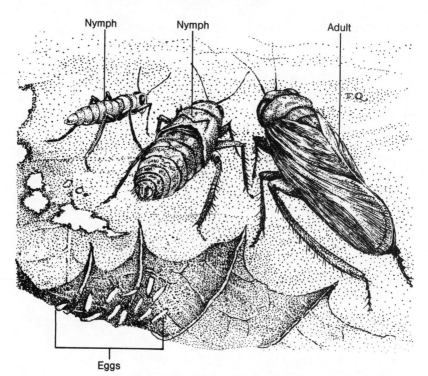

Nymph   Nymph   Adult

Eggs

earwigs, thrips, whiteflies, aphids, and scales pass through three basic forms—*egg, nymph,* and *adult.* This is called *simple* or *incomplete metamorphosis* (see the illustration above). This is because the nymph more or less resembles the adult form, but it does not possess fully developed wings and its coloring may be quite different. After a series of molts in which it increases in size, it molts a final time, acquiring wings and fully developed antennae. It emerges as a full-fledged adult.

Most other insects, including bees, wasps, beetles, butterflies, moths, flies, and lacewings have *complete metamorphosis* (see the illustration on page 8) in which they pass through four distinctly different life stages–*egg, larva, pupa,* and *adult.* Immature forms known as larvae bear no resemblance to the adult form. They are more or less wormlike and may be legged or legless. Sometimes they are covered with spines or tufts of hair. They have chewing mouthparts, even if the adult counterpart has sucking mouthparts. They molt several times, increasing in size but changing very little in form.

After the molt of the last instar, the larva changes into an inactive form called the pupa. It stops feeding, and may even stop moving. Some insects spin a cocoon or web, or roll a leaf around their bodies to protect themselves during this period of vulnerability.

During pupation, the insect changes profoundly from larva to adult. Some structures and tissues such as the plump little false legs dissolve, and new features such as legs, wings, and antennae develop. When the adult features have been formed, the insect splits its pupal chamber and emerges. Later, wings dry, pigmentation develops, and armor hardens.

The adult stage of insects with either type of metamorphosis is usually a relatively short one, geared entirely toward reproduction. Some adult forms, such as male scale insects, do not even have mouths, since they live such a short time and do not need to eat. They mate and die almost immediately afterward.

Although adulthood is usually the shortest period of the insect's life, it is often the one in which the insect is most aware of the world around it. The nervous system is fully developed, and vision is at its best. Respiration, circulation, and, if the insect has mouthparts, digestion are in full swing. Often, insects are most mobile during adulthood.

Breathing. Insects do not have lungs. In almost all species, the blood contains no hemoglobin and is not

COMPLETE METAMORPHOSIS

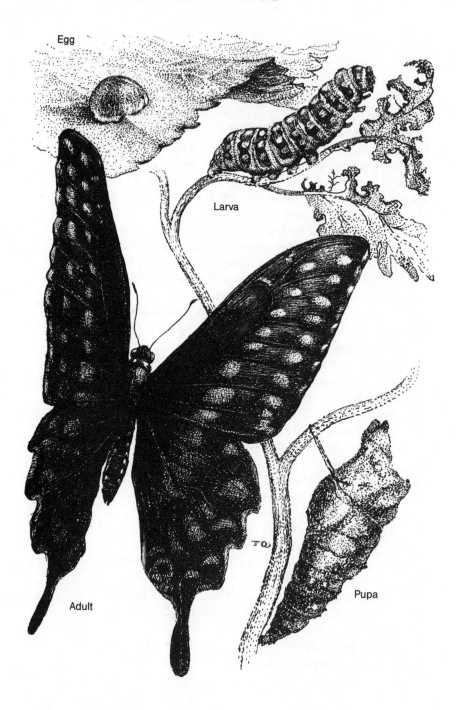

Egg

Larva

Adult

Pupa

used to carry oxygen. Instead, insects breathe through tiny holes or *spiracles* in the thorax and abdomen (see the illustration on page 3). Oxygen passes through a system of branching tubes to all parts of the body. Sometimes the insect pumps its abdominal muscles in order to encourage ventilation.

Circulating the blood. Insect blood is a yellowish-green or clear, thick fluid. It carries food to body organs, stores proteins and water, and picks up waste materials for excretion. It is pumped by a simple, tubular heart located in the middle of the back, just beneath the body wall. Since there are no arteries or veins, blood sloshes through the insect's body cavity, percolating back and forth from the head to the abdomen, bathing every organ. It moves into the wings through rigid tubes.

Eating and digesting. Insects feed on all kinds of things—dead and living plants and animals, paper, trash, and fabrics. Some dine only on blood, or eat just a particular layer of cells in a particular kind of leaf. Others consume anything and everything.

The mouthparts needed to break down these foods are complicated and specialized. There are two basic types—those that chew food and those that suck it. Insects that chew their food have sturdy jaws that move sideways. The jaws are toothed, and can be used to tear food as well as mash and chew it. An additional set of jaws holds the food when the main jaws are open, and serves as a kind of scoop that gets the food into the insect's mouth.

Insects that suck their food have long, styluslike mouthparts. Most garden insects with sucking mouthparts pierce the surface of the plant or animal material with a hollow, jointed beak. One or more tiny needles within this beak make holes in the tissue. Some insects, such as butterflies and moths, lack these piercing organs.

INSECTS
An Overview

They have a long retractable tube or *proboscis* through which nectar is siphoned.

Ingested food passes from the mouth into a simple canal where, if necessary, it is broken down by enzymes. Carbohydrates such as nectar are soluble in water and can be incorporated in body fluids immediately. They provide instant sugar energy, while fats must be digested and carried to storage muscles before they can provide energy. Since insects have fairly dry bodies, they can dissolve only a small amount of sugar and, gram for gram, they get little energy from it. Fat is a much better long-term energy source. Insects that fly at high speeds for long periods of time are usually fat-eaters. Butterflies that fly slowly, and flower flies that move in short jaunts, feed on nectar.

Tasting. Insects have taste organs on lips enclosing their jaws and on special feelerlike organs behind the jaws. Some insects use their antennae to taste things, and certain butterflies have taste buds in their feet. These are so sensitive that, as the insect lands on a flower rich in nectar, the proboscis automatically uncoils.

Butterflies are not the only insects with an acute sense of taste. Most other insects are very sensitive to slight differences in salt or sugar content, or in the particular flavor of their preferred food. Leaves treated with bitter-tasting or acidic substances are rejected by the insects that normally feed on them.

Smelling. The sense of smell is also very acute in most insects. Many secrete substances with odors that repel enemies or attract mates. Although we cannot detect these odors, other insects can and, even in the most infinitesimal amounts, the smells excite them.

Hearing. Insects hear by means of a delicate drum or *tympanum* built into the body wall. This thin membrane connects to special internal organs that carry impulses to the tiny "brain" in the insect's head. Grasshoppers and crickets have very large tympana; others have drums so small they are almost invisible. Sound receptors are also present in the antennae of certain insects or in the tiny hooks of their abdomens.

Touching. Insects have thousands of sensory hairs scattered over the surface of their bodies. These are connected to nerve endings. They tell the insect about its surroundings and inform it about its body position. For instance, when an insect bends its leg, it bends the hairs located there. These send messages to the "brain," informing the insect that the leg is bent. Scales and hairs on the wings of a butterfly or moth tell the insect how to fold its wings when alighting. They also seem to be sensitive to air movements during flight.

Seeing. Insects have extremely large, complicated eyes that take up a large portion of the head, yet are very inefficient. They are made up of many separate hexagonal lenses fitted closely together. Each lens is connected to a cone that directs the light to a series of eye cells. The lens "sees" just a portion of the image. Nerve impulses in the brain build the fragments into a compound picture that has something of a jigsaw puzzle effect.

These eyes can detect movement quite well, but they do not produce a particularly clear picture because there is no focusing mechanism. They are sensitive to color, enabling many pollinating insects to have "favorite" flower colors. Some bees will pollinate only red flowers. Others prefer yellow or blue. Beetles, whose eyesight is quite poor, make few distinctions in color, and are as attracted to white or pale flowers as they are to brightly colored ones. Some insects are so sensitive to color that they can see ultraviolet light that appears black to us.

In addition to compound eyes, most insects possess simple, single-lensed eyes called *ocelli*. These tiny organs

INSECTS
An Overview

perceive light but produce no image. In adults and nymphs, they lie at the base of the antennae or on top of the head. In larvae, ocelli are located on each side of the head. Since they possess no compound eyes, larvae rely entirely on these primitive organs for their vision.

Flying. Insect wings are attached to the thorax by a set of sophisticated flight muscles. The wings themselves, unlike those of birds, contain no muscles. Instead, all movement is controlled by ball-and-socket joints and thoracic muscles that enable the wing to turn in almost any direction and, depending on the species, beat 10 to 1,000 times per second. Insects can loop the loop, swoop, fly upside down, back up in midair, hover, or stop suddenly. Some can move each pair of wings separately, while others move them together. They can even twist the wing surfaces to provide lift and thrust during flight.

Controlling Garden Insects
Once you are aware of the basic ways in which insects function, you can begin to understand their behavior in the garden. You can learn to recognize when they are helping crop production, and to predict when they might become pests. Remember, insects are not pests simply because they eat crop plants: They become pests when their populations get out of hand, and they actually injure plants and interfere with their ability to produce food. With a little care and thought, you can learn to prevent most infestations of possible pests, to tolerate the presence of some plant-eating species, and to control them when they begin to cause intolerable damage.

Garden maintenance. Many of your insect "problems" can be eliminated by proper garden maintenance. Although weeds, trash, diseased plant material, and unplowed soil invite many beneficial insects into the garden, they also encourage pest species. Insects seek shelter in weeds, and lay eggs in and around them. They hibernate in garden trash and in the first few inches of untilled soil. Using a clean mulch and keeping the garden well weeded (but not necessarily weed-free), not only makes for healthier plants, but also controls the growing populations of certain insects. Plowing the soil 9 or 10 inches deep in early spring or fall exposes some of the larvae and pupae to the elements and they die.

Diversified planting. You can help prevent an overpopulation of particular plant-eating insects through diversified planting. Most insects feed on plants belonging to a certain family, and reject unrelated ones. By interplanting favorite host plants with other types, you keep the increase of pest populations at a minimum. For instance, cucumber beetles don't enjoy much except cucumbers, squash, and melons, so plant these crops amidst corn or pole beans. Cabbage loopers may nibble on many different plants, but they rarely stay long on anything other than broccoli, cabbage, kale, and other cucurbits. Avoid planting these crops together. Instead, interplant them with unrelated ones. Some plants, such as aromatic herbs, onion, garlic, and certain flowers, planted around garden crops are believed to repel insects. For more on the fascinating subject of companion planting, see *Good Neighbors: Companion Planting for Gardeners* (Rodale Press, 1985) by Anna Carr.

Crop rotation. Since many insects hibernate or lay overwintering eggs in or on their host plants, it is a good idea not to plant the same crop in the same place each season. Although it is hard to avoid this in a small garden, try to rotate crops as much as possible.

Of course, none of these practices completely eliminate plant-eating insects from your garden. That is the last thing you should do. The idea is not to have an insect-free garden, but merely to limit the number of

INSECTS
An Overview

potentially destructive species so that they can be kept in control by natural predators. All insects are beneficial, even if they seem to be injurious to crop plants. Garden plants can tolerate incredible foliage loss and damage from insects.

Altered planting times. You can alter planting times so that crops grow when they are less likely to be injured by certain insects. Observe insect cycles closely, and keep records of when eggs are laid, when larvae emerge, and when feeding is heaviest. In this way, you can take advantage of insects' natural cycles by planting crops before or after the pests have passed through their hungriest period. Also consider when plants are most susceptible to injury—when they are weakest and most vulnerable—so that their hardiest time coincides with the insect's hungriest period.

Barriers. You can discourage insects in the garden from laying eggs or feeding on certain plants by setting up barriers between them and your plants. Aluminum foil wrapped around a tree trunk prevents borers from crawling up the trunk. A band of a commonly available adhesive such as Stikem or Tanglefoot catches moths and flies as they lay eggs. These sticky bands also prevent some pests and larvae, such as the plum curculio and gypsy moth larvae, from climbing the trunk and infesting the tree. Netting keeps fruit flies away from fruit bushes, and discourages many insects from laying eggs on certain host plants. Floating row covers, such as Reemay, clear plastic, or cheesecloth can be used to protect rows or beds. Paper collars wrapped around the stems of transplants prevent cutworm damage. Tar paper or black plastic on the ground around vegetables keeps root fly maggots from migrating through the soil and onto the plants.

Resistant varieties. If you select resistant varieties of crop plants, chances are few that insects will become serious garden pests. These specially bred horticultural varieties are unattractive to certain potential pests, or are at least able to withstand much more insect injury than other varieties of the species. Of course, no variety is completely resistant to all pests, but some are capable of resisting and tolerating the insects more than others. Check seed catalogs for varieties resistant to the insects that might become problems, and run your own experiments to determine the best varieties for your garden.

Sprays. Insects inevitably get out of hand even after all the preventive measures have been taken. As our tolerance, and the plant's, begin to run low, most of us reach for the spray can. Before applying any kind of poison, we should ask ourselves, is this *really* necessary? Before spraying, try some of these simple, harmless yet effective control measures.

In the home garden, most insects can be picked by hand and dropped into a jar of kerosene or simply squashed or stepped on. Check plants frequently, and eliminate the eggs of pest insects. This is much better than spraying, since it kills only the specific insect in question and allows the beneficial insects to live.

If you *must* spray, try clear water first. Sprayed forcefully on foliage, it helps control aphids, mites, and many other small leaf-eating insects that feed in out-of-the-way places. If this does not work, add a little Fels-Naptha soap to the water, or use an *insecticidal soap* such as Safer's. This will act as a mild contact insecticide and repellent not only to aphids and mites, but some leafhoppers, leafminers, and caterpillars as well. Buttermilk dissolved in water may also reduce populations of some insects, as well as any number of herbal or aromatic plant infusions. A tea made from garlic and water is said to repel some insects. Cedar chips brewed in warm water kills Mexican bean beetles and squash bugs. Flour added to the water controls many different

INSECTS
An Overview

caterpillars and grubs, since it sticks to their soft, damp bodies and eventually smothers them as it dries.

In the orchard, premixed *dormant-oil* sprays help to smother many leaf-eating insects that feed in hard-to-reach places. This mixture is sprayed on trees before buds open in the spring or after leaves have fallen in the autumn. In this way, the delicate buds and young growth are not damaged.

Bacillus thuringiensis (Bt) is a bacterium that can be purchased in most garden stores and used to control various caterpillars. It is sold under the trade names Dipel and Thuricide. Dusted or sprayed (with a soap solution to help the Bt stay on the leaves) on infested plants, it is eaten and enters the insect's stomach, where it penetrates the lining and multiplies in the bloodstream. The caterpillars stop feeding, become paralyzed, and die. For maximum effectiveness, you may have to apply Bt at one- or two-week intervals while the caterpillars are feeding to kill succeeding generations. *Bacillus popilliae,* milky spore disease, is a similar bacterium sold under the trade names Doom and Japidemic. It is primarily used against Japanese beetle grubs, and is applied to turf areas. Unlike Bt, one application of milky spore should continue to provide grub protection for many years, though it's most effective if everyone in a neighborhood applies it to their lawns at the same time.

Diatomaceous earth, sold as Perma-Guard, is made from the ground skeletons of small fossilized animals. When soft-bodied insects such as ants, aphids, beetle grubs, boxelder bugs, caterpillars, fly maggots, mites, slugs, or thrips come in contact with it, its sharp edges lacerate their exoskeletons. This causes the insects to die from dehydration. It is probably the safest, most effective contact insecticide, but is very expensive.

As a last resort, more high-powered, naturally occurring insecticides may be necessary. Although these are not as harmful as most of the chemical poisons, they are nevertheless toxic and should be used only when the situation has truly grown out of hand.

False hellebore is a botanical insecticide that is sold as a dry powder and can be applied as a spray (1 ounce of hellebore dissolved in 2 gallons of water) or a dust mixed with hydrated lime and flour. It works as a stomach poison in many chewing insects such as grasshoppers, beetles, caterpillars, and sawflies.

Pyrethrum is a contact botanical insecticide, not a stomach poison, and is effective against many different insects, including leafhoppers, aphids, caterpillars, bugs, and various beetles. It is a particularly useful orchard spray. Since it is an extremely potent pesticide, use it only when absolutely necessary.

Rotenone is another botanical insecticide that kills many kinds of insects, but does not harm warm-blooded animals. Since it has little lasting effect, it must be applied periodically. A 1 percent solution should kill any insects.

Ryania, made from the roots of a tropical shrub, is a potent insecticide that can be used if all else fails. It is sometimes recommended for use against certain orchard pests, and works against a variety of insects. It is very potent, and should not be used unless other methods have failed.

Sabadilla dust is effective in controlling a number of insects with a minimum of danger, but it is not as easy to find as some of the other plant-derived pesticides. It kills aphids, caterpillars, some beetles, and bugs on contact.

None of these insecticides should be used unless all other control methods have failed. Read about them in garden pest books, such as *The Encyclopedia of Natural Insect and Disease Control* (Rodale Press, 1984), and seek the advice of Extension agents. Even the most "natural" sprays can seriously upset the natural balance in your garden if they are improperly or carelessly applied.

**KEY TO COMMON
GARDEN INSECTS**
Larval Stage

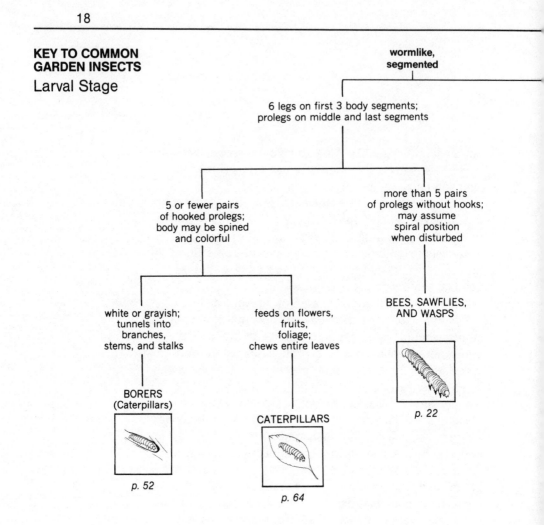

wormlike,
segmented

6 legs on first 3 body segments;
prolegs on middle and last segments

5 or fewer pairs
of hooked prolegs;
body may be spined
and colorful

more than 5 pairs
of prolegs without hooks;
may assume
spiral position
when disturbed

white or grayish;
tunnels into
branches,
stems, and stalks

feeds on flowers,
fruits,
foliage;
chews entire leaves

BEES, SAWFLIES,
AND WASPS

p. 22

BORERS
(Caterpillars)

p. 52

CATERPILLARS

p. 64

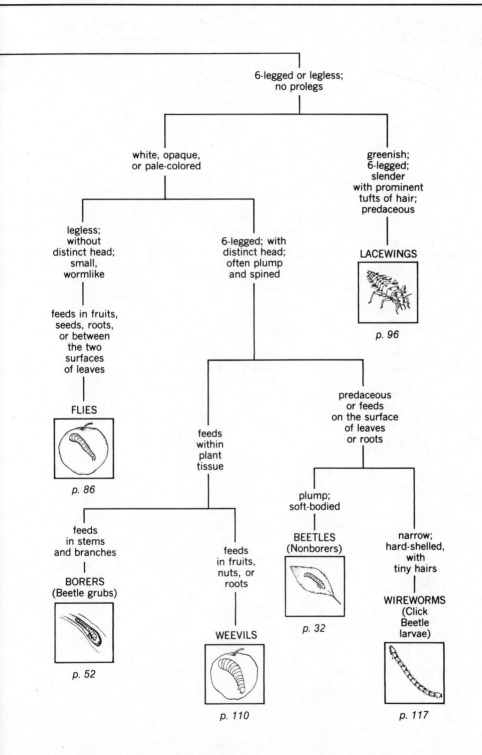

6-legged or legless;
no prolegs

white, opaque,
or pale-colored

greenish;
6-legged;
slender
with prominent
tufts of hair;
predaceous

legless;
without
distinct head;
small,
wormlike

6-legged; with
distinct head;
often plump
and spined

LACEWINGS

feeds in fruits,
seeds, roots,
or between
the two
surfaces
of leaves

p. 96

FLIES

feeds
within
plant
tissue

predaceous
or feeds
on the surface
of leaves
or roots

p. 86

feeds
in stems
and branches

plump;
soft-bodied

narrow;
hard-shelled,
with
tiny hairs

BORERS
(Beetle grubs)

feeds
in fruits,
nuts, or
roots

BEETLES
(Nonborers)

WIREWORMS
(Click
Beetle
larvae)

p. 52

p. 32

WEEVILS

p. 110

p. 117

KEY TO COMMON
GARDEN INSECTS
Adult and
Nymph Stages

**3 body segments, 6 jointed legs,
outer skeleton, winged or wingless**

active fliers and jumpers

4 wings

2 pairs of similar wings

2 pairs of different wings,
one pair may be hidden
beneath a sheath;
oblong or
wedge-shaped body

wings opaque
(except for
clear-winged MOTHS)

wings clear

wings held
above body,
not rooflike

BEES, WASPS

p. 22

wings held sideways
or flat against back

minute,
less
than
1/10"
long;
covered
with
white
powder

broad
wings;
antennae
clearly
visible

MOTHS,
BUTTERFLIES
(Caterpillars)

p. 64

wings
held
rooflike
above
body

hind legs
usually
similar to
front legs;
wings
covered
with hard
sheaths
that form
a straight
line
on the
back

hind legs
adapted
for jumping;
may produce
sound

CRICKETS,
GRASSHOPPERS

p. 80

WHITEFLIES

p. 116

soft-bodied; long,
delicate antennae

armored
body;
stout,
short
antennae

jaws
in
snout

jaws
exposed

BEETLES

LACEWINGS

CICADAS

WEEVILS

p. 32

p. 96

p. 79

p. 110

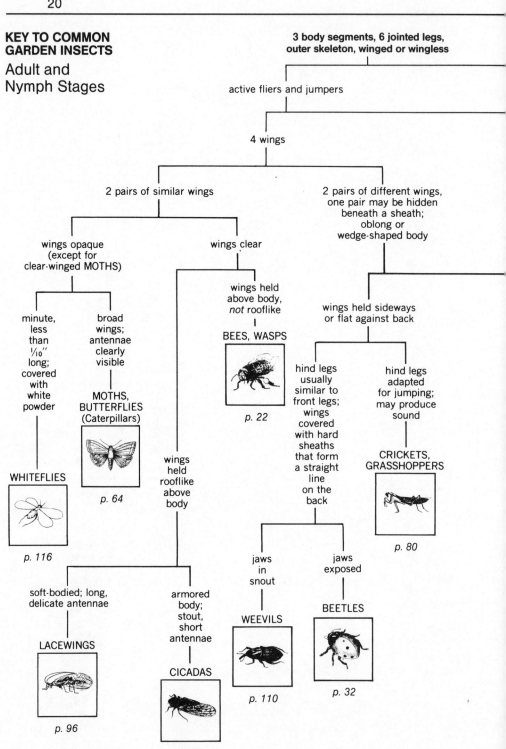

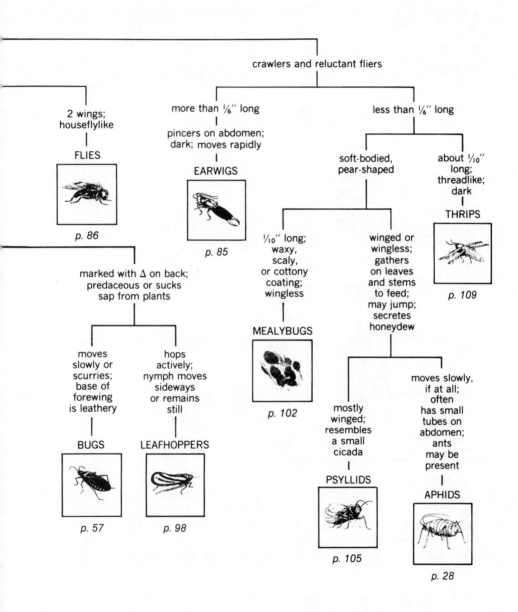

crawlers and reluctant fliers

2 wings;
houseflylike

FLIES

p. 86

more than ⅙″ long

pincers on abdomen;
dark; moves rapidly

EARWIGS

p. 85

less than ⅙″ long

soft-bodied,
pear-shaped

about ¹⁄₁₀″
long;
threadlike;
dark

THRIPS

p. 109

marked with Δ on back;
predaceous or sucks
sap from plants

moves
slowly or
scurries;
base of
forewing
is leathery

BUGS

p. 57

hops
actively;
nymph moves
sideways
or remains
still

LEAFHOPPERS

p. 98

¹⁄₁₀″ long;
waxy,
scaly,
or cottony
coating;
wingless

MEALYBUGS

p. 102

winged or
wingless;
gathers
on leaves
and stems
to feed;
may jump;
secretes
honeydew

mostly
winged;
resembles
a small
cicada

PSYLLIDS

p. 105

moves slowly,
if at all;
often
has small
tubes on
abdomen;
ants
may be
present

APHIDS

p. 28

Also included in book but not on chart: SCALES, *p. 106,* NON-INSECTS, *p. 118*

Ants

FORMICIDAE

—

adult: ¼ inch

Cornfield (red) ant

Carpenter ant

Range: Various species throughout North America.

Description: Adults are black, brown, or reddish; they are wingless or winged with enlarged abdomens. They grow from ⅙ to ¼ inch long.

Life Cycle: Eggs are laid continuously throughout the spring, summer, and fall. Colonies hibernate in the soil or in garden trash.

Feeding Habits: Most garden ants feed on organic matter, although a few species prey on other insects. Many feed on the honeydew secreted by aphids. They may become a nuisance since they "herd" aphids, protecting them from enemies and transporting them to new host plants. Control of aphids will generally eliminate the ant problem.

See photograph, page 265.

Bumblebee
Bombus spp.

adult: 1 inch

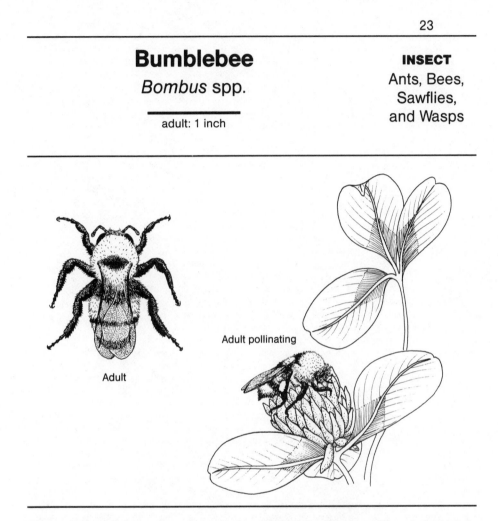

Adult

Adult pollinating

Range: Various species throughout North America.

Description: Adults are black, sometimes with yellow bands on their abdomens. They are fuzzy, with spurs on the hind legs, and are ⅓ to 1 inch long. Eggs are laid on or in the ground.

Life Cycle: There are several broods per year. Most die in winter; only the young queens remain to hibernate in protected spots.

Feeding Habits: Workers feed on nectar of many plants, and are valuable pollinators.

Since they visit many different plant species on each gathering trip, they are less efficient than honeybees.

Similar Insects: Flower flies (page 89).

See photograph, page 266.

INSECT
Ants, Bees,
Sawflies,
and Wasps

Honeybee
Apis mellifera

---

adult: ½ inch

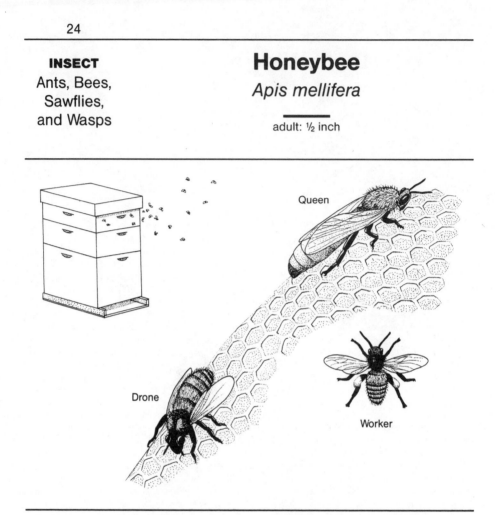

Queen

Drone

Worker

Range: Throughout North America.

Description: Adults are brownish-yellow, with darker thoraxes covered with short hairs. Some species are black. They are ¼ to ½ inch long.

Life Cycle: Eggs are laid continuously except during extremely cold periods. All forms hibernate in the hive.

Feeding Habits: Worker bees feed on nectar from many different plants and, in the process, transfer pollen from one flower to another or from the male to the female flower part. Their pollinating is particularly valuable in orchards.

Similar Insects: Flower flies (page 89).

See photograph, page 266.

European Apple Sawfly

Hoplocampa testudinea

—

adult: ⅕ inch

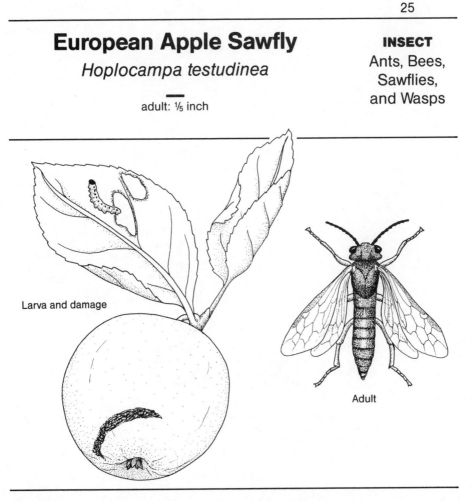

Larva and damage

Adult

Range: Eastern United States, with similar species throughout North America.

Description: Adults are brownish-yellow with a black spot on their heads; they are ⅕ inch long. Eggs, which are laid on blossoms, are white and shiny. Larvae are white to tan with dark brown heads.

Life Cycle: There is one brood per year. This sawfly overwinters in cocoons in the soil.

Host Plant: Apple.

Feeding Habits: Larvae mine fruit, leaving brown sawdust on the surface.

Prevention and Control: For serious problems, spray rotenone as soon as flower petals begin to fall, and repeat two weeks later.

Braconid Wasps

BRACONIDAE

—

adult: ¼ inch

Female parasitizing aphid

Parasitized caterpillar

Adult

Range: Various species throughout North America.

Description: Adults are black, yellowish, or red, and ¹⁄₁₀ to ¼ inch long. Eggs are laid in the bodies of hosts. Larvae are white and wormlike; they develop within the host.

Life Cycle: There are usually several generations per year. Most species overwinter as larvae or pupae in their hosts.

Feeding Habits: Adults lay eggs on the larvae of various caterpillars or aphids.

Larvae may feed within the hosts or on the surface. Often their brown cocoons are seen on the backs of hornworms and other caterpillars.

See photograph, page 267.

Yellow Jacket

Vespula spp.

adult: ¾ inch

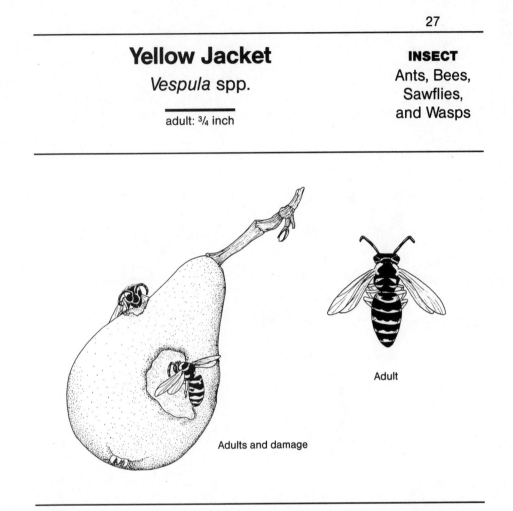

Adult

Adults and damage

Range: Various species throughout North America.

Description: Adults are black and yellow; they are ½ to ¾ inch long, with clear wings folded along the lengths of their bodies when at rest. Eggs are laid in papery cell colonies made of plant materials glued together and formed in hollow logs or stumps.

Life Cycle: Colonies disperse in fall and the young, mated queens hibernate in bark, forming new colonies in the spring.

Feeding Habits: Adults feed on nectar and pollen as well as small insects which they capture to feed their young.

Similar Insects: Flower flies (page 89).

See photograph, page 267.

INSECT
Aphid

Bean Aphid
Aphis fabae

—
adult: 1/12 inch

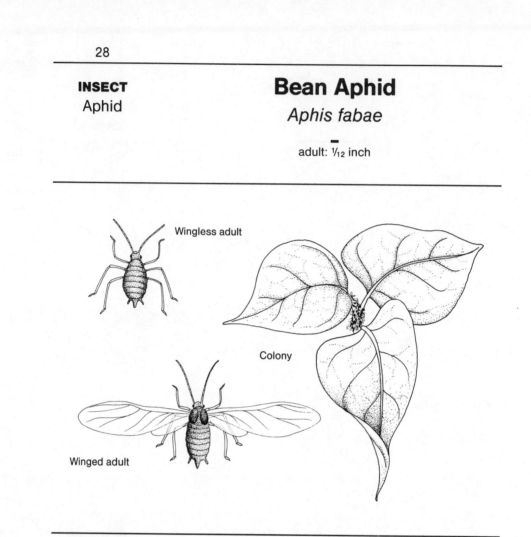

Wingless adult

Colony

Winged adult

Range: This and similar species throughout North America.

Description: Adults are dark green to bluish-black and 1/12 inch long.

Life Cycle: There are many generations per year. This aphid overwinters in the egg stage.

Host Plants: Bean, beet, chard, pea, rhubarb, spinach.

Feeding Habits: Aphids congregate on succulent foliage and stems, depleting them by sucking their juices. The leaves turn yellow, and the plant is generally weakened.

Prevention and Control: Spray foliage with soapy water, then rinse with clear water.

See photograph, page 265.

Green Peach Aphid, Spinach Aphid

Myzus persicae

adult: ▬ ⅕ inch

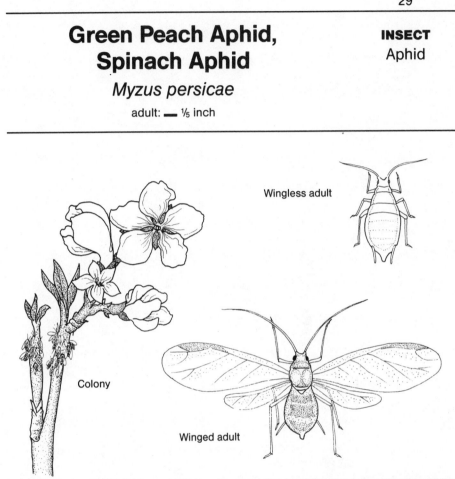

Wingless adult

Colony

Winged adult

Range: Throughout North America.

Description: Adults are greenish to pink or red, or dark brown with wings; they are ¹⁄₁₀ to ⅕ inch long.

Life Cycle: There are innumerable generations per year. In the North, this aphid overwinters in the egg stage; elsewhere females reproduce continuously.

Host Plants: Many small fruits, garden vegetables, and orchard crops.

Feeding Habits: Aphids suck the juices of leaves and stems and transmit viral diseases.

Prevention and Control: Spray foliage with water, soapy water or, for serious infestations, rotenone.

INSECT
Aphid

Pea Aphid
Acyrthosiphon pisum

—

adult: ⅕ inch

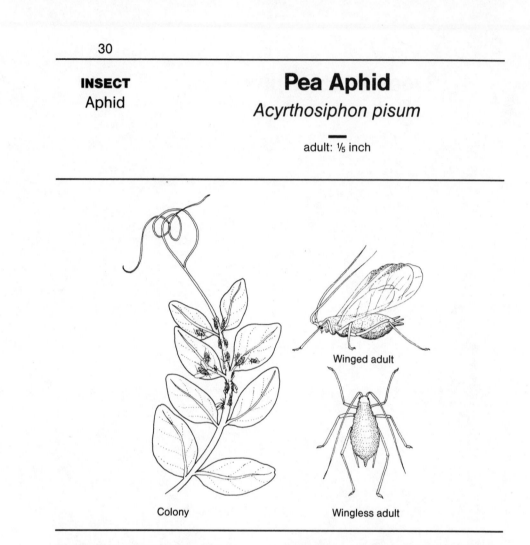

Colony

Winged adult

Wingless adult

Range: Throughout North America.

Description: Adults are green and ⅕ inch long.

Life Cycle: There are 10 to 20 generations per year. Winter is passed in the egg stage on field crops or weeds.

Host Plants: Bean, pea.

Feeding Habits: Aphids can become abundant on plants and can cause serious damage to foliage and pods through heavy feeding.

Prevention and Control: Spray foliage with soapy water, then rinse with clear water.

See photograph, page 265.

Woolly Apple Aphid
Eriosoma lanigerum

—
adult: $\frac{1}{10}$ inch

Winged adult

Damage

Wingless adult

Range: Throughout North America.

Description: Adults are purplish and covered with a bluish-white, cottony substance; they are $\frac{1}{10}$ inch long. The eggs are laid on bark.

Life Cycle: There are many generations per year. Winter is passed in the egg stage.

Host Plants: Apple, pear, quince.

Feeding Habits: Aphids feed on trunk and branches, covering them with cottony material. Twigs become swollen and infested roots develop nodules, causing saplings to become stunted.

Prevention and Control: In early spring, spray trees with dormant-oil spray.

Insect Predator: Chalcid wasp (*Aphelinus mali*).

Similar Insects: Mealybugs (pages 102–4).

Asparagus Beetle
Crioceris asparagi

—

adult: ¼ inch

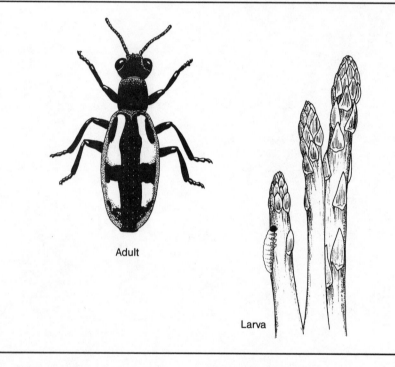

Adult

Larva

Range: Widespread throughout North America.

Description: Adults are metallic blue to black, with four white spots and reddish margins on their wing covers, reddish thoraxes with two spots, and bluish heads. They are slender and ¼ inch long. Eggs, which are laid on young spears, are black and shiny. Larvae are gray or greenish, with black heads and legs. They are plump and less than ⅓ inch long.

Life Cycle: Two to four generations mature each year. Adults overwinter in plant debris.

Host Plant: Asparagus.

Feeding Habits: Adults and larvae chew spears during spring months. In summer, they may defoliate the plants.

Prevention and Control: Apply rotenone for serious infestations.

Insect Predators: Chalcid wasps, lady beetle larvae.

See photograph, page 268.

Bean Leaf Beetle
Cerotoma trifurcata

—

adult: ¼ inch

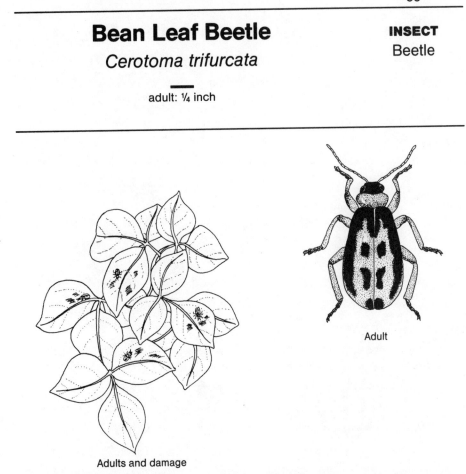

Adult

Adults and damage

Range: Eastern North America, especially in the Southeastern United States.

Description: Adults are reddish-orange and shiny, with black heads and often with black spots. They are ¼ inch long. Eggs are laid on the undersides of leaves. Larvae are white, narrow grubs.

Life Cycle: There are one or two generations per year.

Host Plants: Bean, pea, soybean.

Feeding Habits: Larvae bore into roots and nodules, sometimes girdling the stems.

Adults feed on leaves throughout the summer, but controls are seldom necessary.

Prevention and Control: Apply rotenone or pyrethrum if handpicking does not control the beetles.

See photograph, page 268.

Colorado Potato Beetle

Leptinotarsa decemlineata

—

adult: ⅓ inch

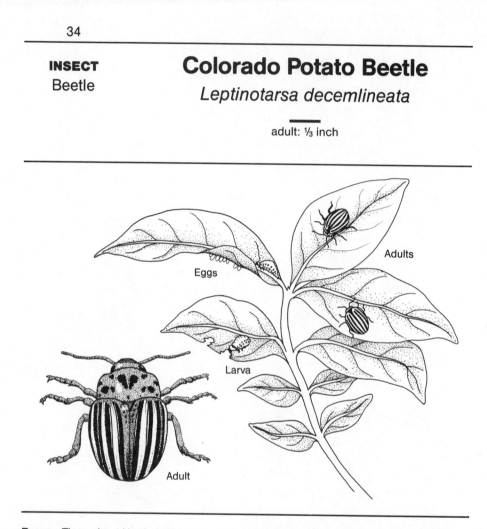

Eggs

Adults

Larva

Adult

Range: Throughout North America, except the South.

Description: Adults are yellow, with black stripes on their wing covers and dark dots just behind their heads. Beetles are ⅓ inch long with hard and very convex shells. Eggs are orange and laid in rows on the undersides of leaves. Larvae are plump and red with black legs and heads, changing to pink or orange with two rows of black spots on each side.

Life Cycle: There are one to three generations per year. Adults overwinter in the soil.

Host Plants: Eggplant, pepper, potato, tomato.

Feeding Habits: Adults and grubs feed on leaves.

Prevention and Control: Mulch well with a 1-foot layer of clean hay or straw. Perma-Guard provides control of first and second instars. Handpicking of eggs (which resemble ladybug eggs, but are larger and more orange) and larvae is an important control. Apply rotenone if necessary.

Insect Predator: Ground beetle (*Harpalus caliginosus*).

See photographs, page 268.

Fig Beetle
Cotinis texana

adult: ½ inch

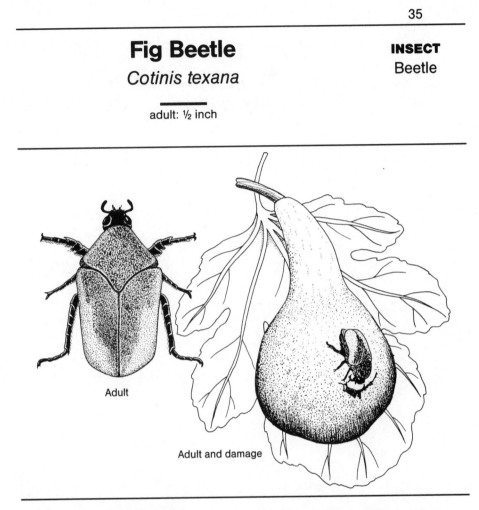

Adult

Adult and damage

Range: Southwestern United States.

Description: Adults are green or coppery with bronze wing-cover margins. They are very large, flat, and broad, reaching ½ inch long. Eggs are gray, oval or round, and are laid in soil rich in organic matter. Larvae are whitish with brown heads. They are thick and up to 2 inches long. They surface in wet weather and tend to crawl on their backs.

Life Cycle: There is one generation per year. Larvae overwinter deep below the soil surface, pupate in early spring, and adults emerge in early or midsummer.

Host Plants: Most tree fruits and berries, as well as corn and other vegetables.

Feeding Habits: Adults chew holes in leaves; larvae disturb roots by tunneling or ruin them by feeding.

Prevention and Control: Clear away piles of compost and grass clippings that are near the orchard.

Similar Insect: June beetle (page 40).

INSECT
Beetle

Flea Beetle,
Striped Flea Beetle
Phyllotreta striolata
adult: ▬ ¹/₁₀ inch

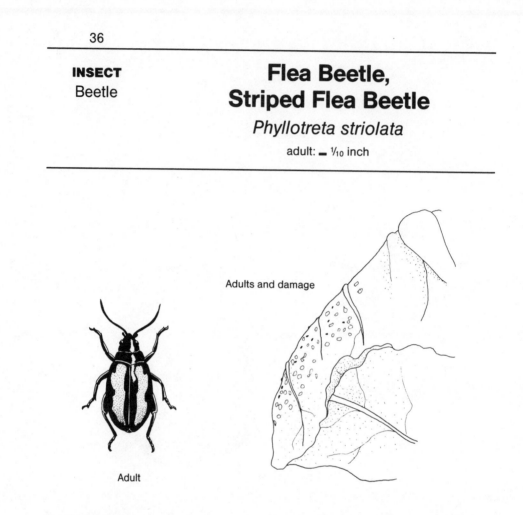

Adults and damage

Adult

Range: Throughout North America.

Description: Adults are black and shiny, with curved yellow or white stripes. They are active, hopping away when disturbed. Flea beetles are ¹/₁₀ inch long. Eggs are whitish, minute, and laid in the soil.

Life Cycle: There are one or two generations per year. Adults overwinter in garden weeds and trash.

Host Plants: Broccoli, cabbage, cauliflower. Similar species on almost every vegetable.

Feeding Habits: Adults and larvae chew tiny holes in leaves and transmit viral and bacterial diseases.

Prevention and Control: Cover crops with floating row covers such as Reemay; seal edges of row cover with soil. Misting with water in the morning and early afternoon may decrease damage. Dust with diatomaceous earth or with rotenone for serious infestations.

See photograph, page 269.

Ground Beetle
Carabus nemoralis

adult: 1 inch

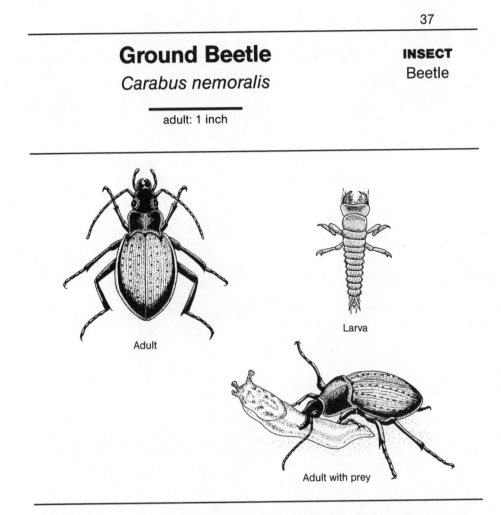

Adult

Larva

Adult with prey

Range: Northern United States and southern Canada, particularly in the western part. Similar species throughout North America.

Description: Adults are black, with tinges of violet on the outer edges of their wing covers. They are heavily armored, long-legged, and nocturnal, reaching 1 inch long. Eggs are laid in the soil. Larvae are whitish to light brown and elongate, with large heads.

Life Cycle: There is one generation per year. Adults hibernate in garden trash.

Feeding Habits: Adults are fierce predators of many kinds of slugs and snails.

Similar Insect: Fiery searcher (page 38).

See photograph, page 269.

INSECT
Beetle

Ground Beetle, Fiery Searcher

Calosoma scrutator

adult: 1 inch

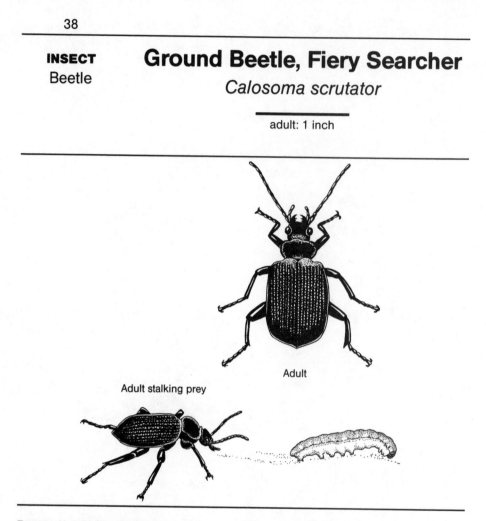

Adult

Adult stalking prey

Range: United States and southern Canada, with many similar species throughout North America.

Description: Adults are blackish-purple with green thoraxes; they are 1 inch long. Eggs are whitish and laid in the soil. Larvae are yellowish-gray to white and flat, with sharp jaws.

Life Cycle: There is one generation per year. Adults hibernate in the soil.

Feeding Habits: Adults feed at night on many soft-bodied larvae, including cankerworms and tent caterpillars.

Similar Insect: Ground beetle (page 37).

See photograph, page 270.

Japanese Beetle
Popillia japonica

———
adult: ½ inch

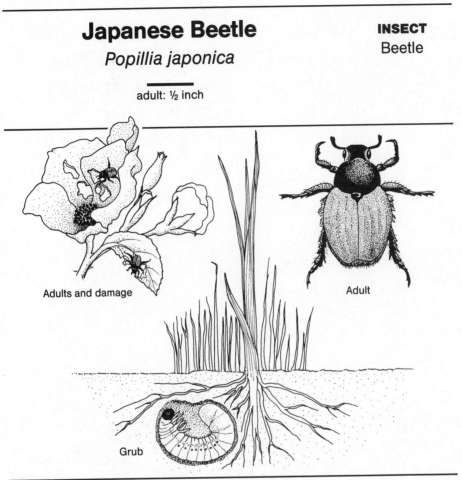

Adults and damage

Adult

Grub

Range: Eastern United States, but is moving westward.

Description: Adults are metallic blue or green with coppery wing covers; they have two small patches of white hair on their abdomens, and five patches on each side below their wing covers. They are ½ inch long. Eggs are white and laid singly or in groups in sod. Larvae are plump and grayish-white with brown heads; they reach ¾ inch long.

Life Cycle: Mature grubs overwinter deep in the soil and begin to move upward in the spring. Pupation occurs in early summer. Adults feed from midsummer to fall. Eggs are laid in late summer. The life cycle is two years.

Host Plants: Apple, cherry, grape, peach, plum, quince, raspberry, rhubarb, rose, and many others.

Feeding Habits: Adults skeletonize leaves and devour flowers. Larvae chew roots.

Prevention and Control: Dust lawn with milky spore disease (Doom or Japidemic) to control grubs; handpicking, rotenone spray or dust, and/or Japanese beetle traps control adults.

See photograph, page 270.

INSECT
Beetle

June Beetle, May Beetle, Daw Bug
Phyllophaga spp.

adult: ———————— 1 inch

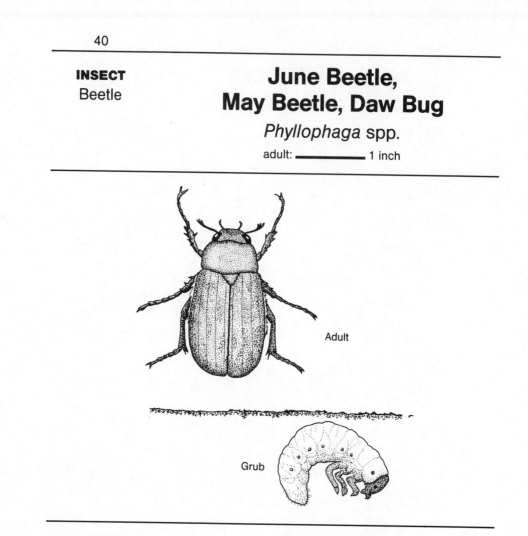

Adult

Grub

Range: Various species found throughout North America.

Description: Adults are reddish-brown or black, robust, hard-shelled, and 1 inch long. Eggs are laid separately several inches below soil surface. Larvae are plump and grayish-white with brown heads.

Life Cycle: There is one generation every three years. Grubs overwinter in soil the first two years; the third winter is spent in the pupal stage.

Host Plants: Potato, strawberry.

Feeding Habits: Grubs feed on underground plant parts during the summer. In spring, they chew roots of garden crops.

Prevention and Control: Control grubs with milky spore disease (Doom or Japidemic).

Similar Insects: Fig beetle (page 35). Grubs are similar to Japanese beetle grubs (page 39).

See photograph, page 272.

Lady Beetle, Ladybug
Hippodamia convergens

adult: ¼ inch

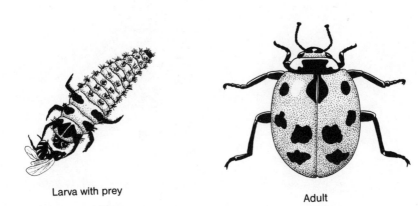

Larva with prey   Adult

Range: Throughout North America.

Description: Adults are orange or red, usually with 12 black spots, and black thoraxes with two white stripes and white rims; they reach ¼ inch long. Eggs are orange and cylindrical. Larvae are black with orange spots. They are slim, flat, and ½ inch long.

Life Cycle: There is one generation per year. In most regions, adults overwinter in garden trash; in the West, adults migrate in fall to hibernate in the mountains.

Feeding Habits: Adults and larvae are important predators of many aphids, and sometimes feed on mealybugs, scales, or other small insects.

Similar Insect: Mexican bean beetle (page 45).

See photograph, page 271.

INSECT
Beetle

Lady Beetle,
Spider Mite Destroyer
Stethorus picipes
adult: . ⅟₃₀ inch

Adult

Larva

Range: Far West, particularly California. Similar species distributed elsewhere in North America.

Description: Adults are round, black, and shiny; they are ⅟₃₀ inch long. Eggs are minute and oval, and are laid on leaves and bark. Larvae are dark gray to black, spined, and ⅟₃₀ inch long.

Life Cycle: There are many generations per year. Adults overwinter in garden litter.

Feeding Habits: Adults and larvae prey on various mites.

Lady Beetle, Vedalia

Rodolia cardinalis

—
adult: ¼ inch

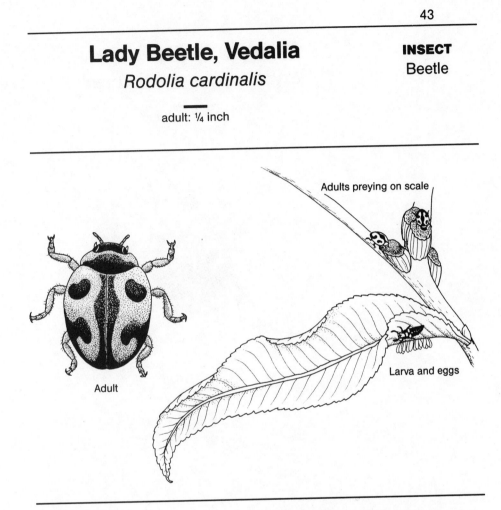

Adults preying on scale

Adult

Larva and eggs

Range: California, Florida.

Description: Adults are red with irregular black marks; in the male, black is the predominant color. They are round, convex, and ¼ inch long. Eggs are red and oval, laid singly or in small groups on the host's egg sac. Larvae are pinkish with black markings. They are wrinkled and spindle-shaped with many soft spines, and about ⅓ inch long.

Life Cycle: There are many generations each season. The beetle overwinters as a pupa on the branches and leaves of citrus trees.

Feeding Habits: Adults and larvae prey upon cottonycushion scale and other soft-bodied insects.

INSECT
Beetle

Mealybug Destroyer
Cryptolaemus montrouzieri

adult: ½ inch

Adult

Larva

Range: California.

Description: Adults are black and shiny, with reddish heads and thoraxes. They are oval and ½ inch long. Eggs are yellow and oval; they are laid singly in the egg sacs of mealybugs. Larvae are yellow and covered with long, white, waxy hairs. They are about ⅓ inch long.

Life Cycle: There may be many generations per season. The beetles overwinter as adults.

Feeding Habits: Both larvae and adults feed on all sorts of mealybugs.

Similar Insects: In the larval stage, they are often confused with mealybugs (pages 102–104).

See photograph, page 271.

Mexican Bean Beetle
Epilachna varivestis

—
adult: ¼ inch

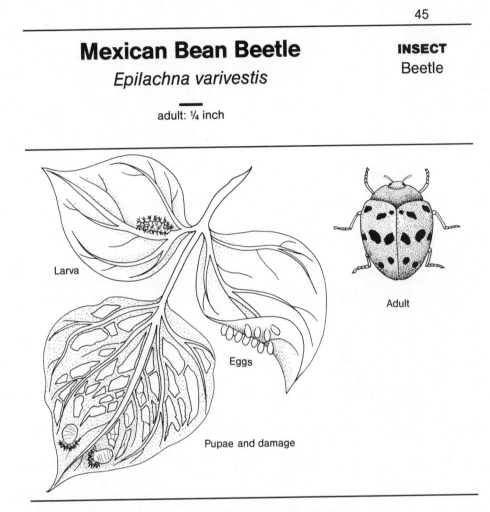

Larva

Adult

Eggs

Pupae and damage

Range: Eastern United States and in parts of Texas, Arizona, Colorado, and Utah. Similar species with different feeding habits found throughout North America.

Description: Adults are yellowish-brown, with 16 black spots on their wing covers. They are round and reach ¼ inch long. Eggs are yellow and are laid in clusters on the undersides of leaves. Larvae are orange, spined, and ⅓ inch long.

Life Cycle: There are one to three generations per year. Adults hibernate in open fields or woods.

Host Plant: Bean.

Feeding Habits: Larvae and adults skeletonize leaves from underneath.

Prevention and Control: Handpick. Apply rotenone or pyrethrum if necessary.

Insect Predators: Various assassin bugs, wasp (*Pediobius foveolatus*).

Similar Insects: Lady beetles (pages 41–43).

See photographs, page 272.

INSECT
Beetle

Northern Corn Rootworm
Diabrotica longicornis

adult: ⅓ inch

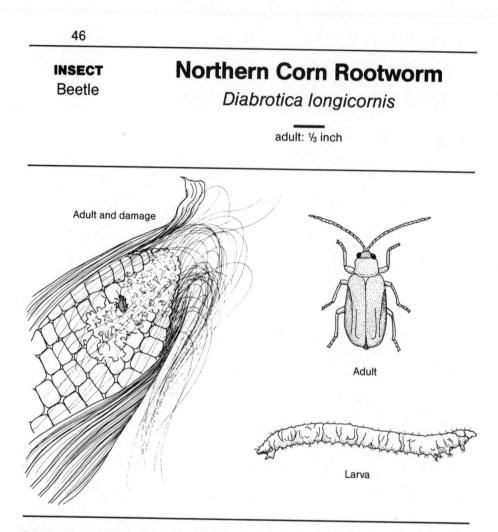

Adult and damage

Adult

Larva

Range: North central United States, and in isolated parts of the East and South.

Description: Adults are bright green to yellowish-green, sometimes with brown heads and thoraxes. They are fast-moving and ⅓ inch long. Eggs are yellow and are laid on the ground near corn roots. Larvae are white worms with brown heads. They are very thin, wrinkled, and up to ½ inch long.

Life Cycle: There is one generation per year. This beetle overwinters in the egg stage. Larvae appear in spring, pupate in the soil in early summer, and emerge as adults in midsummer.

Host Plants: Corn, grains.

Feeding Habits: Adults chew on corn silk and eat the pollen of other plants. Larvae burrow into roots in early summer and do considerable damage.

Prevention and Control: Crop rotation controls the grubs.

Soldier Beetle, Pennsylvania Leather-Wing

Chauliognathus pennsylvanicus

adult: ▬▬ ½ inch

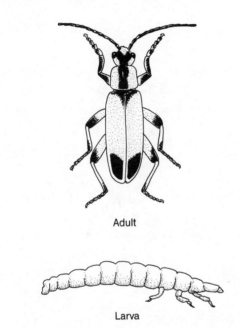

Adult

Larva

Range: Eastern North America.

Description: Adults are golden or dull orange, with black markings on their wing covers and black heads. They are soft-bodied and ½ inch long. Eggs are laid in groups in the soil. Larvae are whitish, flattened and hairy.

Life Cycle: There are two generations per year. Larvae overwinter in garden trash or in the soil.

Feeding Habits: Adults feed on grasshopper eggs, cucumber beetles, and various caterpillars.

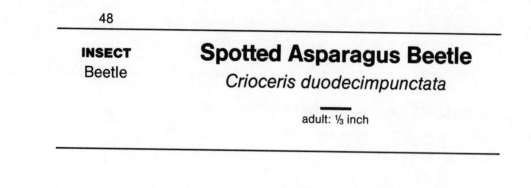

INSECT
Beetle

Spotted Asparagus Beetle
Crioceris duodecimpunctata

adult: ⅓ inch

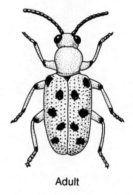

Adult

Range: Throughout most of North America, particularly in the East.

Description: Adults are smooth and shiny red or brownish, with 12 black spots on their backs. They are ⅓ inch long. Eggs are dark brown to greenish and laid on leaves. Larvae are orange, with black heads and legs. They are plump and ⅓ inch long.

Life Cycle: There are one to two generations per year. Adults overwinter in the soil.

Host Plant: Asparagus.

Feeding Habits: Adults feed on spears and leaves in early summer. Larvae do little damage.

Prevention and Control: Apply rotenone.

Insect Predators: Chalcid wasps.

Spotted Cucumber Beetle
Diabrotica undecimpunctata howardi

INSECT
Beetle

—
adult: ¼ inch

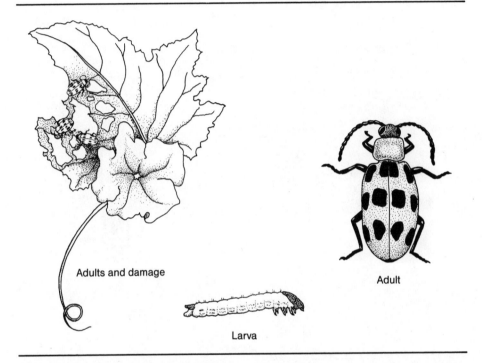

Adults and damage

Adult

Larva

Range: Southern Canada and the eastern United States; a similar species is found in the West.

Description: Adults are greenish-yellow, with small black heads and 11 black spots on their backs. They are ¼ inch long. Eggs are yellow, oval, and laid in the soil at the base of plants. Larvae are beige, with brown heads and a brown spot on their last body segment. They are about ½ inch long.

Life Cycle: In the North, there are one or two generations; in the South, there are up to four. Adults overwinter in plant debris and garden trash.

Host Plants: Corn, cucumber, eggplant, melon, pea, potato, squash, and tomato, as well as many tree fruits.

Feeding Habits: Adults chew holes in plant leaves, flowers, and fruits, and transmit brown rot in stone fruits. Larvae eat roots and stems of plants early in the season.

Prevention and Control: Use rotenone or pyrethrum for serious infestations.

Insect Predator: Tachinid fly (*Celatoria diabrotica*).

See photograph, page 272.

Striped Blister Beetle

Epicauta vittata

adult: ½ inch

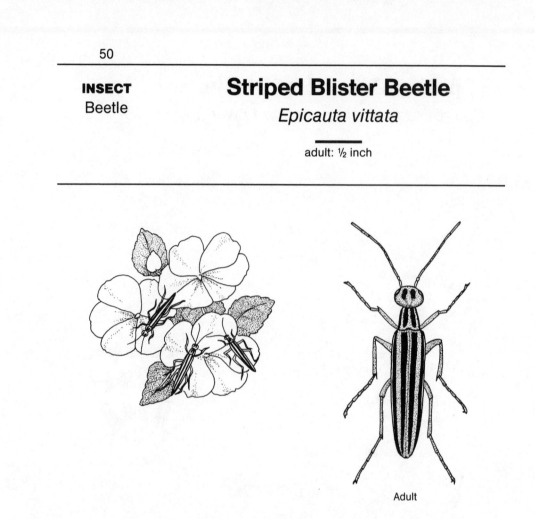

Adult

Range: Eastern North America and central United States.

Description: Adults are yellow with black stripes, black striped heads, and black legs; they are ½ inch long. Eggs are cylindrical and are laid in shallow cells in the soil. The larvae are yellowish to white, with later instars much darker.

Life Cycle: There is one generation per year. Larvae overwinter in the soil.

Host Plants: Bean, beet, melon, pea, potato, tomato, and other vegetable plants.

Feeding Habits: Larvae feed on grasshopper eggs. Adults feed on foliage and fruits.

Prevention and Control: Wear gloves when handpicking, since the insects secrete a harmful substance that may cause blisters to form.

Striped Cucumber Beetle

Acalymma vittata

INSECT
Beetle

adult: ¼ inch

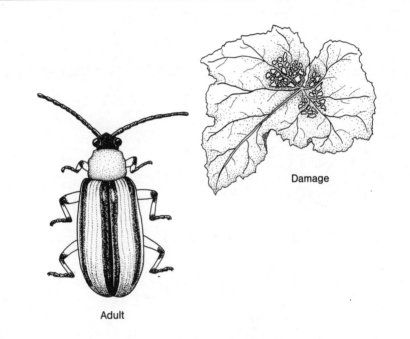

Damage

Adult

Range: Eastern North America.

Description: Adults are pale yellow to orange with three black stripes and black heads; they reach ¼ inch long. Eggs are orange and are laid in the soil at the base of host plants. Larvae are white, slender, and ¼ inch long.

Life Cycle: While there is only one generation in the North, there are two to four in the South. Adults overwinter in plant debris.

Host Plants: Bean, corn, cucumber, melon, pea, pumpkin, squash.

Feeding Habits: Adults chew leaves and flowers, and transmit bacterial wilt and cucumber mosaic. Larvae feed on underground stems and roots.

Prevention and Control: Cover plants with floating row covers, such as Reemay, or with cheesecloth. Use rotenone dusts or sprays for serious infestations.

Insect Predators: Various soldier beetles.

See photograph, page 273.

European Corn Borer
Ostrinia nubilalis

larva: 1 inch

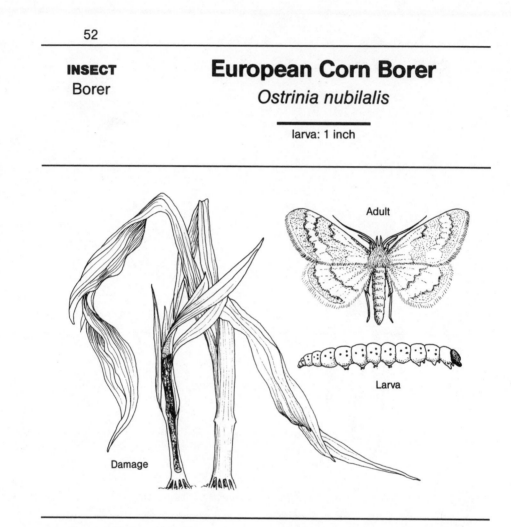

Adult

Larva

Damage

Range: Northern and central United States and southern Canada.

Description: Larvae are grayish-pink caterpillars with dark heads and spots on the top of each segment; they are 1 inch long. Adults are yellowish-brown moths with dark bands on the wings; they are nocturnal and have 1-inch wingspans. Eggs are white and are laid in masses on the undersides of leaves.

Life Cycle: There are one to three generations per year. Larvae hibernate in stalks.

Host Plants: Corn, also many garden crops.

Feeding Habits: Young larvae chew leaves and tassels of corn, and may feed on other plants. Later, they bore into corn stalks and ears, and the stems of garden crops.

Prevention and Control: Split stalks below entrance holes and remove borers.

Insect Predators: Braconid wasp (*Macrocentrus grandi*), tachinid fly (*Lydella stabulans grisescens*).

Similar Insect: Corn earworm (page 67).

See photographs, page 273.

Peachtree Borer

Synanthedon exitiosa

larva: 1 inch

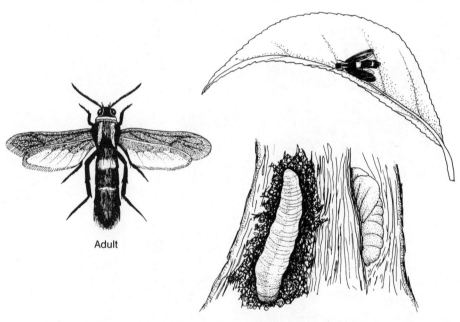

Adult

Larva, pupa, and damage

Range: Throughout North America.

Description: Larvae are pale yellow or whitish caterpillars with brown heads; they are 1 inch long. Adults are steel blue, clear-winged moths with yellow stripes (male) or a wide orange band (female) around their abdomens. Eggs, laid in small groups near the base of trees, are brown or gray.

Life Cycle: There is one generation per year. Larva passes winter in its burrow and pupates in a brown cocoon in the soil each spring.

Host Plants: Apricot, cherry, peach, plum.

Feeding Habits: Borers chew inner bark of lower tree trunks; a mass of gummy sawdust (called frass) appears at the base of injured trees. Vectors of wilt fungus.

Prevention and Control: Each spring, surround base of trees with a ring of tobacco dust 2 inches wide.

Similar Insects: Codling moth (page 66), oriental fruit moth (page 76).

INSECT
Borer

Pickleworm
Diaphania nitidalis

larva: ¾ inch

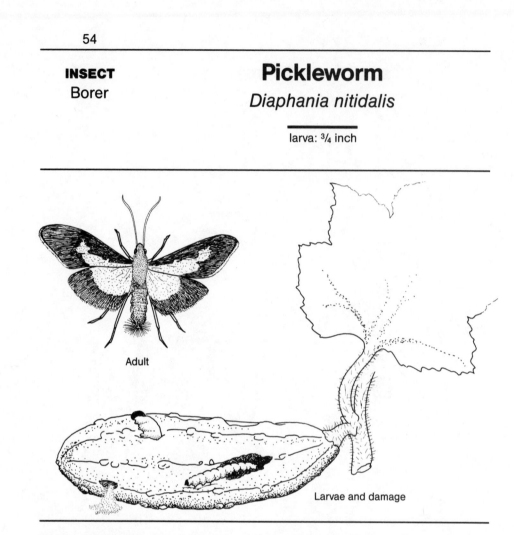

Adult

Larvae and damage

Range: Southeastern United States. Sometimes found north to New York and west to Nebraska.

Description: Larvae are yellowish-white caterpillars with dark spots when young; older larvae are greenish with brown heads and are ¾ inch long. Adults are yellowish-white to tan moths with slender bodies and long, hairy scales on the tips of their abdomens. They have 1¼-inch wingspans. Eggs are white, minute, and laid singly or in small groups on buds, leaves, stalks, and fruits.

Life Cycle: There are one to four broods per year. The pickleworm hibernates as a pupa within a rolled leaf. The adult emerges in late spring.

Host Plants: Cucumber, melon, pumpkin, squash.

Feeding Habits: Larvae enter developing buds and fruits to feed. Each worm may enter several.

Prevention and Control: Slit infested stems and remove the borers, then heap dirt over the injured stem to encourage rooting.

Potato Tuberworm
Phthorimaea operculella

larva: ½ inch

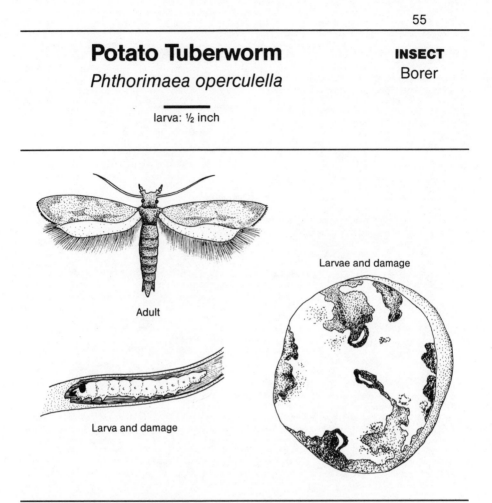

Adult

Larvae and damage

Larva and damage

Range: Southern United States from Florida to California.

Description: Larvae are pinkish-white with brown heads, ½ inch long, and wormlike. Adults are grayish-brown moths marked with darker brown, with very narrow wings and ½-inch wingspans. Eggs are laid singly or in groups on the undersides of leaves or in the eyes of tubers.

Life Cycle: Up to six generations mature per year. Larva pupates in tubers and overwinters in garden trash.

Host Plants: Eggplant, potato, tomato.

Feeding Habits: Larvae tunnel into stems to feed and make silk-lined burrows in the tubers.

Prevention and Control: Clip and destroy infested vines.

INSECT
Borer

Squash Vine Borer
Melittia satyriniformis

larva: 1 inch

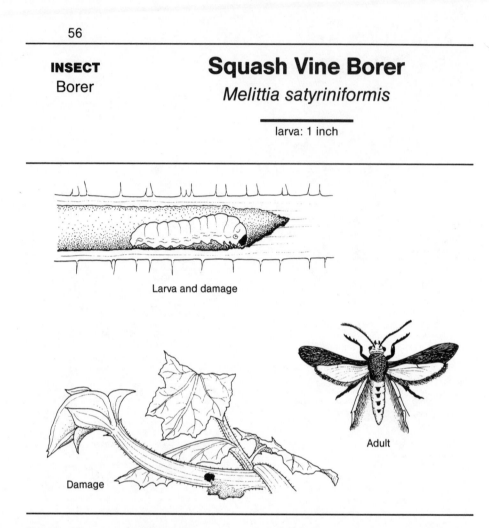

Larva and damage

Adult

Damage

Range: East of the Rocky Mountains, in United States and southern Canada.

Description: Larvae are white caterpillars with brown heads; they are 1 inch long and wrinkled. Adults are orange and black, clear-winged moths with coppery forewings and black stripes around their abdomens. They are 1 to 1½ inches long. Eggs are brown, flat, and oval, laid singly along the stems.

Life Cycle: There are one to two generations. Hibernates as larva or pupa in a cocoon, 1 inch deep in the soil.

Host Plants: Cucumber, gourd, melon, pumpkin, squash.

Feeding Habits: Borers enter base of stems in early summer to feed, causing vines to wilt suddenly and masses of greenish frass to exude from holes in the stems.

Prevention and Control: Slit the stem, remove the borer, and heap dirt over the damaged stalk; alternatively, inject *Bacillus thuringiensis* (Bt) into stem 1 inch above borer hole.

See photograph, page 273.

Assassin Bugs

REDUVIIDAE

INSECT
Bug

adult: ½ inch

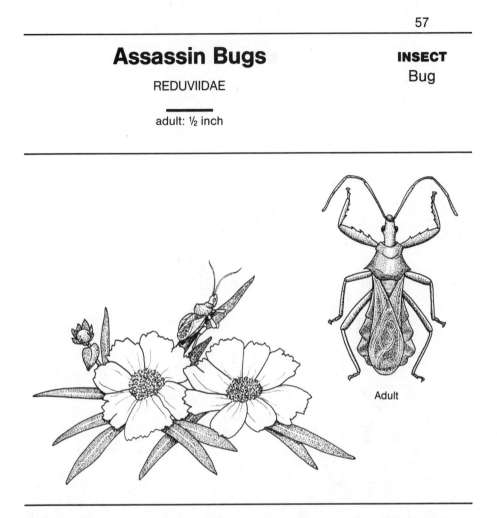

Adult

Range: Various species found throughout North America.

Description: Adults are brown or black and ½ inch long; their bodies are flat and sculptured with a groove that holds the stout beak when at rest. Their abdomens may flare outward beneath their wings; often with peculiar hood or structure behind their heads. Eggs are usually laid in the soil. Nymphs are often brightly colored.

Life Cycle: Various species have different life cycles and habits. In most cases, just one generation occurs each year, with the complete cycle sometimes requiring several years. Some hibernate as nymphs or adults, others pass the winter as eggs.

Feeding Habits: Adults and nymphs feed on larval, and occasionally on adult, forms of many plant-eating insects.

INSECT
Bug

Brown Stink Bug
Euschistus servus

adult: ½ inch

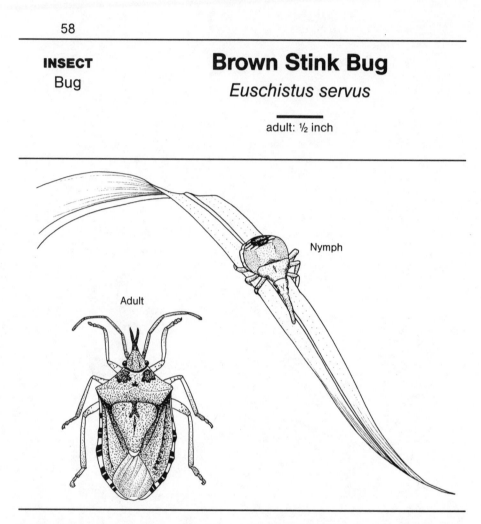

Nymph

Adult

Range: Eastern United States, with similar species in the West and in Canada.

Description: Adults are brown with a checked border beneath their wing covers. They are shield-shaped and ½ inch long. Eggs are laid on leaves and fruits.

Life Cycle: There is one generation per year. Overwinters in the adult or egg stages.

Host Plants: Blackberry, cabbage, corn, peach, tomato.

Feeding Habits: Adults and nymphs puncture fruit skin to feed, causing a gummy substance to appear. Injured fruit has a catfaced or pitted appearance. Many similar stink bugs are predaceous.

Prevention and Control: Weed control is the best preventive measure.

Chinch Bug
Blissus leucopterus

▬
adult: 1/16 inch

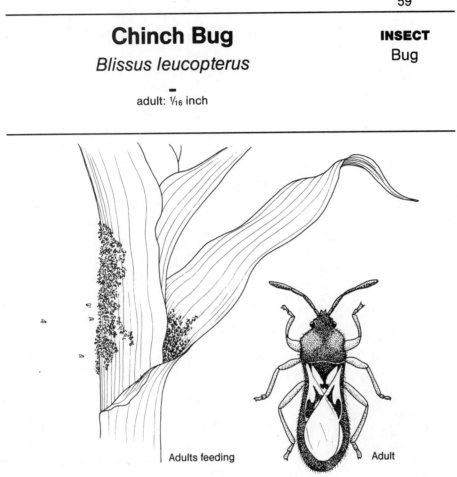

Adults feeding   Adult

Range: Eastern North America.

Description: Adults are black with white or brown forewings, brown legs, and brown antennae; they are 1/16 inch long and emit an offensive odor when crushed. Eggs, which are laid in the soil or on roots, are white to dark red and curved. Nymphs are red with a white stripe across their backs or black with white spots.

Life Cycle: There are two to three generations per year. Adults hibernate in clumps of grass.

Host Plant: Corn.

Feeding Habits: Nymphs and adults feed on corn leaves and stalks.

Prevention and Control: Turn up a ridge of earth around the stalks and pour creosote on top.

INSECT
Bug

Harlequin Bug, Calico Bug
Murgantia histrionica

—
adult: ¼ inch

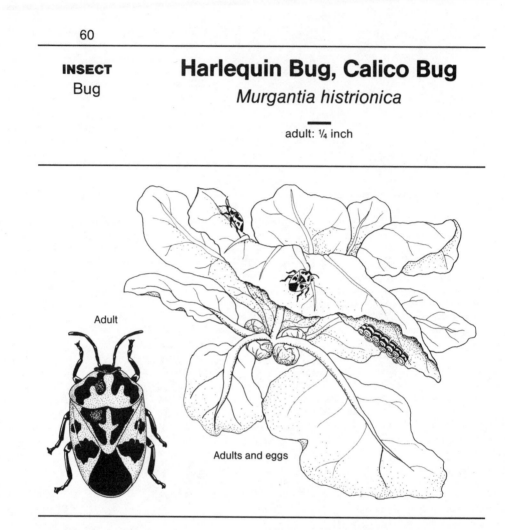

Adult

Adults and eggs

Range: Southern United States.

Description: Adults are ¼ inch long, red and black, shiny, flat, and shield-shaped. Eggs are white with black rings, barrel-shaped, and laid in double rows on the undersides of leaves. Nymphs are red and black and oval.

Life Cycle: There are three to four generations per year, but in the South, it may breed year-round. Adults hibernate in plant debris and litter.

Host Plants: Brussels sprouts, cauliflower, cherry, citrus, collard, horseradish, kohlrabi, mustard, radish, turnip.

Feeding Habits: Nymphs and adults feed on leaves, causing white and yellow blotches to appear.

Prevention and Control: Dust or spray with pyrethrum or sabadilla if the problem is serious.

See photograph, page 274.

Southern Green Stink Bug
Nezara viridula

INSECT
Bug

adult: ½ inch

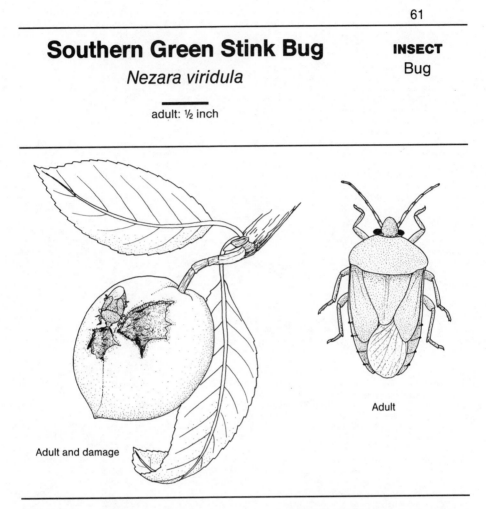

Adult and damage

Adult

Range: Southeastern United States.

Description: Adults are light green and speckled, although the hibernating form may be pinkish; they are ½ inch long. Eggs are glued to leaves. Nymphs are round and bluish-gray with red marks.

Life Cycle: Four to five generations mature per year. Adults hibernate in garden trash.

Host Plants: Bean, citrus, peach, pecan, potato, tomato.

Feeding Habits: Bugs feed on leaves and fruits, causing pods to drop prematurely and nuts to develop black pits.

Prevention and Control: If the damage is intolerable, dust with sabadilla.

INSECT
Bug

Squash Bug
Anasa tristis

——

adult: ½ inch

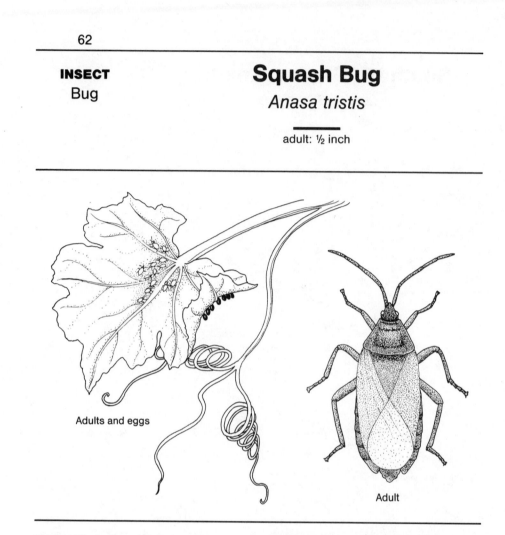

Adults and eggs

Adult

Range: Throughout North America.

Description: Adults are dark brown to black with orange or brown abdominal perimeters; they are ½ inch long and emit a peculiar odor when crushed. Eggs are brown, shiny, and laid in groups or singly on the undersides of leaves and stems. Nymphs are yellowish-green with dark abdomens and thoraxes.

Life Cycle: One generation matures per year. Hibernates as an adult.

Host Plants: Cucumber, melon, pumpkin, squash.

Feeding Habits: Adults and nymphs congregate on leaves to feed, causing them to wilt and blacken.

Prevention and Control: Dust with sabadilla if necessary.

Insect Predator: Tachinid fly (*Trichopoda pennipes*).

See photograph, page 274.

Tarnished Plant Bug
Lygus lineolaris

—
adult: ¼ inch

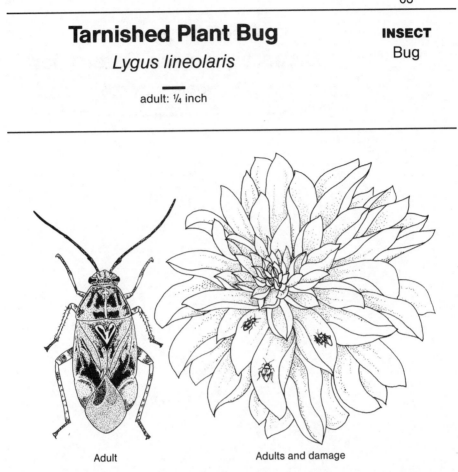

Adult   Adults and damage

Range: Throughout North America.

Description: Adults are greenish-yellow to brown with yellow, brown, and black markings; they are ¼ inch long with a yellow triangle at the end of each forewing. Eggs are elongate and curved; they are inserted in stems, tips, and leaves. Nymphs are pale yellow.

Life Cycle: There are three to five generations per year. Overwinters as an adult or nymph in garden trash.

Host Plants: Most fruits and vegetables.

Feeding Habits: Nymphs and adults suck on stem tips, buds, and fruits. They inject a toxin that deforms roots, blackens terminal shoots, dwarfs and pits fruits, and ruins flowers.

Prevention and Control: Apply ryania or sabadilla dust to serious infestations.

See photograph, page 274.

Beet Armyworm, Asparagus Fern Caterpillar
Spodoptera exigua

larva: —————————————————— 2 inches

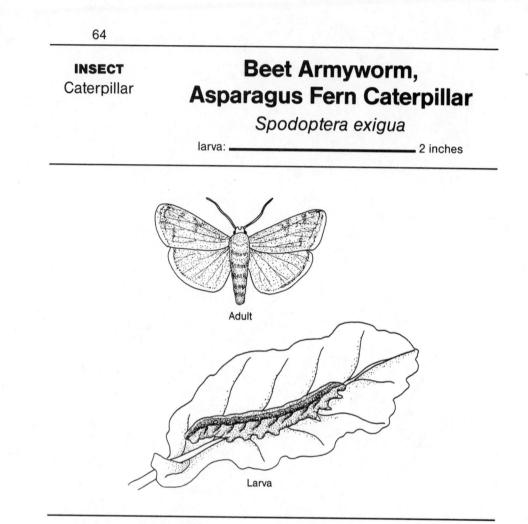

Adult

Larva

Range: Throughout North America.

Description: Larvae are green with yellow undersides and dark green and yellow stripes; they are 1 to 2 inches long. Adults are mottled gray moths with two yellow spots near the centers of their forewings; they are night-flying, with 1-inch wingspans. Eggs are laid on bark in masses and covered with hair.

Life Cycle: Five to six generations mature per year. Adults migrate south in the winter.

Host Plants: Beet, corn, pea, pepper, spinach, tomato.

Feeding Habits: Caterpillars chew foliage and buds. They travel in large groups and may be very destructive.

Prevention and Control: Handpicking is usually adequate, but apply *Bacillus thuringiensis* (Bt) to serious infestations.

Insect Predators: Trichogramma wasps.

Similar Insect: Fall armyworm (page 70).

Cabbage Looper
Trichoplusia ni

larva: 1½ inches

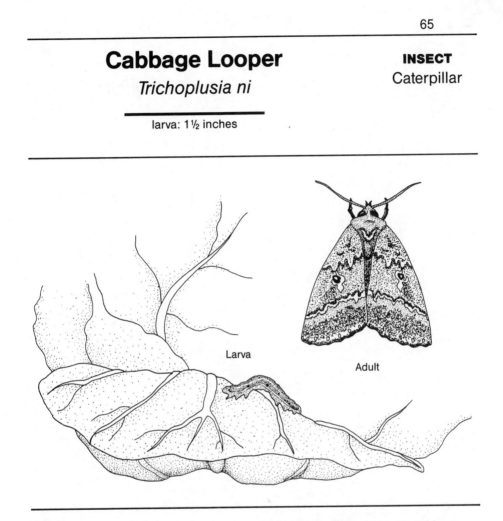

Larva

Adult

Range: United States and southern Canada.

Description: Larvae are 1½ inches long and are green with pale stripes down their backs; they loop their bodies as they crawl. Adults are brownish with a silvery spot in the middle of each forewing; they are night-flying and have 1½-inch wing-spans. Eggs are greenish-white and round, and are laid singly on the upper surface of leaves.

Life Cycle: There are several broods per year. Winter is spent as a pupa attached to a leaf, but in northern regions adults may migrate south for the winter.

Host Plants: Bean, broccoli, cabbage, cauliflower, celery, kale, lettuce, parsley, pea, potato, radish, spinach, tomato.

Feeding Habits: Larvae chew leaves.

Prevention and Control: Use *Bacillus thuringiensis* (Bt) for serious infestations.

Insect Predators: Trichogramma wasps.

Similar Insects: Garden webworm (page 72), imported cabbageworm (page 75).

See photographs, page 275.

INSECT
Caterpillar

Codling Moth

Carpocapsa pomonella

---

larva: 1 inch

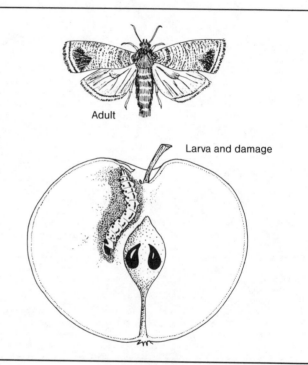

Adult

Larva and damage

Range: Throughout North America.

Description: Larvae are pink with brown heads and are 1 inch long. Adults are grayish-brown moths with lacy brown lines on their forewings and pale, fringed hind wings; they have ³⁄₄-inch wingspans. Eggs are white and flat, and are laid singly on leaves, twigs, or fruit buds.

Life Cycle: There are two generations per year. This caterpillar passes the winter in a cocoon beneath bark or in orchard litter.

Host Plants: Apple, pear, quince, walnut.

Feeding Habits: Larvae enter young apples at the blossom end to feed, and when fully grown, tunnel out, leaving brown excrement on the outside. Later in the season, second-brood larvae enter fruits from any end.

Prevention and Control: In the spring, wrap trunk with corrugated paper. Spray trees with ryania or, during the egg stage, spray with a dormant-oil solution.

Similar Insects: Oriental fruit moth (page 76), peachtree borer (page 53).

See photographs, page 275.

Corn Earworm
Heliothis zea

larva: 1½ inches

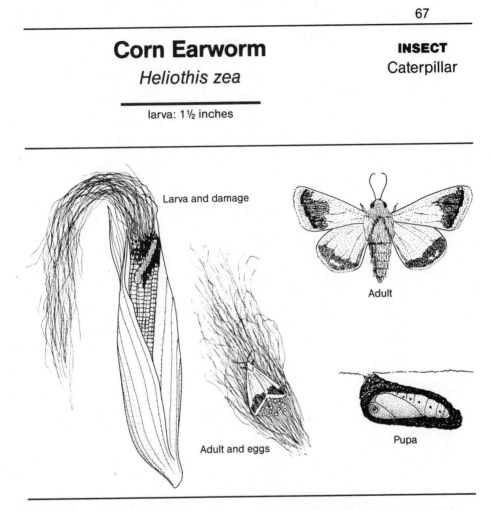

Larva and damage

Adult

Adult and eggs

Pupa

Range: Throughout North America.

Description: The color of larvae varies from white to green and even red. They have four pairs of prolegs, are spined and 1½ inches long. Adults are greenish-gray or brown moths with black markings on the forewings; they are night-flying, with 1½-inch wingspans. Eggs are light brown or yellow, domed and ridged, and laid singly on plant leaves.

Life Cycle: There can be up to seven generations per year. Pupa winters in soil.

Host Plants: Bean, corn, pea, pepper, potato, squash, tomato.

Feeding Habits: Earworms chew buds and leaves, causing plants to be stunted. They enter corn ears at the tip and work their way to the kernels.

Prevention and Control: *Bacillus thuringiensis* (Bt) on vegetables. On corn, apply a drop of mineral oil inside the tip of each ear after silk has wilted.

Similar Insect: European corn borer (page 52).

See photograph, page 276.

INSECT
Caterpillar

Cutworms

NOCTUIDAE

larva: 2 inches

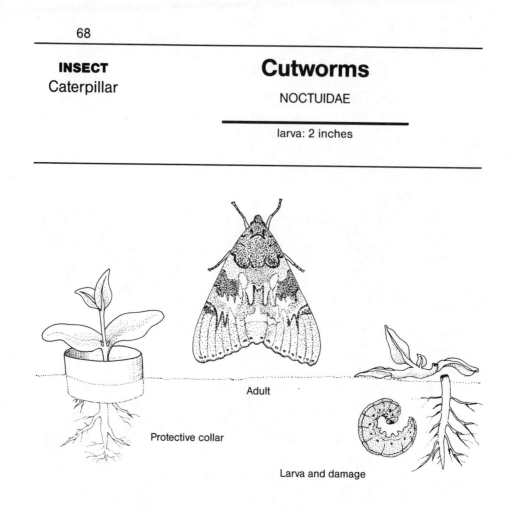

Adult

Protective collar

Larva and damage

Range: Various species throughout North America.

Description: Larvae are 1 to 2 inches long and grayish or brown. They curl up when disturbed and are seldom seen during the day. Adults are gray or brownish moths with paler hind wings. They are night-flying, attracted to lights, and have 1- to 1½-inch wingspans. Eggs are usually laid in the soil.

Life Cycle: There are one to five generations, depending upon species. Winter is passed as a pupa or young larva.

Host Plants: All garden vegetables, particularly seedlings and transplants.

Feeding Habits: Larvae feed near the soil surface, cutting stems several inches below ground level or just above it.

Prevention and Control: Place a collar of stiff paper or cardboard around each plant when it is transplanted to the garden. *Bacillus thuringiensis* (Bt) kills the larvae.

Insect Predators: Trichogramma wasps.

See photograph, page 276.

Eastern Tent Caterpillar
Malacosoma americanum

larva: 2 inches

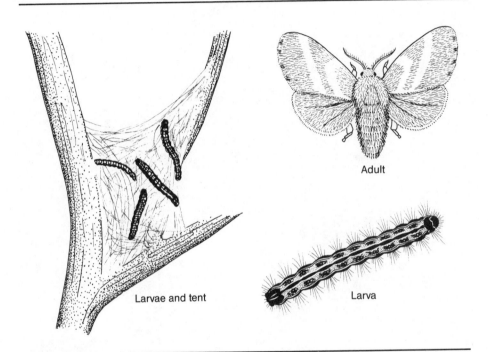

Adult

Larvae and tent

Larva

Range: Eastern and central United States. Similar species in the West.

Description: Larvae are black with white stripes with narrower brown and yellow lines and a row of blue spots on the sides. They are 2 inches long and hairy. Adults are reddish-brown with stripes on the forewings; they have 1- to 1½-inch wingspans. Eggs are laid in a ring around twigs and covered with a shiny, hard surface.

Life Cycle: There is one generation per year. Winter is passed in the egg stage.

Host Plants: Apple, pear, and other fruit trees.

Feeding Habits: Larvae make webbed tents in the forks and crotches of trees and feed within.

Prevention and Control: *Bacillus thuringiensis* (Bt) controls the larvae. Torching the tents also provides control.

Insect Predators: Various ground beetles and predaceous wasps.

Similar Insect: Fall webworm (page 71).

INSECT
Caterpillar

Fall Armyworm, Budworm
Spodoptera frugiperda

larva: 1¾ inches

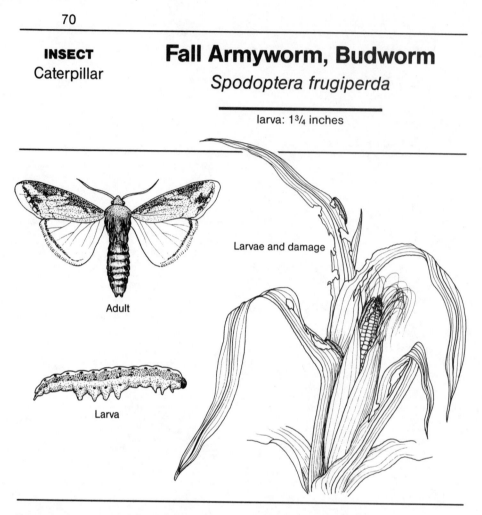

Adult

Larva

Larvae and damage

Range: Most of the United States, except the far North. Similar species throughout North America.

Description: Larvae are brown with black heads. They have yellow stripes down their backs and a V-shaped white mark on the head. They are somewhat hairy. Young white larvae hang from threads or curl up in leaves and are 1¾ inches long. Adults are gray, mottled moths (females with pinkish or white wing margins) with 1½-inch wingspans. Eggs are covered with hair and are laid in groups of 50 to 150 on host plants.

Life Cycle: There are one to six generations per year. Adults migrate south for the winter.

Host Plants: Bean, beet, cabbage, corn, cucumber, potato, spinach, sweet potato, tomato, turnip, and other vegetables.

Feeding Habits: Larvae feed on grasses and corn in early spring, later chewing stems near the ground. Night-feeding.

Prevention and Control: Apply *Bacillus thuringiensis* (Bt) to kill larvae.

Similar Insect: Beet armyworm (page 64).

Fall Webworm
Hyphantria cunea

larva: 1 inch

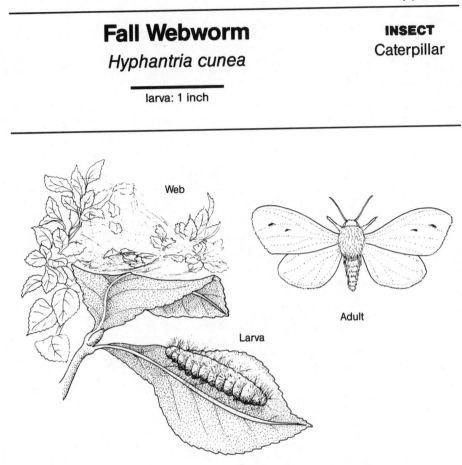

Web

Adult

Larva

Range: United States and southern Canada.

Description: Larvae are pale green or yellow, covered with long, silky hairs attached to small humps, and 1 inch long. Adults are white with brown spots and have 2-inch wingspans. Eggs are laid in masses on the undersides of leaves and covered with hair.

Life Cycle: One to four generations mature per year. Pupae overwinter in cocoons attached to tree bark or orchard trash.

Host Plants: Apple, cherry, peach, pecan, walnut.

Feeding Habits: Caterpillars make silken nests on the ends of branches and feed on leaves.

Prevention and Control: Apply *Bacillus thuringiensis* (Bt) if the damage is intolerable.

Insect Predators: Various trichogramma wasps.

Similar Insect: Eastern tent caterpillar (page 69).

Garden Webworm

Achyra rantalis

larva: ³/₄ inch

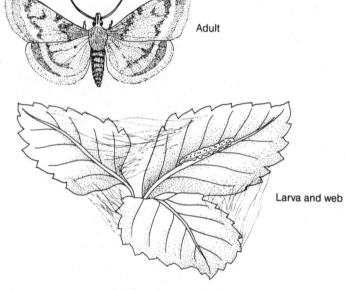

Adult

Larva and web

Range: Throughout North America.

Description: Larvae are green with a light stripe. They are ³/₄ inch long with several hairs on each segment. Adults are brownish-yellow moths with gray and brown markings and ³/₄-inch wingspans. Eggs are laid in clusters on the leaves.

Life Cycle: There are two to four generations a season. Pupae overwinter in the soil.

Host Plants: Bean, beet, corn, pea, strawberry.

Feeding Habits: Larvae spin light webs and feed within, dropping to the ground when disturbed.

Prevention and Control: Use *Bacillus thuringiensis* (Bt) or pyrethrum for intolerable infestations.

Insect Predators: Various trichogramma wasps.

Similar Insects: Cabbage looper (page 65), imported cabbageworm (page 75).

Grapeleaf Skeletonizer
Harrisina spp.

larva: 1 inch

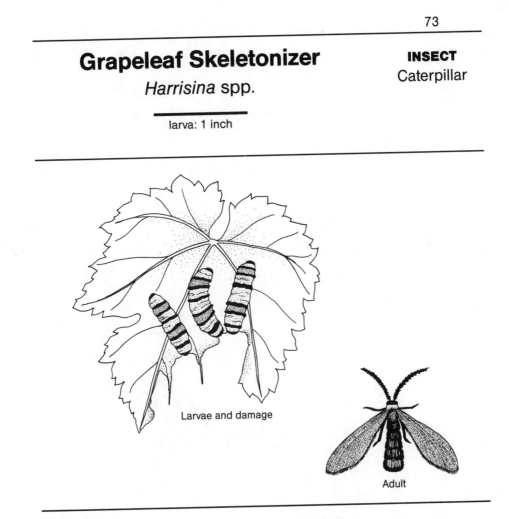

Larvae and damage

Adult

Range: United States and southern Canada.

Description: Larvae are yellow with black bands just behind the head (eastern species with an orange collar). They have long black hairs on each segment and are 1 inch long. Adults are dark gray or metallic blue moths having narrow wings with 1-inch wingspans. Eggs are laid in clusters on leaves.

Life Cycle: There are three generations per year. Pupae overwinter in cocoons in bark or ground litter.

Host Plant: Grape.

Feeding Habits: Larvae feed between the veins on the undersides of leaves. They form neat, compact colonies. Controls are seldom needed.

INSECT
Caterpillar

Gypsy Moth
Lymantria dispar

larva: 2 inches

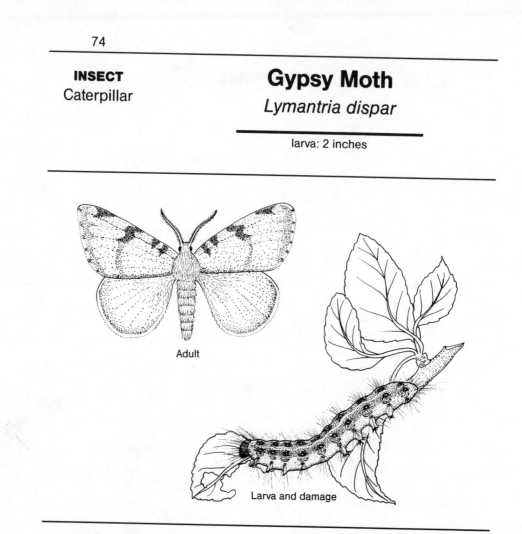

Adult

Larva and damage

Range: Eastern United States.

Description: Larvae are gray with brown hairs, flat, nocturnal, and 2 inches long. Adults are gray (male) or white (female) moths with hairy bodies and 1½- to 2-inch wingspans. Eggs are light brown to yellowish and are laid in groups of approximately 400 and covered with hair.

Life Cycle: One generation matures per year. Winter is passed in the egg stage.

Host Plants: Apple, cherry.

Feeding Habits: Masses of caterpillars feed on foliage at night, hiding in orchard litter during the day.

Prevention and Control: Apply *Bacillus thuringiensis* (Bt) to control the caterpillars. Tanglefoot around the trunk will keep larvae from crawling up into the tree.

Insect Predators: Trichogramma wasps eat the eggs.

Imported Cabbageworm

Pieris rapae

INSECT
Caterpillar

larva: 1¼ inches

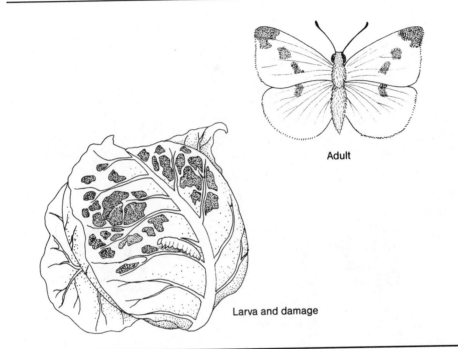

Adult

Larva and damage

Range: Throughout North America.

Description: Larvae are velvety pale green with a yellow stripe and are 1¼ inches long. They leave behind dark green pellets of excrement. Adults are white moths with a black tip on their forewings and two or three black spots. They have 1- to 2-inch wingspans. Eggs are yellowish, bullet-shaped, ridged, and laid singly on the leaves.

Life Cycle: There are two to three generations per year. Overwinters in the pupal stage.

Host Plants: Cabbage, cauliflower, kale, kohlrabi, mustard, radish, turnip.

Feeding Habits: Caterpillars feed on leaves, chewing huge holes in them.

Prevention and Control: *Bacillus thuringiensis* (Bt) can be used on a large scale, but first try dusting with a flour-and-salt mixture or spraying leaves with sour milk or a garlic infusion.

Insect Predators: Various trichogramma wasps.

Similar Insects: Cabbage looper (page 65), garden webworm (page 72).

See photographs, page 276.

Oriental Fruit Moth

Grapholitha molesta

larva: ½ inch

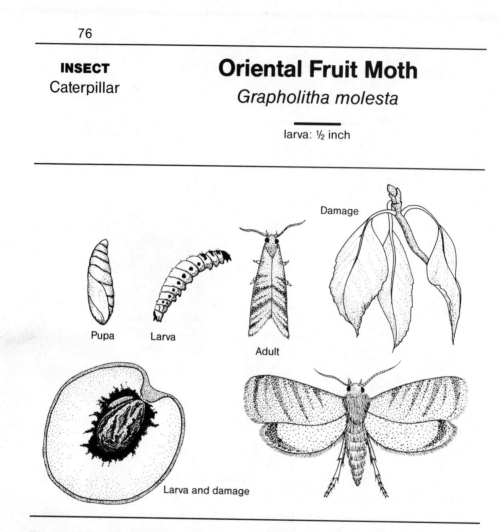

Damage

Pupa   Larva

Adult

Larva and damage

Range: Eastern North America and the Pacific Northwest.

Description: Larvae are grayish-white to pink with brown heads and brown markings on their thoraxes, usually in white webs, and are ½ inch long. Adults are gray moths with brown markings and have ½-inch wingspans. Eggs are white, flat, and are laid on the undersides of leaves or on twigs.

Life Cycle: Four to seven generations mature per year. Hibernates in its cocoon in tree bark or on the ground.

Host Plants: Almond, apple, apricot, cherry, peach, pear, plum.

Feeding Habits: Larvae bore into young twigs and later enter fruits at the stem end to feed. There is no external damage to fruits, only tunneling within.

Prevention and Control: Cultivate the soil 4 inches deep several weeks before trees bloom. Use *Bacillus thuringiensis* (Bt) to kill larvae.

Insect Predators: Braconid wasp (*Macrocentrus ancylivorus*), trichogramma wasp (*Trichogramma minutum*).

Similar Insects: Codling moth (page 66), peachtree borer (page 53).

Parsleyworm, Celeryworm, Black Swallowtail Butterfly

Papilio polyxenes asterius

INSECT
Caterpillar

larva: ━━━━━━━━━━━━ 2 inches

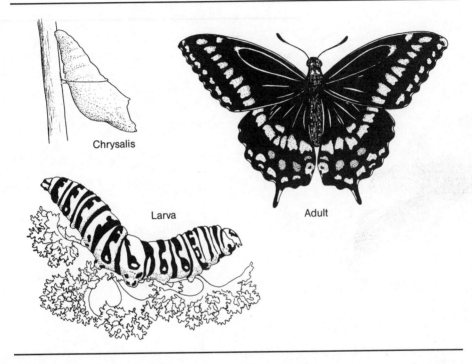

Chrysalis

Larva

Adult

Range: Throughout North America.

Description: Larvae are brown with white on the middles of their backs; later green with a white-spotted black band on each segment and two orange horns that project when the insects are disturbed. They are 2 inches long. Adults are black butterflies with yellow spots on the edges of their wings, a taillike projection on the hind wings, and 3-inch wingspans. Eggs are white and are laid singly on leaves of host plants.

Life Cycle: There are two to four generations per year. Passes the winter as a pupa or, in the South, as an adult.

Host Plants: Carrot, celery, parsley, parsnip.

Feeding Habits: Larvae chew leaves and stems but, since few are present, they do little damage.

Prevention and Control: Apply *Bacillus thuringiensis* (Bt) if handpicking is not adequate.

See photographs, page 277.

INSECT
Caterpillar

Tomato Hornworm
Manduca quinquemaculata

larva: 4 inches

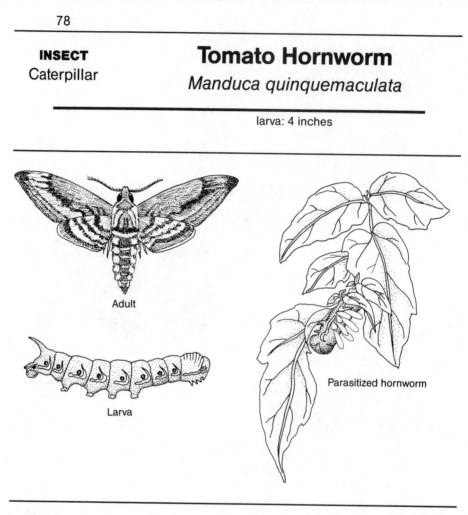

Adult

Larva

Parasitized hornworm

Range: Throughout North America.

Description: Larvae are green with seven or eight white stripes, and a black horn projecting from the rear of their bodies. They are 3 to 4 inches long. A similar species, the tobacco hornworm (*M. sexta*), has a red horn. Adults are grayish or brownish moths with white zigzags on the rear wings and orange or brownish spots on their bodies. They have 4- to 5-inch wingspans. Eggs are greenish-yellow and are laid on the undersides of leaves.

Life Cycle: There are one to two generations per year. Winter is passed in the pupal stage.

Host Plants: Eggplant, pepper, potato, tomato.

Feeding Habits: Larvae chew leaves and fruits.

Prevention and Control: Plants can tolerate some feeding, but if the caterpillars become a problem, remove them by hand.

Insect Predators: Braconid wasps lay eggs on caterpillars, often forming small white cocoons on the skin. Trichogramma wasps parasitize hornworms in the egg stage.

See photograph, page 277.

Periodical Cicada
Magicicada septendecim

adult: 1 ½ inches

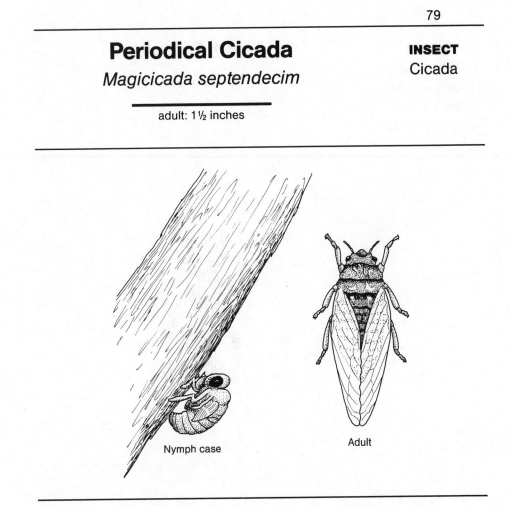

Nymph case

Adult

Range: Thirteen-year race found in the eastern United States; 17-year race found mainly in the Southeast.

Description: Adults are brown to blackish with orange legs and transparent wings. They are wedge-shaped and 1 to 1½ inches long. Eggs are inserted in slits made in the bark of twigs. Nymphs are small, resembling brown ants when young, later they are brown to black and stout-bodied.

Life Cycle: Thirteen or 17 years are required to complete the life cycle.

Nymphs remain underground until adulthood.

Host Plants: Apple, many woody ornamentals.

Feeding Habits: Nymphs chew tree roots and adults suck sap from limbs and twigs, but neither do any damage. Injury comes from egglaying slits that may cause the tips of twigs to die.

Prevention and Control: Remove injured twigs as soon as possible.

INSECT
Crickets,
Grasshoppers,
Mantids, and
Walkingsticks

Field Cricket
Gryllus spp.

adult: 1 inch

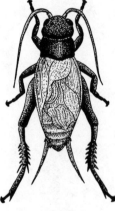

Adult

Range: Throughout North America.

Description: Adults are ¾ to 1 inch long and are dark brown or black with long antennae and wings folded flat along their sides. Eggs are laid in damp soil.

Life Cycle: One to three generations mature per year. In the South, winter is passed in the nymph or adult stage; elsewhere in the egg stage.

Host Plants: Bean, cucumber, melon, squash, tomato.

Feeding Habits: Adults and nymphs chew foliage and flowers of young vegetable crops, but controls are rarely necessary.

Grasshoppers, Locusts

ACRIDIDAE

adult: 2 inches

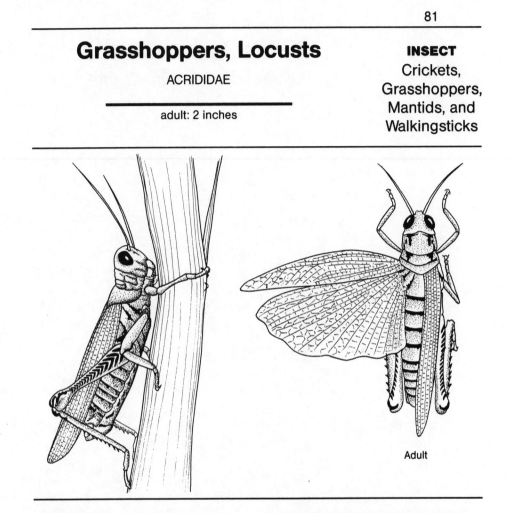

Adult

Range: Various species throughout North America.

Description: Adults are brown to reddish-yellow or green. They have long bodies with prominent jaws and short antennae. They are 1 to 2 inches long and have enlarged hind legs for jumping. Eggs are laid in egg pods in soil and weeds.

Life Cycle: There is one generation per year. Overwinters in the egg stage.

Host Plants: Most vegetable crops.

Feeding Habits: Grasshoppers feed during the day on leaves and stems, often defoliating plants during dry periods.

Prevention and Control: Trap grasshoppers in Mason jars partially filled with molasses and water and buried in the garden. Sprays of hot pepper, soap, and water may repel the insects. A protozoan parasite of grasshoppers, *Neosema locustae*, is commercially available. It takes several years to control grasshopper populations, but is highly effective.

See photograph, page 278.

Broadwinged Katydid
Microcentrum rhombifolium

adult: 1½ inches

Adult

Range: Most of the United States, except the North.

Description: Adults are green with large angular wings and are 1½ inches long. Eggs are grayish-brown, flat, and laid in double rows on twigs.

Life Cycle: One generation matures per year. Winter is passed in the egg stage.

Host Plants: Many orchard trees.

Feeding Habits: Katydids feed on foliage, but since there are few of them, they do no significant damage.

See photograph, page 279.

Praying Mantids

MANTIDAE

adult: 2½ inches

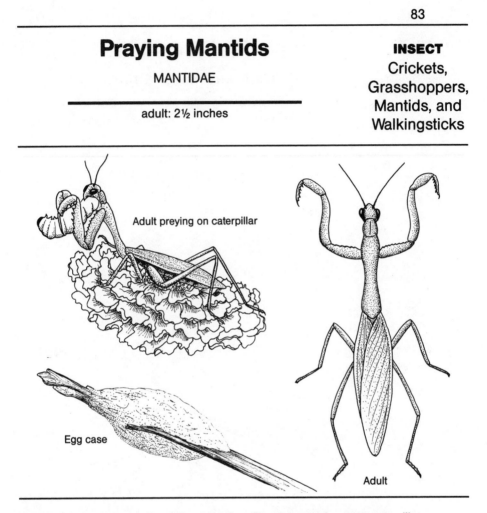

Adult preying on caterpillar

Egg case

Adult

Range: Various species throughout North America.

Description: Adults are green or brownish and have long bodies with papery wings and enlarged front legs adapted for grasping. They are 2½ inches long. Eggs are white or light brown; masses are glued to stems and twigs.

Life Cycle: There is one generation per year. Winter is passed in the egg stage.

Feeding Habits: Nymphs and adults feed on aphids, beetles, bugs, leafhoppers, flies, bees and wasps, caterpillars, butterflies, and each other.

See photograph, page 278.

INSECT
Crickets,
Grasshoppers,
Mantids, and
Walkingsticks

Walkingstick
Diapheromera femorata

adult: 3 inches

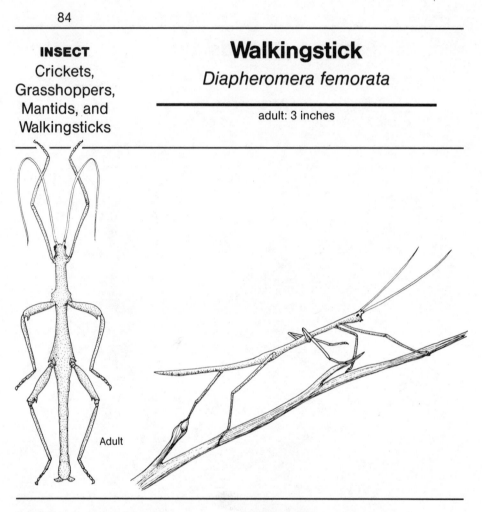

Adult

Range: Eastern United States.

Description: Adults are brown or dark green with thin, sticklike bodies. Though they are 3 inches long, they are easily camouflaged in trees and shrubs. Eggs are black and are deposited on the ground.

Life Cycle: There is one generation per year. Winter is passed in the egg stage.

Host Plant: Cherry.

Feeding Habits: Nymphs may feed extensively on foliage, but damage is never serious.

European Earwig
Forficula auricularia

adult: ¾ inch

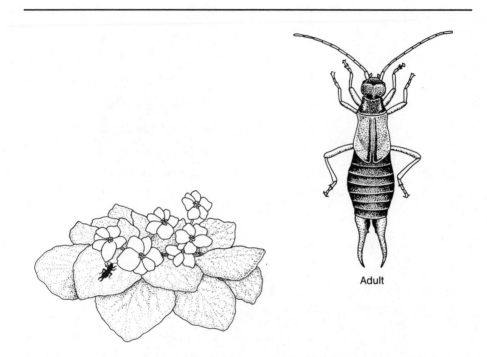

Adult

Range: Eastern North America, with similar species throughout North America.

Description: Adults are reddish-brown with short, leathery forewings. They are straight and thin, reaching ¾ inch long, with pincers on the tips of their abdomens. Eggs are white, round, and laid in the soil.

Life Cycle: One to two generations mature per year. Overwinters in the egg stage.

Host Plants: Many young garden plants and fruit trees.

Feeding Habits: Nymphs feed on plant shoots and eat holes in foliage and flowers. Sometimes ripening fruits are infested, but damage is tolerable.

Insect Predator: Tachinid fly (*Bigonicheta spinipennis*).

INSECT
Fly

Apple Maggot
Rhagoletis pomonella

—

larva: ¼ inch

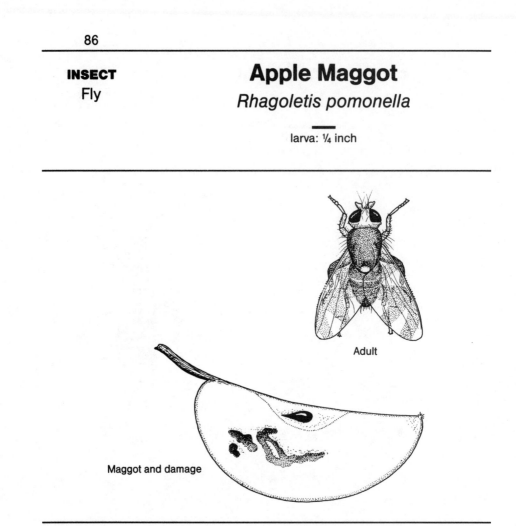

Adult

Maggot and damage

Range: Eastern United States and southern Canada.

Description: Adults are black with yellow legs, yellow markings across their abdomens, and zigzag bands across their wings; they are ¼ inch long. Eggs are laid singly in punctures in the apple skin. Larvae are white or yellowish and ¼ inch long.

Life Cycle: There are one to two generations per year. Brown pupae hibernate in the soil.

Host Plants: Apple, blueberry, cherry, plum.

Feeding Habits: Adults puncture fruit skin during egglaying. Larvae form winding tunnels while feeding within fruit pulp, often causing the entire fruit to rot.

Prevention and Control: Trap flies in jars filled with 1 part blackstrap molasses and 9 parts water. Hang jars in tree branches.

Cabbage Maggot
Hylemya brassicae

—

larva: ¼ inch

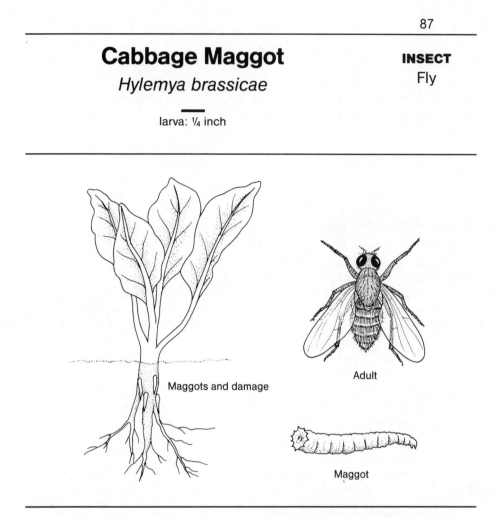

Maggots and damage

Adult

Maggot

Range: Western United States.

Description: Adults are gray with black stripes on their thoraxes, resembling houseflies. They are ¼ inch long. Eggs are white and are laid on plants near the soil surface. Larvae are white, blunt-ended, and ¼ inch long.

Life Cycle: There are two to three broods per year. Winter is passed as a pupa in the soil.

Host Plants: Broccoli, Brussels sprouts, cabbage, cauliflower, radish, turnip.

Feeding Habits: Maggots tunnel into roots and stems while feeding, causing plants to wilt and become susceptible to bacterial or fungal diseases.

Prevention and Control: Protect seedlings with a square of tar paper laid flat on the ground around the stem, or cover with screening. Dust with rock phosphate or with diatomaceous earth.

Insect Predators: Rove beetles.

Carrot Rust Fly
Psila rosae

larva: ⅓ inch

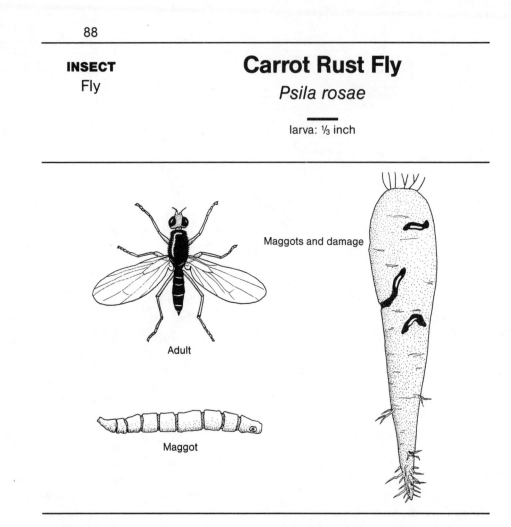

Adult

Maggots and damage

Maggot

Range: Throughout most of North America.

Description: Adults are black or green with yellow hair and yellow heads and legs; they reach ⅕ inch long. Eggs are laid in the crowns of plants. Larvae are yellow to white and ⅓ inch long.

Life Cycle: Two to three generations mature per year. Maggots or pupae hibernate in the soil.

Host Plants: Carrot, celery, parsley, parsnip.

Feeding Habits: Larvae chew roots, leaving reddish-brown excrement in their tunnels. Injured plants are dwarfed and often infested with soft-rot bacteria. They decompose quickly. Early plantings are particularly susceptible.

Prevention and Control: Sprinkle rock phosphate around the base of plants. Rotate. Do not plant alternate hosts for the flies to eat. A serious infestation may take up to seven years to eradicate.

Flower Flies, Hover Flies

SYRPHIDAE

adult: ½ inch

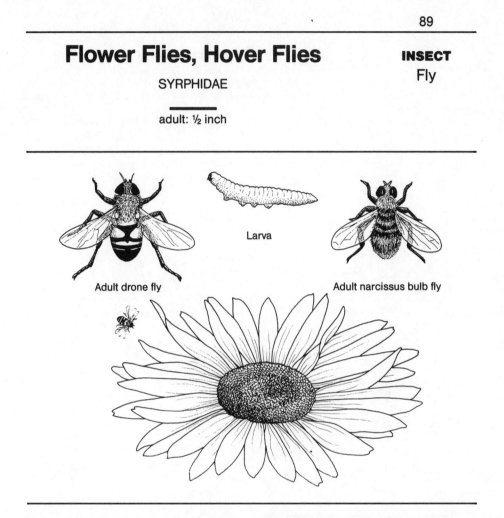

Larva

Adult drone fly

Adult narcissus bulb fly

Range: Various species throughout North America.

Description: Adults are black with yellow bands and are ⅓ to ½ inch long. They hover over flowers and dart away quickly. Eggs are white, oval, and laid singly or in groups on foliage. Larvae are green to gray or brown and ½ inch long.

Life Cycle: There are several generations per year. Most species hibernate in the pupal stage.

Feeding Habits: Adults feed on nectar. The larvae of most species feed on aphids, mealybugs, and other small insects.

Similar Insects: Bees and wasps (pages 23–27).

See photograph, page 279.

INSECT
Fly

Leafminers
Liriomyza spp.

—
adult: $\frac{1}{10}$ inch

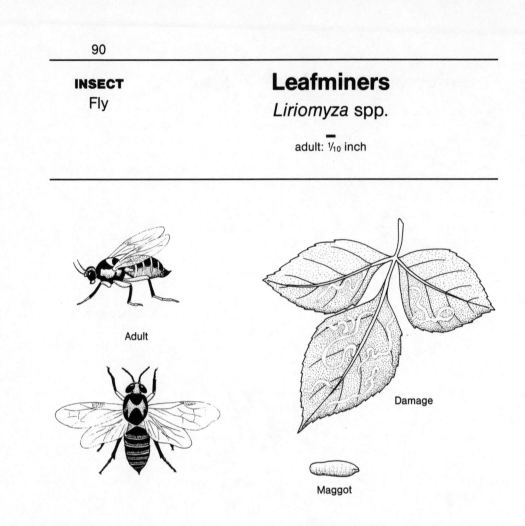

Adult

Maggot

Damage

Range: Various species throughout North America.

Description: Adults are black with yellow stripes and are $\frac{1}{10}$ inch long. Eggs are laid on leaf surfaces. Larvae are yellowish, stout, and wormlike.

Life Cycle: There are several generations per year. Leafminers hibernate in cocoons in the soil.

Host Plants: Bean, blackberry, cabbage, lettuce, pepper, potato, spinach, turnip.

Feeding Habits: Maggots mine beneath the surface of leaves, causing white tunnels to form. Related leafminers may chew until blotched areas form in the leaves.

Prevention and Control: Cover plants with floating row covers, such as Reemay, burying the edges in the soil. If this is impractical, remove and destroy infested leaves.

Mediterranean Fruit Fly
Ceratitis capitata

INSECT
Fly

larva: ¼ inch

Adult

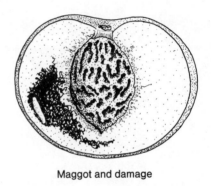

Maggot and damage

Maggot

Range: Southern half of United States.

Description: Adults are black with yellow abdomens and yellowish marks on their thoraxes; their wings are also banded with yellow. They reach ¼ inch long. Eggs are white and are deposited in holes in fruit rind. Larvae are whitish, legless, and ¼ inch long.

Life Cycle: There can be from 1 to 12 generations per year. Pupae or adults overwinter in the soil or in protected spots.

Host Plants: Many orchard fruit crops.

Feeding Habits: Maggots burrow into fruit pulp to feed, causing it to rot. Although infestations occasionally occur, a government control program has virtually eliminated the insects.

INSECT
Fly

Onion Maggot

Hylemya antiqua

---

larva: ⅓ inch

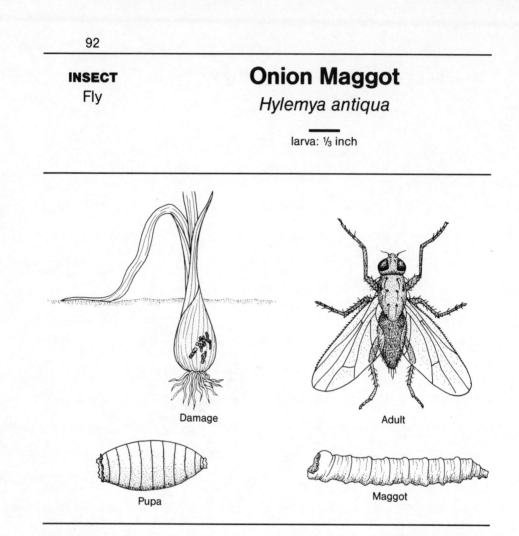

Damage

Adult

Pupa

Maggot

Range: Northern United States and southern Canada.

Description: Adults are gray or brown with humped backs and large wings and are ¼ inch long. Eggs are white and cylindrical, and are laid at the base of plants or in bulbs. Larvae are white, blunt-ended, and ⅓ inch long.

Life Cycle: There are two to three generations per year. The onion maggot hibernates as a pupa in the soil.

Host Plant: Onion.

Feeding Habits: Larvae tunnel into bulbs to feed, ruining crops and often killing young onions. Most damage is done in spring.

Prevention and Control: Apply diatomaceous earth to the base of the plants.

Pepper Maggot
Zonosemata electa

INSECT
Fly

—
adult: ⅓ inch

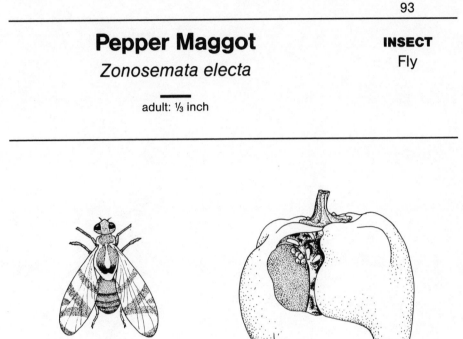

Adult

Maggot

Maggots and damage

Range: Eastern and southwestern United States.

Description: Adults are yellow with brown stripes on their wings and are ⅓ inch long. Eggs are white and curved, and are deposited in developing peppers. Larvae are white to yellow, small, and pointed.

Life Cycle: One generation matures per year. Winter is passed as a pupa in the soil.

Host Plants: Eggplant, pepper, tomato.

Feeding Habits: Maggots feed within peppers, causing them to decay or drop.

Prevention and Control: Sprinkle talc, diatomaceous earth, or rock phosphate on the fruits during egglaying periods. Remove and destroy infested fruits.

Robber Flies

ASILIDAE

adult: ¾ inch

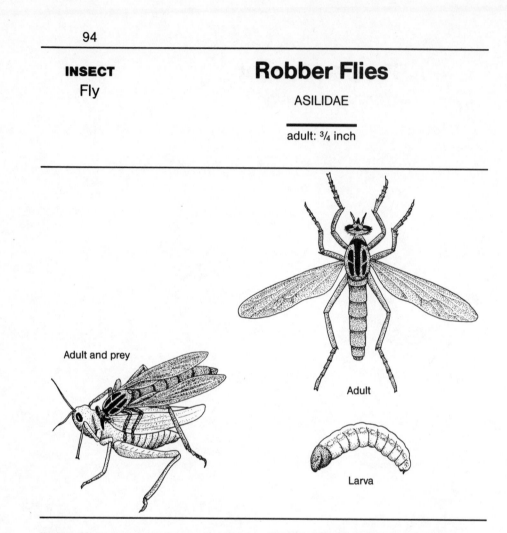

Adult and prey

Adult

Larva

Range: Various species throughout North America.

Description: Adults are gray (rarely, yellow and black) with stout beaks and hairy mouths. They produce a loud buzzing sound and are ½ to ¾ inch long. Eggs are whitish and are laid in the soil or on plants. Larvae are white, flat, and cylindrical.

Life Cycle: There is one generation per year, the life cycle requiring at least one year for completion. Most species hibernate as larvae in the soil.

Feeding Habits: Adults capture flying insects such as beetles, leafhoppers, butterflies, flies, and bugs. Larvae prey on white grubs or beetle pupae and sometimes feed on grasshopper eggs.

Tachinid Flies

TACHINIDAE

adult: ½ inch

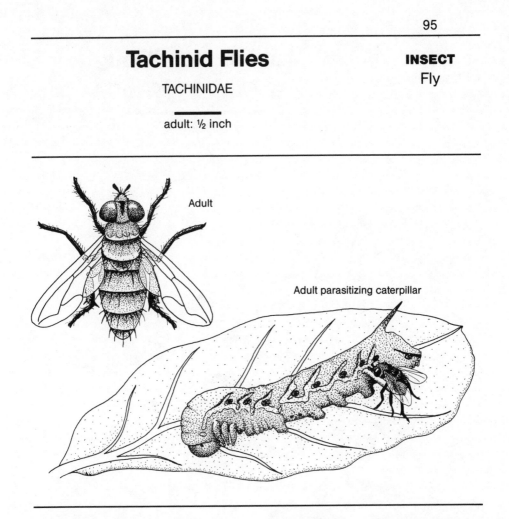

Adult

Adult parasitizing caterpillar

Range: Various species throughout North America.

Description: Adults are gray or brown with pale markings and are ⅓ to ½ inch long. They are strong fliers that walk rapidly on plant surfaces. Eggs are white and are deposited on foliage or on the body of the host. Larvae are grayish to greenish-white, thick-bodied, and spined.

Life Cycle: There are usually many generations per year. Larvae hibernate in the body of the host.

Feeding Habits: Larvae are internal parasites of many beetles, grasshoppers, bugs, caterpillars, and sawflies. They feed within the body of the host, sucking its body fluids and eventually killing the insect.

See photograph, page 279.

INSECT
Lacewing

Antlion, Doodlebug
Hesperoleon abdominalis

adult: 1½ inches

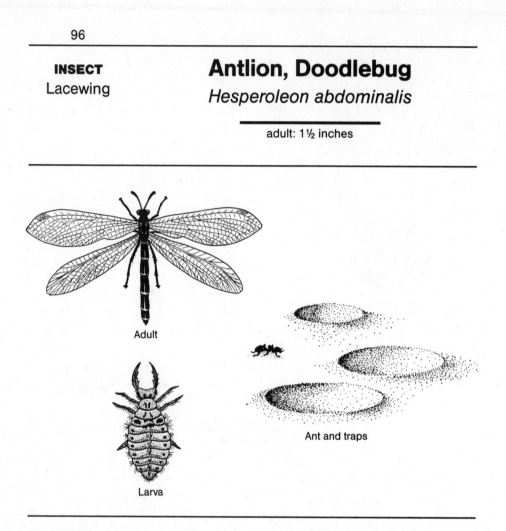

Adult

Larva

Ant and traps

Range: Various species throughout North America.

Description: Adults are dark brown with yellow just behind their heads; they have long, membranous wings and clubbed antennae, and are 1½ inches long. Eggs are laid in sand. Larvae are brown or grayish with plump abdomens and narrow thoraxes and heads; they build pits and walk backward.

Life Cycle: There is one generation per year. Life cycle may require up to two years. Eggs and larvae overwinter in sand.

Feeding Habits: Larvae trap and eat ants and other small insects.

See photograph, page 280.

Green Lacewing

Chrysopa spp.

adult: ¾ inch

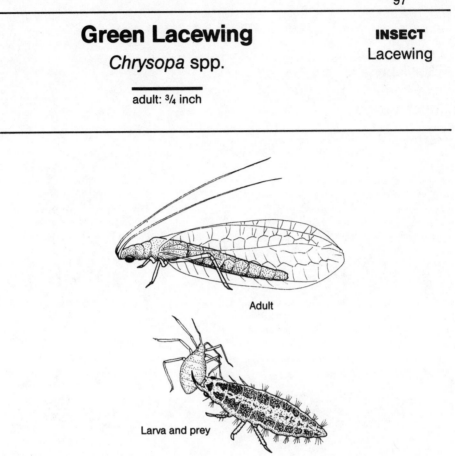

Adult

Larva and prey

Range: Various species throughout North America.

Description: Adults are pale green with slender bodies and delicate, long green wings. They reach ½ to ¾ inch long. Eggs are white and are laid on slender stalks on the undersides of leaves. Larvae are yellowish-gray with brown marks, tufts of hair, and long jaws.

Life Cycle: Three to four generations mature per year. The green lacewing passes the winter in the pupal stage.

Feeding Habits: Many adults and larvae prey on aphids, various larvae, and the eggs of other insects.

Beet Leafhopper
Circulifer tenellus

—

adult: ⅕ inch

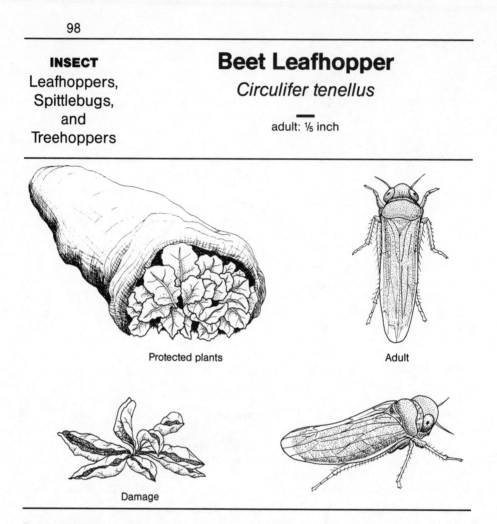

Protected plants

Adult

Damage

Range: Western North America, with similar species found elsewhere.

Description: Adults are greenish-yellow to brown, with darker irregular markings; they reach ⅕ inch long. Eggs are yellowish and are deposited in plant stems. Nymphs are pale green and are similar to the adults.

Life Cycle: There are several generations per year. Adults hibernate in weeds.

Host Plants: Beet, potato, tomato.

Feeding Habits: Adults and nymphs transmit curly top and tomato yellows while feeding, causing plants to be stunted and deformed.

Prevention and Control: Cover crops with floating row covers such as Reemay, burying the edges in the soil. If this is impractical, dust plants lightly with diatomaceous earth.

Insect Predators: Bigeyed bugs, some flies, and various wasps.

Similar Insect: Potato leafhopper (page 99).

Potato Leafhopper
Empoasca fabae

—
adult: ⅕ inch

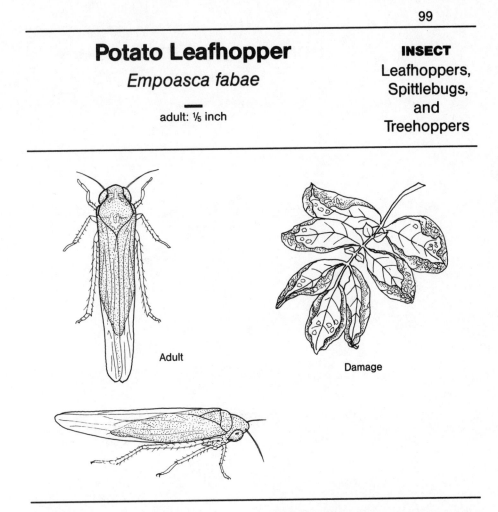

Adult

Damage

Range: Eastern North America.

Description: Adults are green with white spots on their heads, wings, and part of their thoraxes; they reach ⅕ inch long. Eggs are yellowish-white and are laid in veins on the undersides of leaves.

Life Cycle: There are two to four generations per year. Adults hibernate in garden trash and weeds.

Host Plants: Bean, celery, citrus, eggplant, potato, rhubarb.

Feeding Habits: Adults and nymphs transmit viral diseases to host plants while feeding. Infected leaves are curled and stippled or stunted and bleached. Citrus fruit rinds may be punctured or blemished.

Prevention and Control: Cover plants with floating row covers or netting in early summer. Diatomaceous earth may control the hoppers.

Similar Insect: Beet leafhopper (page 98).

INSECT
Leafhoppers,
Spittlebugs,
and
Treehoppers

Spittlebugs, Froghoppers

CERCOPIDAE

—

adult: ⅓ inch

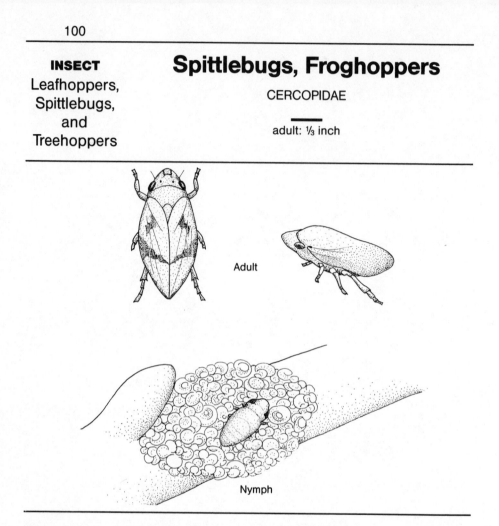

Adult

Nymph

Range: Various species throughout North America.

Description: Adults are brownish or green (often with stripes or bands on their wings), triangular, and ¼ to ⅓ inch long. Eggs are laid in grasses between the leaves and main stems. Nymphs are green and are surrounded by masses of froth.

Life Cycle: One generation matures per year. Winter is passed in the egg stage.

Host Plants: Corn, many garden vegetables, and small fruits.

Feeding Habits: Nymphs and adults may feed on some plants, but they are harmless.

Buffalo Treehopper
Stictocephala bubalus

—

adult: ¼ inch

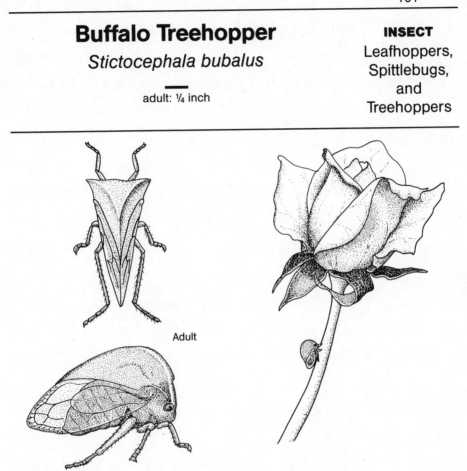

Adult

Range: Throughout North America.

Description: Adults are green with a hard, triangular hood covering the head and part of the abdomen. They are ¼ inch long. Eggs are yellow and are laid in C-shaped slits in bark. Nymphs are light green and spined.

Life Cycle: There is one generation per year. Eggs overwinter in bark and hatch the following spring.

Host Plants: Most fruit trees, potato, tomato.

Feeding Habits: Though treehopper feeding usually doesn't cause much damage, egg slits may seriously injure young fruit trees. Infested trees are scaly, cracked, and dwarfed.

Prevention and Control: Apply dormant-oil spray in early spring or dust foliage with diatomaceous earth.

Citrus Mealybug
Planococcus citri

—

adult: ¹/₁₀ inch

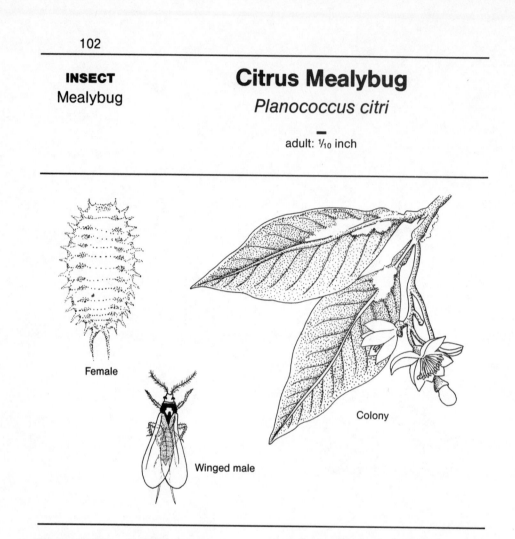

Female

Winged male

Colony

Range: Southern United States and California.

Description: Adults are yellowish and ¹/₁₀ inch long. They are covered with dense white powder and have short, irregular filaments of equal length around their bodies.

Life Cycle: Two to three generations mature per year. Winter is passed in the egg stage.

Host Plants: Avocado, citrus, potato.

Feeding Habits: Adults and nymphs feed on cell sap in twigs and foliage.

Prevention and Control: Spray fruit trees with water, soapy water, insecticidal soap, or kerosene emulsion.

Insect Predator: Mealybug destroyer.

Similar Insects: Mealybug destroyer (page 44), woolly apple aphid (page 31).

Comstock Mealybug
Pseudococcus comstocki

adult: ¼ inch

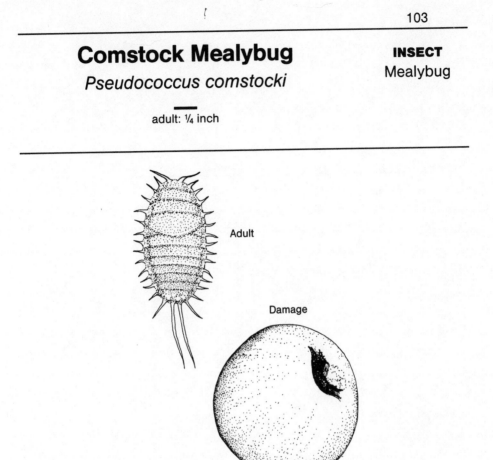

Adult

Damage

Range: Eastern United States and California. Other species throughout North America.

Description: Adults are white with short waxy spines, elliptically shaped, and ¼ inch long. Eggs are laid under bark.

Host Plants: Apple, grape, peach, pear.

Feeding Habits: Infested fruits are disfigured by feeding and may be covered with dark mold. Branches are infested near pruning scars, causing galls to form.

Prevention and Control: Spray foliage with water, soapy water, or insecticidal soap.

Insect Predators: Various chalcid wasps control the insects on grape.

Similar Insects: Mealybug destroyer (page 44), woolly apple aphid (page 31).

INSECT
Mealybug

Longtailed Mealybug
Pseudococcus adonidum

—
adult: 1/10 inch

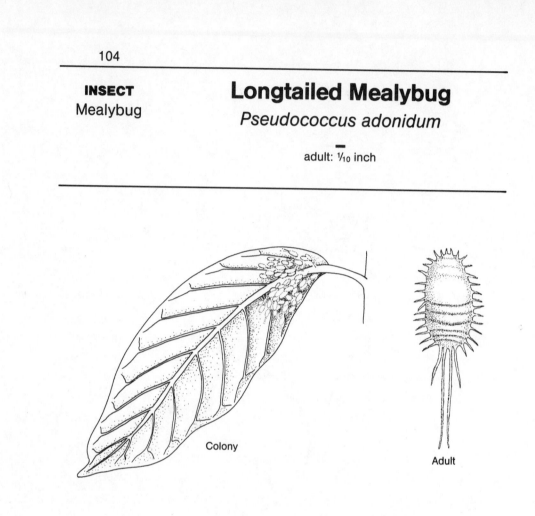

Colony

Adult

Range: Throughout North America, particularly in the South.

Description: Adults are white, waxy, and cottony, with very long anal filaments; they are 1/10 inch long. The young are born live.

Life Cycle: There are many generations per year. Winter is passed in all stages.

Host Plants: Avocado, banana, citrus, plum.

Feeding Habits: Mealybugs feed on fruits, foliage, and stems.

Prevention and Control: Spray plants with water, soapy water, or insecticidal soap.

Insect Predators: Chalcid wasps (*Anarhopus sydneyensis, Hungariella peregrina*).

Similar Insects: Mealybug destroyer (page 44), woolly apple aphid (page 31).

See photograph, page 280.

Pear Psylla
Psylla pyricola

—
adult: 1/10 inch

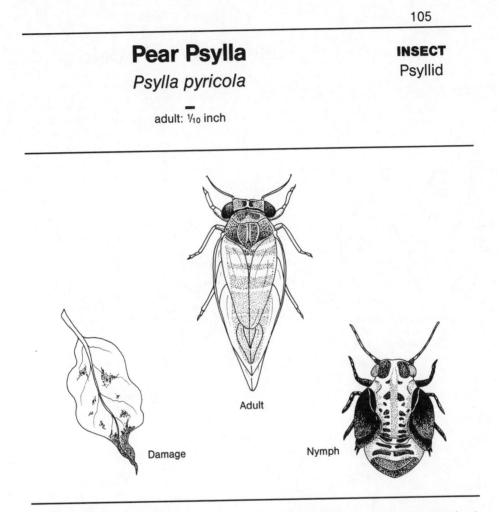

Adult

Damage

Nymph

Range: Eastern United States and the Pacific Northwest. Similar species distributed elsewhere.

Description: Adults are reddish-brown with green or red markings and transparent wings. They are 1/10 inch long. Eggs are yellowish and are laid at the base of buds, on twigs, or on the upper surfaces of leaves near the veins.

Life Cycle: There are three to five generations per year. Adults hibernate in garden litter.

Host Plants: Pear, quince; similar species attack potato, tomato.

Feeding Habits: Nymphs and adults feed on foliage and fruits, excreting honeydew which encourages the growth of sooty mold. Infested leaves develop brown spots; fruits are scarred and buds may fail to develop.

Prevention and Control: Spray trees with dormant oil in the spring or, if pests are well established, dust with limestone or diatomaceous earth.

Insect Predator: Chalcid wasp (*Trechnites insidiosus*).

California Red Scale
Aonidiella aurantii

—
adult: $\frac{1}{12}$ inch

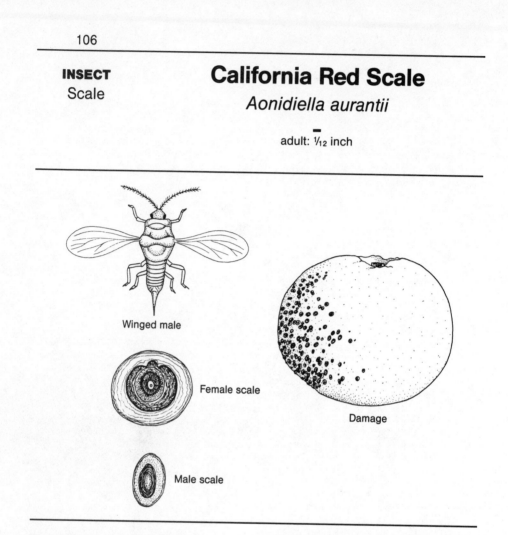

Winged male

Female scale

Male scale

Damage

Range: Southern United States.

Description: Adults are reddish-brown, tortoise-shaped, with a small nipple at the center of the caplike coverings, and $\frac{1}{12}$ inch long. Nymphs are brown. They are borne live and move about for several hours before beginning to feed.

Life Cycle: There are many broods. Winter is passed in all stages.

Host Plants: Citrus, fig, grape, walnut.

Feeding Habits: Scales feed on all parts of trees, including fruits. They inject a toxic substance, causing leaves and fruits to develop yellow spots. Citrus is particularly susceptible to serious injury.

Prevention and Control: Apply a dormant-oil spray in early spring.

Insect Predators: Various chalcid wasps (*Aphytis lingnanensis, A. melinus,* and *Prospaltella perniciosi*).

Cottonycushion Scale
Icerya purchasi

—
adult: ⅕ inch

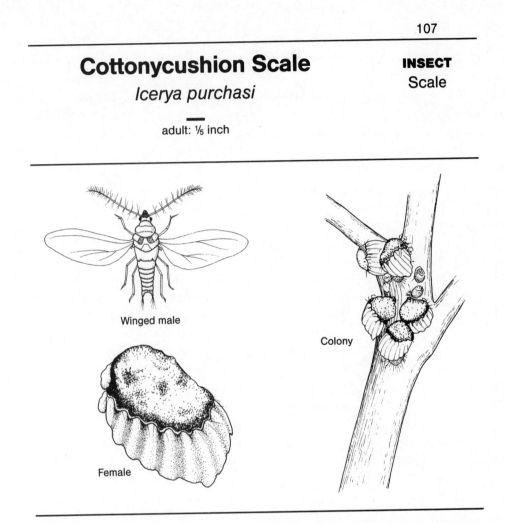

Winged male

Female

Colony

Range: Southern United States.

Description: Adults are reddish-brown and ⅕ inch long. Females are covered with a white, ridged mass that holds up to 800 red eggs. Nymphs are red with black legs, antennae, and long hairs.

Life Cycle: There are three generations per year. Winter is passed in all stages.

Host Plants: Almond, apple, apricot, citrus, fig, peach, pecan, pepper, potato, quince, walnut.

Feeding Habits: Scales attach themselves to stems and bark to feed.

Prevention and Control: Spray with dormant oil early in spring, before growth begins.

Insect Predators: Many lady beetles, particularly vedalia.

See photograph, page 280.

San Jose Scale

Quadraspidiotus perniciosus

—

adult: $\frac{1}{12}$ inch

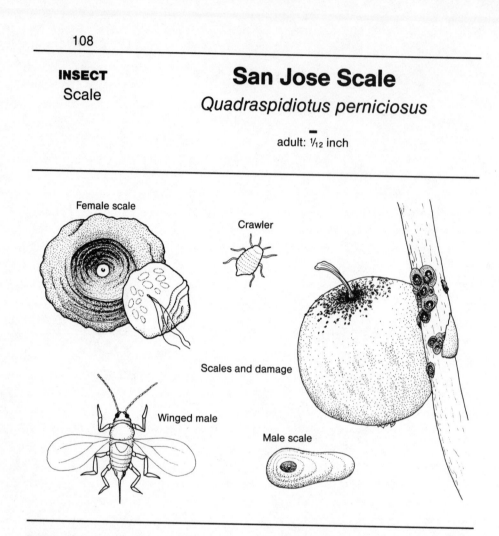

Female scale

Crawler

Scales and damage

Winged male

Male scale

Range: United States and southern Canada.

Description: Adults are grayish, with a dark projection in the centers and small yellow pouches beneath. Nymphs are yellow and borne live.

Life Cycle: Up to six generations mature per year. Dark nymphs overwinter on bark.

Host Plants: Apple, cherry, peach, pear, pecan, quince.

Feeding Habits: Compact colonies feed on bark and fruits, often causing a red, inflamed area to form around them. If left unchecked, trees may die.

Prevention and Control: Spray with dormant oil in early spring, just before blossoms open.

Citrus Thrips
Scirtothrips citri

·
adult: ¹⁄₅₀ inch

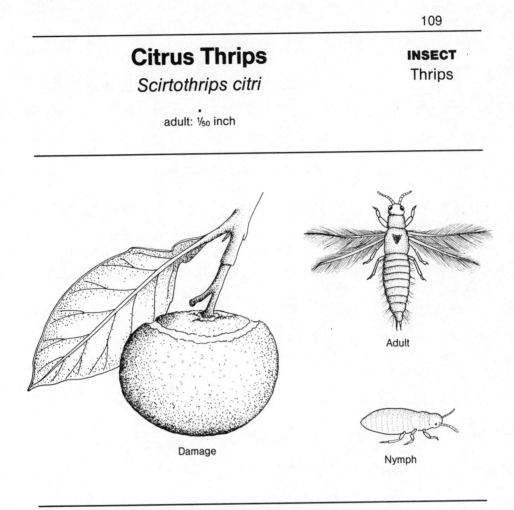

Damage

Adult

Nymph

Range: Southwestern United States.

Description: Adults are brownish-orange with dark hoods and abdominal margins (similar species are black) and reach ¹⁄₅₀ inch long. Eggs are kidney-shaped and are thrust into young leaves, stems, twigs, or fruits. Nymphs are yellowish-orange with red eyes.

Life Cycle: There are many generations per year, a new one emerging every two or three weeks. Overwinters in the egg stage, except in the warmest regions where it breeds year-round.

Host Plants: Citrus, date, grape, peach.

Feeding Habits: Thrips suck juices from plant tissue, causing flowers to become streaked with brown and wither prematurely. Fruit develops a ring around the blossom end.

Prevention and Control: Apply a dust of sulfur or diatomaceous earth if the thrips are truly injuring fruit crops. Usually this is unnecessary.

INSECT
Weevil

Apple Curculio
Tachypterellus quadrigibbus

—

adult: 1/10 inch

Adult

Adults and damage

Range: Eastern North America.

Description: Adults are brownish-red and are humped with long snouts; they are 1/10 inch long. Eggs are laid in punctures placed close together on the fruit surface. Larvae are white or grayish and wormlike.

Life Cycle: One generation matures per year. Adults hibernate in sheltered spots.

Host Plants: Apple, pear, quince.

Feeding Habits: Larvae feed and pupate in fallen fruit or injured fruit still on the tree.

Prevention and Control: Shake branches and collect curculios as they fall on a sheet below, or dust with diatomaceous earth.

Similar Insect: Plum curculio (page 114).

Bean Weevil
Acanthoscelides obtectus

adult: ⅕ inch

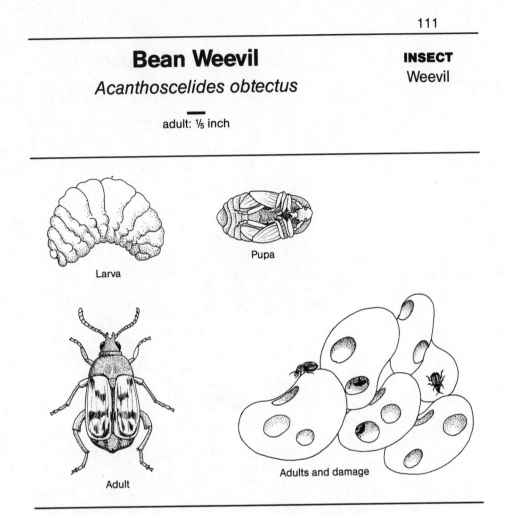

Larva

Pupa

Adult

Adults and damage

Range: Throughout North America.

Description: Adults are brown or dark green with darker mottling; they are flat and reach ¹⁄₁₀ to ⅕ inch long. Eggs are white and are laid on beans. Larvae are whitish.

Life Cycle: Outdoors, there is one brood per season; in stored beans, weevils breed continuously. Outdoors, adults hibernate under garden trash.

Host Plants: Bean, pea.

Feeding Habits: Many larvae feed within each bean seed, pupate, then emerge through a small hole.

Prevention and Control: Dry seed, then freeze for 48 hours after harvesting, or heat at 135°F for 3 to 4 hours.

INSECT
Weevil

Cabbage Curculio
Ceutorhynchus rapae

—
adult: ⅛ inch

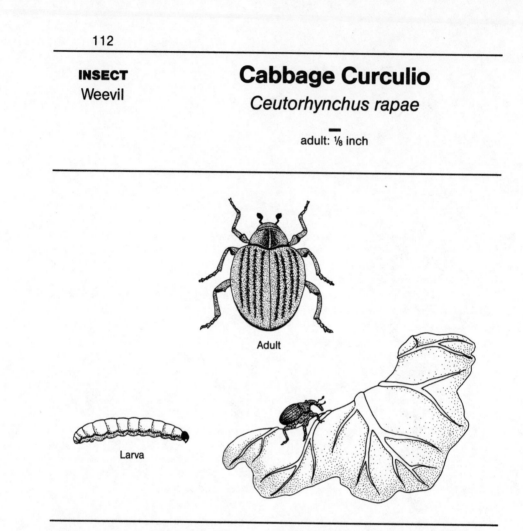

Adult

Larva

Range: Throughout North America.

Description: Adults are black with bluish or yellowish hairs; they have curved, slender beaks with antennae in the middle and grow to ⅛ inch long. Eggs are gray, oval, and are inserted in plant stems. Larvae are whitish.

Life Cycle: There are several generations per year. Adults hibernate in the soil.

Host Plants: Broccoli, cabbage, cauliflower, turnip.

Feeding Habits: Adults and grubs mine stalks and feed on leaves, but controls are seldom necessary.

Carrot Weevil

Listronotus oregonensis

—
adult: ⅕ inch

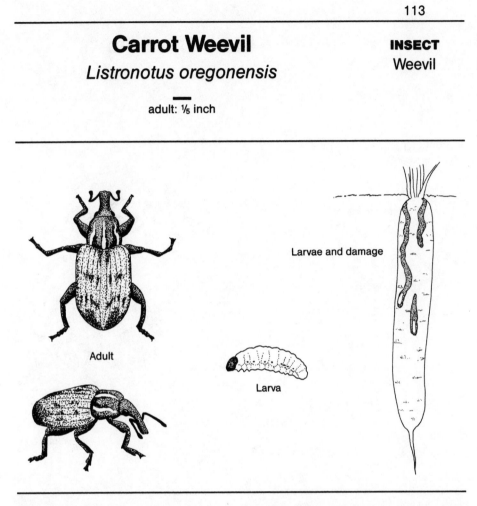

Adult

Larva

Larvae and damage

Range: Eastern and central North America.

Description: Adults are dark brown to coppery, hard-shelled, and ⅕ inch long. Eggs are white and are deposited in the stalks of leaves. Larvae are white with brown heads, curved, and legless.

Life Cycle: There are two generations per year. Adult beetles overwinter in grass and garden litter.

Host Plants: Carrot, celery, dill, parsley.

Feeding Habits: Grubs mine into the tops of carrot roots or into celery hearts to feed. Their zigzag paths destroy much of the plant's tissue.

Prevention and Control: Crop rotation and cultivation are the only effective organic controls.

Similar Insect: Vegetable weevil (page 115).

INSECT
Weevil

Plum Curculio
Conotrachelus nenuphar

—

adult: ¼ inch

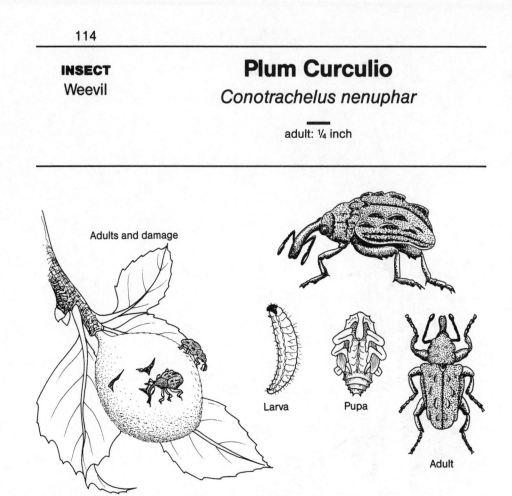

Adults and damage

Larva   Pupa

Adult

Range: Eastern North America.

Description: Adults are dark brown with fine, white hairs on their bodies; they have sculptured wing covers and slightly curved, thick beaks. They grow to ¼ inch long. Eggs are white to gray, elliptical, and are laid beneath crescent-shaped slits in the skin of fruits.

Life Cycle: There are one to two generations per year. Adults hibernate in the soil.

Host Plants: Apple, blueberry, cherry, peach, pear, plum, quince.

Feeding Habits: Adults damage fruits during egglaying. Larvae mine within fruits to feed for several weeks before leaving to pupate in the soil. Brown rot develops, causing fruits to be deformed or to drop prematurely.

Prevention and Control: Knock weevils from the trees onto a sheet. Pick up and destroy dropped fruits. Tanglefoot around trunks helps keep the curculios out of the trees.

Similar Insect: Apple curculio (page 110).

See photograph, page 281.

Vegetable Weevil

Listroderes costirostris obliquus

adult: ½ inch

Larvae and damage

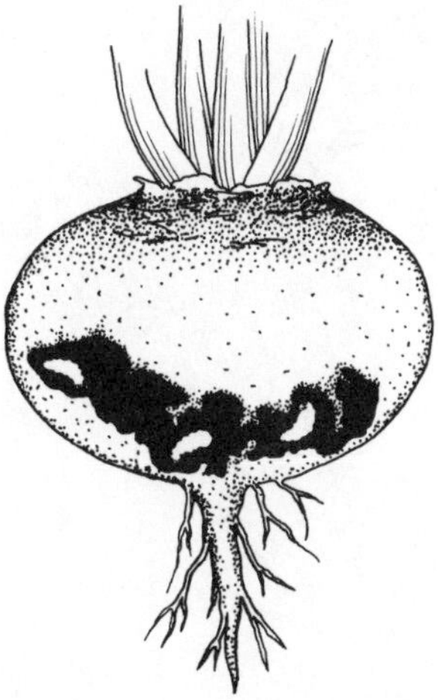

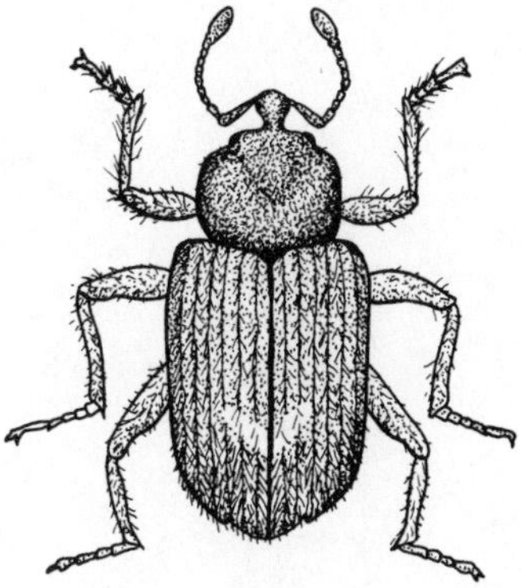

Adult

Range: Southern United States.

Description: Adults are gray to brownish with a lighter V-shaped mark near the tips of their wing covers; they are ½ inch long. Eggs are laid on stems and crowns of plants. Larvae are greenish, sluglike, and ¼ inch long.

Life Cycle: There is one generation per year. Adults pass the winter sheltered by garden litter and weeds.

Host Plants: Beet, cabbage, carrot, lettuce, onion, potato, radish, spinach, tomato, turnip.

Feeding Habits: Grubs and adults begin feeding on the crowns of plants, then chew foliage, leaving only stems.

Prevention and Control: Dust plants with a small amount of diatomaceous earth.

Similar Insect: Carrot weevil (page 113).

INSECT
Whitefly

Greenhouse Whitefly
Trialeurodes vaporariorum

—
adult: 1/12 inch

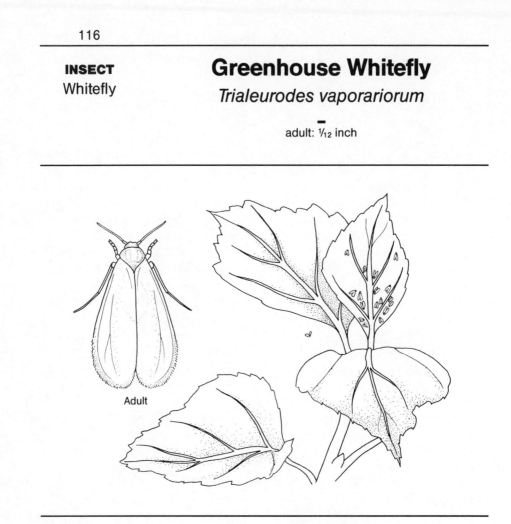

Adult

Range: Southern and coastal United States.

Description: Adults are white, covered with a powdery substance, mothlike, and 1/20 to 1/12 inch long. Eggs are yellow, cone-shaped, and are laid on small projections on the undersides of leaves. Nymphs are green, translucent, and flat, with fine waxy filaments.

Life Cycle: There are many broods each year. The greenhouse whitefly hibernates in the nymph stage.

Host Plants: Most fruits and vegetables.

Feeding Habits: Nymphs and adults suck the juices from succulent new growth and cause plants to become weak and susceptible to disease.

Prevention and Control: Dust with tobacco dust or spray with tobacco tea. Use the commercially available parasite, *Encarsia formosa,* to control whiteflies in the garden and greenhouse. Yellow sticky traps also provide control.

See photograph, page 281.

Eastern Field Wireworm
Limonius agonus

larva: ½ inch

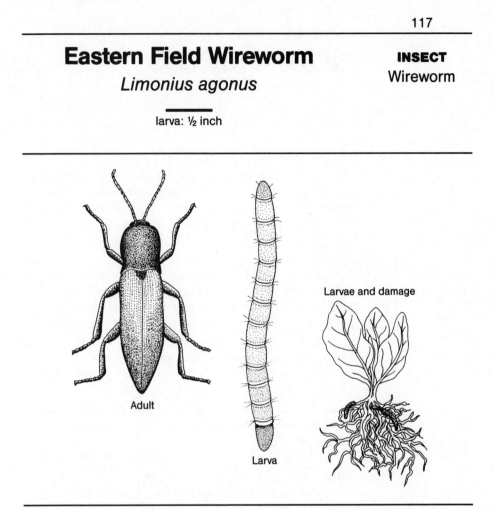

Adult

Larva

Larvae and damage

Range: Eastern North America. Similar species throughout North America.

Description: Larvae are brown to yellowish with shiny, hard skin. They are cylindrical and reach ⅓ to ½ inch long. Adults are black to grayish or brown with dark spots on their heads and bands across their wing covers; they are ½ inch long. Eggs are laid in damp soil several inches beneath the surface.

Life Cycle: There is one generation per year, the life cycle requiring one to six years to complete. Adult beetles overwinter in cells in the soil.

Host Plants: Bean, beet, carrot, corn, lettuce, onion, pea, potato, strawberry.

Feeding Habits: Larvae chew seed, feed on underground roots and tubers, and burrow into other plant parts.

Prevention and Control: Trap wireworms in pieces of potato scattered around the garden. Do not follow sod with strawberries.

Similar Insects: Millipedes (page 120).

Non-Insects

There are a number of small creatures in the garden that crawl about as insects, feed as insects, and even resemble insects, but when you look closely, you realize they are *not* insects. Some belong to a different class in the phylum Arthropoda, while others, lacking a segmented body or hard exoskeleton, are members of an entirely different phylum.

Centipedes are close relatives of insects. They have antennae, and they breathe through spiracles and a system of branched tubes. They have a distinct head and jointed legs. But they have only two body parts, no wings and, instead of 6 legs, they have 30 or more. Therefore they are members of the class Chilopoda, not Insecta.

Millipedes, with up to 400 legs, are also close relatives of insects. They make up an entirely different class, Diplopoda. They live in the soil and feed primarily on dead plant material, although they will occasionally eat roots, tubers, and fruits.

Mites are the smallest creatures you can actually see in the garden. If you were to look at one under a microscope, you would see that they have four pairs of legs, no antennae, and no thorax. They resemble tiny ticks and, with those insects, belong to the class Arachnida.

Slugs and *snails* are the largest soil-dwelling creatures that might be mistaken for insects. They tend to feed on plants and they have tiny projections that roughly resemble antennae, but, since they are soft-bodied and without legs at any time in their life cycle, they are classed in a separate phylum, Mollusca.

Garden Centipede, Garden Symphylan

Scutigerella immaculata

adad NON-INSECT

adult: ▬ ¼ inch

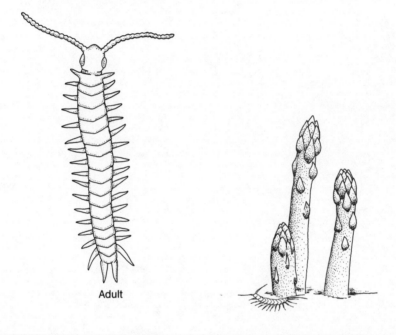

Adult

Range: Throughout North America.

Description: Adults are white, flat, and 12-legged, with long antennae. They are active and reach ¼ inch long. Eggs are white and are laid in clusters 1 foot deep in the soil.

Life Cycle: There are many generations per year. Winter is spent in the adult stage in the soil.

Host Plants: Asparagus, cucumber, lettuce, radish, tomato.

Feeding Habits: Symphylans sever small roots and scar underground plant parts as they feed. Plants become stunted and may even die.

Prevention and Control: Flooding may control them, or try a tobacco infusion poured into the soil.

NON-INSECT

Millipedes

DIPLOPODA

———

adult: ½ inch

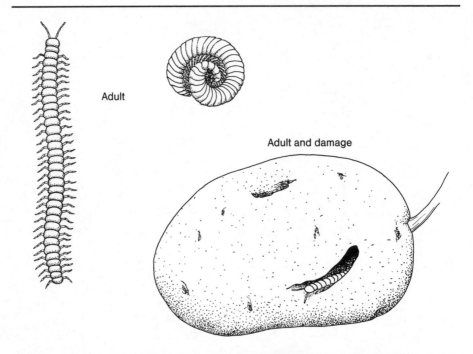

Adult

Adult and damage

Range: Throughout North America.

Description: Adults are brown to pinkish-brown or gray; their long, round, wormlike bodies have many segments, with two or more legs per segment. They are found coiled like a spring and are ½ inch long. Eggs are translucent, sticky, and are laid in clusters in or on the soil.

Life Cycle: There is one generation per year. Winter is passed in the soil.

Host Plants: Bean, cabbage, carrot, corn, potato, strawberry, tomato, turnip.

Feeding Habits: Most species feed on decayed plant material, but they may eat plant roots or enter fruits and tubers in or on damp soil. Seedlings are often severed. Fungal diseases attack larger plants. Some millipedes are predators that eat many kinds of soil insects.

Prevention and Control: Drench infested soil with tobacco tea if millipedes become a problem.

Similar Insect: Eastern field wireworm (page 117).

Mites, Spider Mites

ARACHNIDA

adult: ¹⁄₅₀ inch

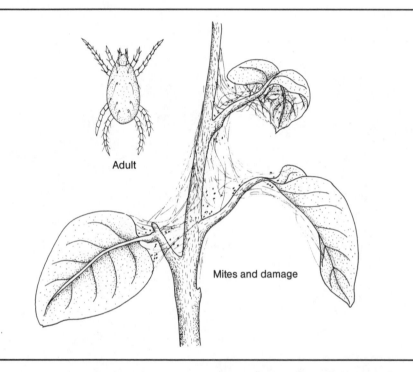

Adult

Mites and damage

Range: Throughout North America.

Description: Adults are reddish-brown or pale in color. They are spiderlike, with eight legs and no antennae, thoraxes, or wings. They reach about ¹⁄₁₅₀ to ¹⁄₅₀ inch long. Eggs are laid at the base of plants or on leaves and buds.

Life Cycle: There are many generations per year, the life cycle often requiring only a few days. Adult mites hibernate in debris or under bark.

Host Plants: Many, particularly fruit trees and various small fruits.

Feeding Habits: Mites feed on leaves, fruits, and roots. Infested leaves become silvery and may turn yellow. They curl and may be covered with a fine web. Fruit may be russeted, dry, and rough or deformed. A few species of mites form blisters on young leaves.

Prevention and Control: Spray cold water on leaves, or try a slurry of wheat flour, buttermilk, and water.

Insect Predators: Lacewings, lady beetles, predatory mites. All of these are also commercially available.

NON-INSECT

Slugs and Snails

MOLLUSCA

---

adult: 3 inches

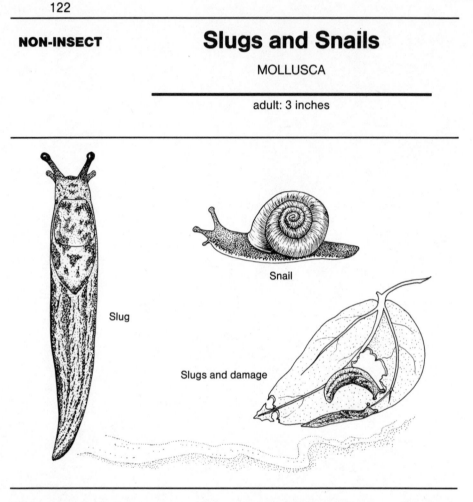

Slug

Snail

Slugs and damage

Range: Various species throughout North America.

Description: Adults are gray to black or brown, soft-bodied, often with a soft hump in their centers, and have eyes at the tips of small tentacles. Two other tentacles are used for smelling. They reach from ½ inch to 3 inches long. Snails have a single shell; slugs have none.

Life Cycle: Several years are required to complete the life cycle. Winter is spent in the soil or in garden litter.

Host Plants: Many.

Feeding Habits: Most slugs and snails feed at night, spending the day beneath decaying boards or in garden trash. They scrape holes in foliage, and may cause extensive damage.

Prevention and Control: Handpick slugs and snails when they emerge in the evenings. Place shallow saucers of stale beer in the garden to drown them. Dust with diatomaceous earth for more serious infestations.

Non-Insect Predators: Predatory snails.

See photograph, page 281.

Diseases

An Overview

Plant diseases are distressing. Identifying problems caused by insects, poor nutrition, and even environmental stresses seems much easier than identifying diseases. Potato beetles are quite visible, after all, but no one can see a virus or most fungi and bacteria. Besides, as good gardeners know, if soils are healthy and the year is good, diseases just aren't a big problem.

If you keep your soil fertile and friable, time plantings well, rotate intelligently, and use careful cultural practices, you won't see many diseases in the garden. Ignoring diseases and deciding that it's better to work on the soil than pore over descriptions of diseases and their symptoms is sometimes a perfectly reasonable course of action. However, if a disease is persistent, if it recurs year after year on crop after crop, you would be wise to learn what it is, how it works, and how to eliminate or discourage it.

This section is intended to help guide you through that tricky process. Using a fair amount of observation, some thought, an occasional good guess or two, and plenty of page turning, you should be able to drastically reduce or avoid disease occurrence. You may not always be certain whether a tomato plant is hosting fusarium wilt fungi or bacterial blight, for example, but at least you'll be able to narrow the problem down to these two diseases and know which actions are likely to be effective in both the long and short term. The table on pages 136–139, Common Diseases of Garden Vegetables, should help. Now let's look at the major types of disease.

Bacteria
Bacteria are microscopic primitive plants. Most are one-celled, though some have more than one cell. They reproduce by division of their nuclei. The cell wall is surrounded by a material called slime, a capsule, or a

microcapsule. This material is very often the cause of disease in the host.

While bacteria do not reproduce sexually, and thus cannot evolve as a consequence of hybridization, they do mutate easily in response to factors such as exposure to ultraviolet light and the chemical composition of their environment. This mutation can create new diseases and complicate control.

Bacteria enter plants through openings such as pores and wounds. They cause three major types of plant disease: *wilting,* as a consequence of invading and plugging the vascular system; excessive and abnormal growth, as exemplified by *galls;* and death of plant tissue, as shown by *rots, spots,* and *internal blights.*

Fungi
Fungi cause the majority of plant diseases. As a group, these plants are distinguished by their lack of chlorophyll. Since they can't make food for themselves, they, like us, rely on the nutrition contained in other organisms.

Some fungi, called *saprophytes,* live only on organic matter that is already dead. Many are allies in your compost pile and soil, organisms that ingest and break down organic material into forms that other organisms can use. While true saprophytes don't cause plant disease, some pathogenic (disease-causing) fungi are referred to as saprophytic in action because they produce byproducts that kill cells in advance of their spread through the plant. Once the cells have been killed, the nutrients they contain are available to the invading fungus. Some fungi are *facultative saprophytes,* meaning that while they normally prey on living organisms, they can also live on dead material. Pathogens that live all summer in garden plants but overwinter on dead litter are facultative saprophytes.

Parasites are dependent on living organisms. A

DISEASES
An Overview

facultative parasite can live on both dead and living material but, unlike a facultative saprophyte, spends more time preying on dead than living matter. By contrast, *obligate parasites* live only on living material.

Fungi have bodies composed of branching filaments, or cylindrical tubes, called *hyphae.* The outer cell walls of hyphae are rigid and contain chitin or cellulose. Growth of hyphae occurs at their tips. A group of hyphae form a *mycelium,* and a group of mycelia is called a *thallus.* Some fungi reproduce asexually from the growth of sections of hyphae called *sclerotia,* while others make reproductive units called *spores.* Asexual spores are formed by the division of cell nuclei, while sexual spores are formed by the union of two gene cells.

Most fungi reproduce both sexually and asexually, making different spores to guarantee their survival in almost any situation. In general, asexual spores are produced in the best growing conditions. These spores, sometimes called *summer spores,* are ready to begin growth alomst immediately upon their release from the parent organism. Wind, rain, or animals transport them to new sites where, if conditions are favorable, they germinate and begin to feed.

Spores that can remain alive, although dormant, until they encounter good germinating conditions and an appropriate host are called *resting spores.* Most resting spores are formed sexually, and some fungi don't produce them until signaled by the environment that winter or hard times are approaching. Some dormant spores can remain viable, or capable of germination, for 20 years or more.

Fungal diseases that are soilborne and spend most of their lives on roots and debris underground very often produce swimming spores, or *zoospores.* But aboveground pathogens also produce swimming spores that navigate

DISEASES
An Overview

through dew and rain. These fungi also produce wind-borne spores, *conidiospores,* in drier conditions.

When a spore lands on an appropriate host, it can germinate in an hour or two, or wait for better growing conditions such as a film of water, daylight, correct temperatures, or optimum humidity. A germ tube, or hypha, grows from the spore and usually enters the plant through a wound or natural opening. Some fungi exude a chemical that breaks down surface cells, allowing the pathogen to enter. Others form a *penetration peg,* a strong hypha that is anchored to the leaf with a sticky substance. The anchor gives the free tip enough leverage so that it can bore into the plant tissue.

Pathogenic fungi that kill cells in leaves often restrict photosynthesis and metabolic activities. Many release toxins or enzymes that break down cell structure, producing rot in seeds, roots, and fruits. Others plug the *xylem,* or water-carrying vessels, by destroying the cell walls or building up such large populations that the fungus itself fills the vessel. Galls and smuts often attack plant *meristems,* the areas where new growth occurs.

Nematodes

Nematodes are actually microscopic animals, but their mode of action and control warrant their inclusion in the disease section. They have unsegmented, muscular, wormlike bodies. Of the several thousand species now identified, only a few hundred are injurious to plants. As obligate parasites, they only reproduce in living organisms. However, they can remain dormant for long periods of time—more than 30 years in some species.

Nematodes have stylets that pierce plant tissue. Some species excrete a digestive juice that rots cells prior to feeding. Others exude substances that stimulate adjacent cells to enlarge or multiply abnormally. As

DISEASES
An Overview

vectors, they carry many viral diseases. But even when they don't carry disease, the small holes they make are open wounds that allow many secondary organisms to enter the plant.

Nematodes reproduce both sexually and parthenogenically, or without benefit of males. Eggs are released in the soil or plant tissue. Larvae hatch from the eggs, reaching adult status within a few days to a few weeks. Parthenogenic nematodes don't reach sexual maturity until they feed on a living host. In cold climates, they overwinter as eggs or larvae.

Although they can move, nematodes are so tiny that they rarely travel more than a foot through the soil. They are usually introduced to a piece of land by infected planting stock, infested soil, or running water.

Viruses
Viruses are composed of genetic material (DNA or RNA) and a protein casing. They do not divide to reproduce. Instead, their genetic material causes host cells to make more viruses. Viruses are obligate parasites: Reproduction or, more accurately, multiplication, can only occur in a living host. But even when inactive, some viruses can remain in a viable state for as long as 50 years in dead plant material.

Most viruses are carried by insect vectors. Nematodes also carry them, and a fungus transmits the virus that gives lettuce a disease called big vein. Dodder, a parasitic weed, transmits viruses as it spreads from host to host. Seeds may carry viruses, and infected propagating stock is certain to produce infected progeny. Mechanical transmission is also possible.

More than 300 viruses have been identified, but the tendency of viruses to mutate allows for numerous strains. As a result, plant resistance to a particular virus may be only a temporary condition. The three broad symptoms of viral infection are *yellowing, stunting,* and *malformations.*

DISEASES
An Overview

Mosaic patterns, ring spots, and more uniform paleness are all forms of yellowing. Stunting can be generalized or confined to one type of organ or location. Malformations include leaf rolls, puckering, and "shoestring" (extremely narrow leaves).

Using the Entries

Diseases listed here are the most common in the United States and southern Canada. They are categorized by type of causative organism (bacterium, fungus, nematode, or virus) and alphabetized by common name(s) within each category. To avoid confusion, Latin names are also given for each organism.

A list of host plants is given, but it can't always be complete. Some diseases affect so many plants that a full list would fill the page. However, when an organism affects members of different families, these crops are listed. This information is important not only for identification but for planning rotations. If the same organism causes diseases in both lettuce and potatoes, for example, rotating these crops only serves to build populations by providing a continuous host.

Descriptions of symptoms are as graphic as possible. 'Signs' are included with symptoms. A disease sign is the visible presence of the organism. For example, you can see the spreading white body of a powdery mildew or the slimy bacterial mass of a blight. These visible portions are signs. Symptoms are effects. The wilting, drooping leaves of a plant with bacterial blight, or yellowed dwarfing caused by a virus, are symptoms.

Symptoms are variable. A given disease can't be eliminated from consideration simply because the written description differs a bit from what you are seeing. For one thing, we all perceive differently; what looks yucky and slimy to you may only look slightly wet to me. The same disease can also look very different depending on envi-

DISEASES
An Overview

ronmental conditions, age and general health of the host plant, and even sub-species, or race, of the disease organism itself. Spots caused by the same organism can look large and distinct on plants in one area, but small and vaguely defined in another. However, if a pathogen is said to produce spots and a plant is unmarred, you'd be wise to continue looking for the cause of the trouble.

Environmental and nutritional factors often set the stage for disease attack. In some cases, you can prevent further outbreaks by manipulating these elements. If plants contract a disease that is most common when nitrogen levels are too high, for example, subsequent plantings can be made in areas where nitrogen levels are lower. Plants can also be afflicted with "diseases" that are actually *disorders* caused by environmental fluctuations or nutritional deficiencies. Refer to the table on the facing page, Common Disorders of Vegetable Crops, for help in identifying these disorders.

The prevention and control measures listed range from instructions as simple as removing affected leaves to the bother of changing rotational patterns. Throughout, the suggestions assume a desire to permanently rid your plants of the pathogen while saving as much of the crop as possible or feasible. In those cases where tolerating a disease for the sake of a small yield is not sensible in the long term, the gardener is advised to pull the whole plant, sometimes including roots and surrounding soil, and remove it from the garden. Similarly, if an organism can reproduce after being subjected to a hot compost (one that sustains temperatures of 160°F for three to four days), burn the host or throw it out with the trash.

Terminology

Unfamiliar words can be intimidating. Plant pathology is normally discussed in language that few people have in their working vocabularies. Most of the unfamiliar words

COMMON DISORDERS OF VEGETABLE CROPS

Condition	Crop	Symptoms	Cause
Black Heart	Beet, Turnip	Darkening in center, sometimes hollow	Boron deficiency; sometimes potassium or phosphorus deficiency
	Potato	Same	Lack of oxygen
	Celery	Same	Fluctuating soil moisture; calcium deficiency
Blasting	All Flowers	Buds or flowers drop prematurely	Soil too wet or dry
	Onion	Leaf tips bleach, brown and wither	Bright light after cloudy, wet conditions
Blossom-End Rot	Tomato, Pepper, Cucurbits	Dark, sunken area at blossom end of fruit	Dry conditions after wet; calcium deficiency
Cracked Stem	Celery	Stem cracks	Boron deficiency
Hollow Heart	Crucifers	Hollow stem	Boron deficiency
Sunscald	Tomato, Pepper	White area appears, blisters before secondary rotting occurs	Excessive loss of foliage; heavy pruning or trellising of tomatoes
Tipburn	Lettuce, Potato	Leaf tips brown	Bright light after cloudy, wet conditions; potassium deficiency; calcium imbalance

you'll find in the disease entries are descriptive. Plant pathologists use these terms because they carry a fairly complete meaning in the smallest possible package. For example, it's easier to use the word *haustorium* rather than say that the fungus in question has a specialized

DISEASES
An Overview

kind of hypha, or filament, which penetrates the cells of the host plant and absorbs nutrition from them.

The disease entries have been compiled with an attempt to strike a middle approach on terminology. If an entry is understandable without an unfamiliar term, the term doesn't appear. But if the language and ideas bogged down when the term was deleted, it does appear. The disease glossary starts on page 301.

The Spread of Disease
Insects carry diseases caused by fungi, viruses, and bacteria. Some pathogens live inside the insect organism for part of their life cycle, while others are carried along in the cell sap that the insect sucks up. As the insect moves from site to site, the pathogen is released in its saliva. Mechanical transmission is also common; by tracking through a patch of infective material, such as spores or bacterial slime, and then wandering over an uninfected leaf or plant, the insect spreads the disease. Birds, animals, and gardeners also transmit diseases mechanically.

People carry more disease spores around than an army of aphids do. Touching first one and then another plant spreads disease. Using an uncleaned tool in various parts of the garden accomplishes the same task. Make it a rule: If diseases are in your garden, do not move from a diseased plant or area to a healthy one without washing hands, tools, and the bottom of your shoes. And even if you don't think diseases are present, never move from plant to plant when humidity is high enough to leave a film of moisture on leaves. Of all the *vectors,* or disease carriers, in your garden, you are probably the most proficient.

Immunity, Resistance, and Susceptibility
Immunity implies that a pathogen simply can't feed on a particular host. For example, potatoes are immune to

corn smut fungi, and corn is immune to late blight fungi. In contrast, *resistance* means that the plant is relatively susceptible to the pathogen, but is able to fight against it to a greater or lesser degree.

Resistance is often inborn, or genetic. Chemical characteristics can make plants resistant by making the host unattractive to the pathogen. Other genetic qualities that give resistance may be functional, as in a case where stomates (leaf pores) open at a time of day when spores are not stimulated to germinate.

Morphological resistance, or resistance conferred by the formation of plant tissue, can be genetic, a product of the environment, or caused by the interaction of these two factors. For example, a plant variety may have a tendency to form cuticles thick enough to repel germinating spores. However, low light levels can inhibit this characteristic, allowing pathogens to attack. *Escape* can also be a product of either genetic characteristics or environmental conditions; a plant that matures before a pathogen builds to damaging populations "escapes" infection.

Hypersensitivity, or extreme susceptibility to a pathogen, can also make a plant somewhat resistant; if cells around a spot of infection die very quickly, the pathogen may not be able to spread through the plant. This form of resistance can also be termed *tolerance.* Tolerant plants are those that can be infected, but not appreciably disabled, by a disease organism.

Susceptibility is sometimes determined by the age of the host. In general, plants are more likely to be disabled by parasitic diseases in their youth and decay organisms as they age. This action explains why one planting of a crop succumbs to disease attack and another resists it.

Prevention and Control
Gardeners protect against disease attack by trying to eliminate the pathogen, exclude it, avoid it, or minimize

DISEASES
An Overview

the damage it creates. Although these approaches seem distinct, the boundaries between them merge, and gardeners are wise to use as many strategies as possible.

Total elimination is rarely achieved. However, some techniques do serve to decrease populations to manageable levels. It's often effective to remove infected plants and, in some cases, the soil around their roots, then burn or compost them. Farmers or growers with large plantings can flame stubble that contains overwintering organisms. Keep the garden and adjacent areas weeded to control alternate hosts. Hot-water treatments kill pathogens on infected seed.

Exclusion techniques include using certified disease-free seed and planting stock. Cleaning all tools and implements, as well as shoes and hands, when moving from one area to another may also exclude harmful organisms. If a disease is insect-vectored, screening out or controlling the insect carrier can exclude the disease.

Rotations serve to first avoid pathogens that overwinter in soil or plant debris and then, if carried out for long enough, eliminate them by not providing a host. For example, growing African, French, and golden marigolds (or 'Nemagold' marigold mix) as a cover crop, then turning them under at the end of the season, controls nematodes.

Resistant varieties also avoid attack, so choose them when ordering or buying seeds or transplants whenever possible. Seed catalogs follow the names of tomato varieties with "V" to show resistance to verticillium and "F" to show resistance to fusarium wilt. While other crops lack this convenient coding, a glance at the entries will reveal phrases such as "resistant to powdery mildew," "tolerant of anthracnose," and "scab-resistant."

Damage is minimized when both soils and plants are healthy. Decomposing organic matter supports numerous organisms that feed on pathogens. By green-manuring

and applying compost, gardeners can decrease pathogenic populations. Providing good drainage and increasing the air circulation between plants by wider spacings
thwarts the spread of many fungi. Plants growing in
healthy soils and under appropriate conditions are much
more resistant to or tolerant of attack than unhealthy crops.

On Being Complete

This section is in no way a complete and exhaustive
discussion of plant diseases and their causative organisms.
For most gardeners, entries will enable them to solve
common disease problems in the garden. However, if you
find that you want to learn more about a particular
disease or organism, or that you have become interested
in the subject as a whole, please refer to the Bibliography
on page 311.

A Word of Encouragement

Plant pathologists have to travel extensively to see a good
selection of diseases. In your own garden, you probably
won't have the chance to get to know more than a few;
disease incidence on well-managed land is simply not
that common.

But "well-managed" is the operative term. To keep
disease incidence low, you do have to take care of your
soil, amend with discretion, rotate wisely, and practice
good sanitation techniques. Space in this book can't
accommodate a full discussion of good growing practices,
but fortunately, many good books and instructional materials
are available. And it *is* true that as your soils and cultural practices improve, disease incidence decreases.
Healthy plants, growing in a healthful environment, have
resistance and/or tolerance to even the most virulent pathogens.

COMMON DISEASES OF GARDEN VEGETABLES

Crop	Disease	Symptoms
Alliums (Garlic, Leek, Onion)	Downy Mildew	Early symptoms are sunken spots on leaves; later, a purplish mold develops over spots
	Pink Rot	Roots turn pinkish or red, eventually rot; plant is stunted, with wilted tops
	Smut	Black spots on leaves and between the sections of the bulbs; young plants may have twisted leaves; common in northern regions
Asparagus	Asparagus Rust	Reddish-yellow spots on stems, branches; gradually entire plant yellows, weakens, and eventually dies
	Fusarium Wilt	Wilted, stunted spears with brownish surface color
Bean, Lima	Bacterial Spot	Reddish-brown lesions on stem, leaves, and pods; young diseased pods may fall from plant
	Downy Mildew	Pods are mottled with white, fuzzy fungus strands on them
Bean, Snap	Anthracnose	Dark red, sunken spots on leaves and stems; pinkish-red spots on pods; seeds are often black
	Bacterial Blight	Large brown blotches on leaves, possibly bordered with yellow or red; water-soaked spots on pods; seed may be discolored
	Mosaic	Leaves crinkled with mottled areas; pods may be rough, misshapen
	Rust	Many small, reddish-orange to brown spore masses on leaves and possibly stem; leaves rapidly yellow, dry up, and drop
Beet	Leaf Spot	Small, round, tan to brown spots on leaves and stems; later leaves turn yellow and drop
Brassicas (Broccoli, Brussels Sprouts, Cabbage, Cauliflower, Turnip)	Black Rot	Leaves yellow, veins become black; plant becomes stunted and heads of cabbage, cauliflower, or Brussels sprouts are one-sided or nonexistent; stem cross section shows a brown, woody ring

Crop	Disease	Symptoms
Carrot	Leaf Blight	Yellow to whitish spots on leaves; girdling of roots; water-soaked spots or lesions on roots
	Root-Knot Nematode	Small galls on lateral rootlets; pimple-sized swellings on main root; plants may be yellow and stunted
Celery	Blights (Early and Late)	Greenish or water-soaked spots on leaves; sunken lesions possible on stalks; growth may be visible in wet weather
	Fusarium Wilt (Celery Yellows)	Reddish tissue on stalks and leaves; yellowing of foliage
	Pink Rot	Water-soaked spots on stalks; bitter-tasting, rotted stems; damping-off may occur in an infected seedbed
Corn	Bacterial Wilt	Pale, streaked leaves; yellow, sticky substance exudes from a cut stem
	Corn Smut	Large galls develop on stalk, ears, and roots; later, grayish galls blacken and release spores; ripened spores appear oily or powdery
Cucurbits (Cucumber, Pumpkin, Squash)	Anthracnose	Small, dark spots on leaves; eventually spots grow together and entire leaf is destroyed; fruits may blacken and drop; problem develops in warm, moist conditions
	Bacterial Wilt	Leaves wilt quickly, possibly while still green; white, sticky material might be seen when a stem is cut
	Downy Mildew	Yellow to purplish spots start on leaves, gradually cover entire plant
	Mosaic	Leaves of cucumber and squash develop rough, mottled surface; cucumber fruit may be entirely white; plant may be stunted and yellow in several places
	Powdery Mildew	Round, white spots on undersides of leaves; eventually entire leaf is covered with powder; fruits ripen prematurely and have poor flavor and texture

(continued)

COMMON DISEASES OF GARDEN VEGETABLES—*Continued*

Crop	Disease	Symptoms
Cucurbits—*continued*	Scab	Dark spots on fruit of cucumber and pumpkin; leaves may have water spots and stems may have shallow lesions; sap oozes from fruits, then greenish mold develops
Eggplant	Fruit Rot	Brownish spots on leaves; damage is particularly bad during wet weather when fruit may develop small, tannish cankers which later rot
	Verticillium Wilt	Yellowing of foliage and gradual defoliation; plants may become stunted
Pea	Ascochyta Blight	Leaves shrivel and die; roots and lower stems may blacken and rot; disease overwinters on plant debris
	Bacterial Blight	Brownish or yellow blotches form on leaves and pods; stems may turn purplish; leaves eventually yellow
	Powdery Mildew	Stems, leaves, and pods dusted with white powdery mold; black specks appear later in the season; plants are stunted and vines shriveled
	Root Rot	Yellowed, gangly plants with rotting roots and lower stems; plant may die before pods form
Pepper	Anthracnose	Dark, round spots on fruit; entire pepper may rot or dry up; serious problem particularly in southern and central regions
	Bacterial Spot	In dry areas, leaves develop yellowish spots with darker margins; older leaves eventually drop
Potato	Blackleg	In warm, moist climates, plants become stunted and leaves yellow and roll; stem base develops brown, rotted areas on the inside; inside of tubers shows darkened blotches and a soft rot that worsens during storage
	Early Blight	Spots develop in rings on leaves; eventually leaves may die; tubers develop puckered skin and shallow rough lesions; mold may result

Crop	Disease	Symptoms
	Mosaic	Mottled, crinkled foliage; brown specks appear on tubers, and plants may droop and die prematurely
	Rhizoctonia	Dark brown cankers appear on young sprouts; mature stalks may become brown; tubers are covered with hard, black "scurfs"; tubers may also be roughened in a cross-patched pattern
	Verticillium Wilt	Late in season, older leaves yellow; affected vines die prematurely; stem tissue discolors from base; tubers may be pinkish
Spinach (also Swiss Chard)	Blight	Yellowish, curled leaves; stunted leaves and plants
	Downy Mildew	In moist areas, leaves develop yellow spots with fuzzy, purplish growth beneath
Sweet Potato	Black Rot	Small, round, brown spots on potato tubers; stem may also show decay
	Soft Rot	Soft, watery rot on stored tubers
	Stem Rot	Young infected plants may die after transplanting; survivors develop bright yellow leaves, and later stems rot; harvest is of poor quality
Tomato	Anthracnose	Fruits develop small, round, water-soaked spots; later, fruits darken and rot
	Blights (early and late)	Irregular, water-soaked spots may develop on leaves; plant becomes partly defoliated; seedlings may girdle; stem end of fruit becomes grayish-green; blossoms or young fruits may drop
	Fusarium Wilt	Leaves yellow and droop; cross section of stem shows brownish liquid within; fruit usually decays and drops
	Mosaic	Mottled leaves; young leaves are bunched or puckered; plants are stunted; yield is reduced; in some types of mosaic, fruit is also mottled

DISEASES
Bacteria

Angular Leaf Spot

Pseudomonas lachrymans

BACTERIUM

Range: Throughout United States and Canada, particularly severe in humid areas.

Description: The first symptoms of angular leaf spot are small, water-soaked spots on leaves and stems. Because the spots spread no farther than the veins surrounding them, they are irregularly angular. They turn yellow to tan or brown, and may exude a brown bacterial ooze on the underside of the leaf. When the bacterial ooze dries, a white residue is left behind. The spots may drop out after they dry, leaving ragged holes and areas in affected leaves. On fruit, spots are small, round, and white. Under the spot, the fruit rots deeply.

Life Cycle: If not carried on the seed coat, these bacteria infect stems, leaves, and fruit resting on infected soil, or are carried from one plant to the next by gardeners. They attack through stomates (leaf pores) or wounds. Overwintering occurs on plant refuse or on seed coats from infected fruit.

Host Plants: All cucurbits, but most severe on cucumber, muskmelon, and summer squash.

Transmission: Seed-, soil- and rain-borne. Transmitted by people in the field.

Prevention and Control: Do not work with cucurbits before the dew has dried or in rainy weather. If infection is slight, prune off and burn affected leaves or whole plants, preferably before the bacterial ooze has formed on the underside of the leaf. Use three- to four-year rotations on cucurbits. At the end of the season, bury all refuse, even if disease has not been noticed. In the case of diseased plants, remove and compost or burn.

Notes: This disease grows most abundantly in warm, moist weather, and is also spread by rain and dripping dew.

See photograph, page 282.

Bacterial Bean Blight

Xanthomonas phaseoli

BACTERIUM

Range: Throughout United States and southern Canada, but less common in the Far West of both countries.

Description: Small, water-soaked spots on foliage are the first symptom of bean blight. These spots enlarge and coalesce before browning and drying. Dried areas of the leaf may drop out. A yellow or light green margin is sometimes visible around the spots. On stems, lesions are long and initially water-soaked before turning reddish-brown with age. On pods, the disease shows as small, irregularly shaped sunken areas. If bacterial ooze is emitted from spots or lesions, it dries to a yellowish powder.

Life Cycle: Infection occurs through natural openings or wounds in plant tissue. Once feeding on plant tissue, the disease moves rapidly through the plant, but does not usually kill it or prevent seed from forming. It overwinters on seed from infected pods or within crop debris.

Host Plants: Beans.

Transmission: Seed-, soil-, and rain-borne. Spread by gardeners in the field.

Prevention and Control: Do not work with beans in moist conditions. A three-year rotation is effective against soilborne residues. If the disease is apparent, pull vines and compost hot or burn. Do not save seed if any plants have shown symptoms of the disease. Western-grown seed is less likely to carry the disease.

Notes: Moist, cool weather favors this disease. Cool, nighttime dew is particularly conducive to its spread and ability to infect.

See photograph, page 282.

Bacterial Blight of Pea
Pseudomonas pisi
BACTERIUM

Range: Throughout United States and Canada, particularly severe in the East and South.

Description: Foliage displays dark green, water-soaked spots as the first symptom. These areas brown and dry, sometimes dropping and making the leaf look ragged. On stems, brown or very dark green streaks show. When severe, a cream-colored bacterial slime may ooze from spots or streaks. Flowers may be killed or pods may be covered with brown or dark green, water-soaked spots. Occasionally pods wither. Seeds inside infected pods feel unusually slippery as a consequence of accumulated bacterial slime.

Life Cycle: Bacterial blight may enter uninfected plants through stomates (leaf pores) or wounds, but is more commonly carried on the seed. The organism attacks the plant progressively and, if it reaches the vascular system, causes wilting before the plant dies. Plants infected from seed often die before setting seed themselves. This disease overwinters in crop debris and can remain viable for about three years in the soil.

DISEASES
Bacteria

Host Plant: Pea.

Transmission: Seed-, soil-, and rain-borne.

Prevention and Control: Plant peas in nutrient-rich soil with good drainage, giving them a four-year rotation. Use western-grown seed or seed that is certified to be disease-free. If any disease has been present, remove the vines at the end of the season. A hot compost (one that reaches 160°F for three or four days) or burning will kill the organism.

Notes: High humidity favors the growth and subsequent spread of this disease.

See photograph, page 282.

Bacterial Blight of Tomato
Corynebacterium michiganense
BACTERIUM

Range: Throughout United States and southern Canada.

Description: Stunted seedlings are the first sign of bacterial blight transmitted through infected seed. When bacterial blight attacks older plants, wilt is the first sign of the disease. Wilting often shows up first in the margins of only one side of a leaflet. The leaflet may curl before the wilted tissues brown and die. The disease often proceeds up one side of the plant first, affecting the other side only after the tissues on the first side are damaged beyond repair. On fruits, small, raised white spots signal the disease. Even after the centers of the fruit spots turn dark, a white halo may surround them. Fruits may also be stunted or malformed.

Life Cycle: The bacteria persist in soil for two years, and enter plants through wounds or small, natural openings. After gaining entry, the bacteria travel to the vascular system of the plant where they live and reproduce, infecting plant tissues as they move through the plant. Seeds from infected plants may carry the bacteria either on their surfaces or internally.

Host Plant: Tomato.

Transmission: Soil-, seed-, and rain-borne.

Prevention and Control: Three-year rotations are effective against bacterial blight. However, if you see a plant with signs of the disease during the season, pull it, taking as much of the surrounding soil as possible. Composting plant debris at 160°F for three or four days kills the organism. Use commerically produced seed, or treat saved seed at 122°F for 25 minutes.

Notes: Bacterial blight is infective at any temperature range tolerable to tomato plants. However, tolerance and subsequent resistance are higher among healthy, unwounded plants than those that are sickly.

See photograph, page 282.

Bacterial Leaf Spot

Pseudomonas maculicola

BACTERIUM

Range: Primarily Northeastern and Mid-Atlantic United States.

Description: Small spots on foliage are the first sign of this disease. The spots may have a brown or purple coloration and can become quite copious. When a leaf looks spatter-painted, it yellows and may drop. The plant suffers from its diminished vitality and reduced chlorophyll-producing potential.

Life Cycle: Once the bacteria begin to feed on plant tissue, they reproduce rapidly. Symptoms may not be apparent for three to six days, but by that time, a new outbreak of infectious bacteria is ready to be moved by rain or gardeners to uninfected plants. The bacteria enter through wounds or natural openings. Commonly, the disease lives on because it is transmitted by seed or overwinters in infected plant debris.

Host Plants: Crucifers, particularly oriental greens, turnip, cauliflower, and cabbage.

Transmission: Seed-, soil-, and rain-borne, and mechanically transmitted.

Prevention and Control: Rotate plantings on a three-year cycle. Start all seedlings to be transplanted in nutritionally rich seedbeds that have not carried crucifers for at least three years. If spots appear on any plants, remove them immediately and destroy by burning, or by composting at 160°F for three to four days.

Notes: Young plants, no matter what the weather, are most susceptible to these bacteria. Provide good nutrition for hasty and vigorous growth.

See photograph, page 282.

Bacterial Spot

Xanthomonas vesicatoria

BACTERIUM

Range: Throughout United States and Canada.

DISEASES
Bacteria

Description: The first symptoms are dark, water-soaked spots on the top surfaces of leaves. On the undersides, the spots may be slightly raised. The tiny spots darken and look greasy as the disease progresses. On stems, streaks are dark and sunken. Spots on immature fruit are very obvious. Beginning as small, translucent areas, they raise above the surface slightly as they increase in size and darken. Later they sink, making the skin over them look wrinkled. Secondary organisms often invade.

Life Cycle: The disease enters through natural openings and wounds. Although it doesn't travel through the vascular system, inoculum is easily spread from one portion of the plant to another. Overwintering occurs in crop debris and on seed from infected plants.

Host Plants: Tomato, sweet pepper.

Transmission: Seed-, rain-, and wind-borne.

Prevention and Control: Rotate all tomatoes and peppers on a minimum of a three-year cycle. If infection shows, pull the plant and compost at 160°F for three or four days or burn. Do not save seed from infected plants.

Notes: Warm, wet weather favors the spread and infective ability of this disease.

See photograph, page 283.

Bacterial Wilt of Cucurbits
Erwinia tracheiphila
BACTERIUM

Range: Midwestern, north central, and Northeastern United States. Rare in the South or Far West.

Description: Individual leaves show the disease first. Large, irregular patches on the leaves lose turgidity before the whole leaf begins to wilt. As the disease spreads, whole stems and then branches wilt during midday before browning and shriveling. Eventually, the whole plant may wither and die. More resistant plants show slight daily wilting and general stunting. Infected stems emit a thick bacterial mass when cut and squeezed.

Life Cycle: This organism overwinters within the digestive system of the cucumber beetle. In the spring, when the insect feeds on young plants, the bacteria are released in the beetle's excrement, which is dropped on leaves. The organism travels into the plant through stomates (leaf pores) or small wounds. Once there, it begins to feed and reproduce within the vascular system. Feeding cucumber beetles ingest it for another safe winter season.

Host Plants: All cucurbits except watermelon.

Transmission: Cucumber beetle.

Prevention and Control: Covering young plants with screens, plastic, or floating row covers often prevents the beetles from landing on them. Because these beetles overwinter in the soil, rotation is extremely important: Separate subsequent plantings as far as possible.

Notes: This disease can infect plants in any environmental or nutritional regime in which the plants will grow.

See photograph, page 283.

Blackleg of Potato, Soft Rot of Tomato
Erwinia atroseptica
BACTERIUM

Range: Throughout United States and southern Canada.

Description: One or more stems on infected potato plants blacken and look slightly rotted near, or several inches above, the soil line. Lower leaves on infected stems yellow and curl upward before browning and dropping. The whole stem may fall over if the basal rot progresses too far. The plant is usually more erect and less spreading than the normal habit. Dark bacterial slime is sometimes apparent on the outside of infected stems. Tubers can become infected at the stem end and appear soft and rotted once the disease takes hold. On tomatoes, this rot is most noticeable on the fruit that develops water-soaked or dark spots. Skin over the spots sometimes blisters as a consequence of slight accumulation of gas produced by the organism. Decay is rapid.

Life Cycle: Blackleg persists in soil for many years after hosts have been present. The disease enters the plant when biting or chewing insects transmit it, or through small wounds or natural openings near or below the soil line. It gradually moves both upward to the foliage and downward to the roots and/or tubers. If the infection in the tuber is slight, it may go unnoticed and be spread by the cutting knife prior to planting.

Host Plants: Potato and, less commonly, tomato.

Transmission: Soilborne, seed-borne, insect-vectored, and (most commonly on potatoes) spread by a cutting knife.

Prevention and Control: Use only certified, disease-free seed, and look carefully for infection as you cut tubers into seed pieces. Rotations of four or five years are

DISEASES
Bacteria

usually effective. Sterilize cutting knives as described for prevention of potato ring rot, page 149. Remove all portions of infected plants as well as surrounding soil, and burn or compost at 160°F for a minimum of three or four days.

Notes: Blackleg infection is encouraged by warm, moist weather.

See photograph, page 283.

Black Rot
Xanthomonas campestris
BACTERIUM

Range: Throughout United States and southern Canada, but less common in the Far West of both countries.

Description: The first signs of black rot are chlorotic (yellowed), generally V-shaped wedges from leaf margins to an interior vein, with the apex of the triangle at the leaf margin and the tip at the interior vein. Later, the veins show a dark discoloration which is echoed by darkened vascular systems seen when the stem is cut. Leaves with a great deal of damage dry and drop, leaving a bare stem. Sometimes, infection first shows on only one side of the plant. Affected seedlings usually die before maturity. If a cut stem of a severely affected plant is squeezed, a yellowish bacterial ooze is apparent. Although black rot produces a dry and odorless decay, invasion by secondary rotting organisms is common, and affected plants may become slimy and smell offensive.

Life Cycle: Coming in contact with a susceptible plant, these bacteria move through the outer pores at the leaf margins, the stomates (leaf pores), or wounds, and then move to the vascular system. Growing there, they damage and plug the vascular system. Overwintering occurs in diseased crop debris or in the slight bacterial slime on seeds.

Host Plants: All crucifers.

Transmission: Seed-, soil-, and rain-borne.

Prevention and Control: Give all cruciferous crops a three-year rotation before growing again in the same garden area. Buy western-grown certified disease-free seed, or treat homegrown seed for 30 minutes in a 122°F hot-water bath. Provide good drainage and high nutrition in all growing areas.

Notes: Black rot is most serious in warm, moist seasons. High humidity and nighttime dew favor its spread.

See photograph, page 283.

Brown Rot, Southern Bacterial Wilt

Pseudomonas solanacearum

BACTERIUM

Range: Primarily southern United States, from Maryland southward.

Description: Wilting is the predominant symptom of brown rot. Before that, you may notice a slight stunting. The first wilting occurs at midday, and plants seem to recover overnight. However, the wilting becomes progressively more severe and lasting. On stems, brown, water-soaked streaks and lesions may appear, and a dark bacterial ooze is sometimes evident. Potato tubers often show a darkened vascular ring about ½ to ¾ inch below the skin. Cutting into the stem of any severely affected plant reveals a darkened vascular system and some bacterial ooze.

Life Cycle: Brown rot persists in soil for six years without a living host. Infecting plants that come in contact with it, the bacteria invade through wounds and natural openings, and often move into the vascular system. Wilting is a consequence of damaged or clogged vascular tubes in the plant.

Host Plants: Many. But especially important to potato, beans, beet, carrot, sweet potato, nightshade crops, and rhubarb, as well as both annual and perennial flowers.

Transmission: Soil- and water-borne. Mechanically transmitted by gardeners and tools.

Prevention and Control: Because so many crops are susceptible to this disease and its viability without a living host is so long, rotations must be planned carefully to avoid encouraging it. Lettuce, crucifers, corn, and cucurbits are not susceptible to this species of *Pseudomonas,* and should form the basis of the rotation after a crop with this disease. Use northern-grown seed potatoes because they don't carry the organism. Rogue all plants that show wilting and darkened vascular systems, and compost (at a minimum of 160°F for three to four days) or burn.

Notes: This disease loves warm weather. Below 55°F, the disease is repressed, but it spreads and reproduces well as soon as ambient air temperatures are in the high 70s to high 90s.

See photograph, page 283.

Crown Gall
Agrobacterium tumefaciens
BACTERIUM

Range: Throughout United States and southern Canada.

Description: Large, irregularly shaped soft galls, usually fairly near the soil line on either roots or stems. The galls may look outwardly firm, but are soft on the inside. A rough-looking overgrowth of plant tissue may cover the gall. Secondary organisms attack galls, often causing decay. Plants may wither and look sickly before most gardeners explore far enough to discover the galls characteristic of this disease.

Life Cycle: Although previously believed to remain viable for many years, crown gall bacteria are now known to live only two to three years without living hosts. More often, infected seedlings or infected irrigation water brings the disease to your garden. Plants are infected through wounds and bruises. The bacteria feed in intercellular spaces, and exude acetic acids and other substances that promote abnormal and excessive division of nearby cells. As the gall grows, the bacteria invade farther through stressed and broken cell walls, enlarging the infected area.

Host Plants: Many, including brambles, grape, fruit and nut trees, and ornamentals, especially rose, aster, chrysanthemum, and daisies. Vegetables most often infected include beet, turnip, and tomato.

Transmission: Soil- and water-borne. Insect-vectored.

Prevention and Control: The best preventive for crown gall is exclusion. Check the roots of all imported stock carefully and discard those that show abnormal galls or thickenings. Should you find crown gall in a planting, dig the plant with all roots and surrounding soil, and destroy by composting hot (160°F for three to four days) or burn.

Notes: Crown gall is most serious when the weather is warm, but doesn't infect tomatoes at temperatures consistently above 85°F. Because it is most prevalent when plants have wounds, nematodes and other root-damaging or leaf-and stem-chewing organisms promote its spread.

See photograph, page 284.

Potato Ring Rot
Corynebacterium spedonicum
BACTERIUM

Range: Throughout United States and Canada.

Description: The first sign of ring rot is wilting of foliage late in the season. Often only a few branches of the plant wilt. Lower leaves on wilted stems yellow between veins, and leaf margins may curl upward. Cutting through the stem on heavily damaged plants reveals a cream-colored, oozing bacterial mass within the vascular system. Tubers from infected plants do not show damage until they have been stored for a few weeks to two months. Cutting into them, the darkened vascular system which encircles the tuber about ½ to ¾ inch beneath the skin is immediately visible. A thickened and creamy-colored material can be squeezed out of the vascular region if the disease has progressed beyond the first browning. Tubers left for storage through the winter may show dry cankers before becoming brown and withered. Their lack of health makes them vulnerable to secondary rot organisms, which may cause them to become soft and slimy.

Life Cycle: Ring rot does not enter the plant through stomates (leaf pores) or other natural openings. Rather, it relies on wounds or infected seed pieces for transmission. Once inside the plant, it lives and reproduces within the vascular system. It can remain viable for several years on equipment and bins that have come in contact with infected plants.

Host Plant: Potato.

Transmission: Through infected seed pieces, contaminated knives, and infected equipment.

Prevention and Control: The best prevention is avoidance. Use only seed potatoes certified to be disease-free, and check the vascular system as you cut them into pieces. Additionally, rotate knives when cutting seed pieces, dropping them first into a 10% bleach solution after a cut, and then into a clean water solution before reusing. Sterilize all storage bins as they are emptied. Watch for signs of disease in the field, removing roots and tubers as well as the tops of infected plants.

Notes: This organism lives well under all conditions tolerated by its host plant.

See photograph, page 284.

Scab
Streptomyces scabies
BACTERIUM

Range: Throughout United States and southern Canada. Most prevalent in potato-growing areas.

Description: Warty or corky scabs or brown, sunken depressions form on the skin of the root crop. The infection does not penetrate far into the root, nor does it affect flavor. However, scab-infected crops

DISEASES
Bacteria

do not store well; secondary organisms find it easy to penetrate scabby areas.

Life Cycle: *Streptomyces* has some characteristics of a fungus, some of a bacterium. Like a fungus, it grows as a mycelium and develops spores. It can also live in the soil for a number of years without a host.

Host Plants: Potato, beet, carrot, parsnip, radish, rutabaga, turnip.

Transmission: Soilborne.

Prevention and Control: Do not apply alkaline materials such as lime or wood ashes to soil before planting root crops. Similarly, apply only composted manure; *Streptomyces* passes unharmed through animals' digestive systems. Rotate crops with legumes. Maintain a low soil pH and good soil moisture levels. If the problem is severe, green-manure the area with soybeans or another legume and till in the residue to increase soil activity. Use resistant varieties, and when choosing seed potatoes, look for a thick skin.

Notes: Scab does not grow well in soils with a pH of 5.2 or below. High soil-moisture levels appear to inhibit it as well, and gardeners using good-quality compost report very low incidence, probably because parasites and predators are so abundant.

See photograph, page 288.

Soft Rot
Erwinia carotovora
BACTERIUM

Range: Throughout United States and southern Canada.

Description: Produces a soft, watery rot on both growing and stored crops. The predominant symptom, aside from the rot, is an offensive odor. In plants such as lettuce, the bacteria often invade dead tissue such as old leaves or leaf tips suffering from tipburn.

Life Cycle: Soft rot enters the plant through wounds and bruises, or when a carrier insect bites into the plant. Once in contact with plant tissue, the organism exudes enzymes and toxins that decompose the cementing layer between cells, making the released nutrients available for the bacteria. They ingest the material and move on to new tissue as it is infected. Not only does this bacterial ooze give off an offensive smell, it also provides an inoculum for infecting new plants or stored crops. Unfortunately, these bacteria can subsist on dead organic matter in the soil.

Host Plants: Many. Most vegetables and many ornamentals, including iris and other popular perennials.

Transmission: Soilborne and vectored by root-chewing maggots, especially cabbage maggot and carrot rust fly maggot.

Prevention and Control: No resistant varieties of any crop are known. Be gentle when harvesting, and check all storage vegetables for signs of decay. Store vegetables at the lowest recommended temperature. After harvest, let the soil clinging to root crops dry before placing them in storage areas. Under no circumstances should vegetables be washed before going into storage. In the field, the best prevention is very good drainage and soil full of beneficial organisms such as those coming in on compost.

Notes: Warm temperatures and moisture favor the spread of this disease.

See photograph, page 284.

Alternaria Blight
Alternaria Blight of Carrots
Alternaria dauci

Alternaria Blight of Cucurbits
Alternaria cucumerina

FUNGUS

Range: United States and southern Canada.

Description: In carrots, the older leaves are attacked first. Irregular brown spots with yellowish centers show near leaf margins and petioles (leaf stems). Leaves turn yellow, then brown and die. In cucurbits, circular brown spots with concentric rings appear on upper surfaces of older leaves. Dark brown to black filaments and spores are apparent on both leaf surfaces. Leaves curl, dry, and die. Fruits have sunken spots on which dusky green spores grow.

Life Cycle: *Alternaria* species persist in soil, living on infected plant debris between cropping seasons. Germination occurs over a wide temperature range, depending on the species. Generally, hosts of warm-weather crops produce spores most readily at temperatures of 80°F or above, while those of cool-weather plants reproduce at 70°F. Several spore generations occur each season.

Host Plants: Carrot, parsley, cucurbits, beans, onion, ginseng, and many ornamentals. *A. solani* is responsible for early blight on nightshade crops (see page 159).

Transmission: Spores may be seed-borne or, more commonly, wind-borne from infected plant debris or crops in the field.

Prevention and Control: Prune off and destroy affected plant parts before spores form. Remove diseased plant debris from the garden. Rotate crops.

Notes: Warm, humid weather favors the spread of the disease.

See photograph, page 285.

DISEASES
Fungi

Anthracnose

Colletotrichum spp.,
Gloeosporium spp.

FUNGUS

Range: Eastern and central United States and southeastern Canada.

Description: These imperfect fungi can be recognized by their distinctive flesh-toned to light pink spore masses that ooze out of lesions. Spores are particularly noticeable in damp weather. The first symptoms are lesions on the stem, leaf, or fruit. On bean plants, lesions on cotyledons (seed leaves), stems and petioles (leaf stems) are dark and circular, spots on leaves are often elongated and angular and may follow the veins. On pods, dark brown spots with a lighter border often enlarge to 1 centimeter or more in size. On melon leaves, circular spots begin as light brown and turn reddish-brown on muskmelons, black on watermelons. Spots may enlarge and coalesce before shattering. The whole leaf may shrivel and die. Water-soaked, elongated lesions on stems and petioles become sunken and brown. Melon and cucumber fruits have dark, sunken lesions. Tomato fruit shows dark, depressed spots with tan centers. Concentric rings are often visible in the spots. In potatoes, anthracnose is known as black dot and usually follows other diseases. Lesions often start on the stem just below the soil surface. The black dots in the skin of tubers are sclerotia which can overwinter in the soil. Rhubarb anthracnose, also called stalk rot, shows as water-soaked spots on the stems and petioles. Turnips, mustard, radishes, and Chinese cabbage in the Southeast show small, round gray spots on leaves and elongated spots on stems. Only Southeastern strawberries are affected; anthracnose girdles the stems of runners, often before they root.

Life Cycle: This parasitic fungus overwinters as mycelium in seeds and crop debris in the field. Spores formed in the spring are splashed onto hosts where they germinate, forming a penetration peg at the end of the hyphae. The penetration peg mechanically invades plant tissue through the cuticle. Spores formed during the growing season can infect other plants immediately.

Host Plants: Many cultivated and wild plants are susceptible to one or another *Colletotrichum* or *Gloeosporium* species. Beans, bramble fruits, Chinese cabbage, cucumber, melons, mustard, nightshade crops, pea, rhubarb, strawberry, and turnip are often infected.

Transmission: Spores are soilborne and carried by windblown rain or on seed.

Prevention and Control: Rotate crops. Remove infected plants from the field. Work in the garden only when leaves are dry. Plant only western-grown bean seeds, and discard any with wrinkled or discolored seed coats. Burn diseased seedlings.

Notes: Spores germinate only in a water film, so moist or rainy weather favors the growth and spread of anthracnose. The disease grows well over a wide temperature range (59–77°F).

See photograph, page 285.

Ascochyta Blight

Ascochyta spp.,
Mycosphaerella pinodes
FUNGUS

Range: United States and southern Canada, but more important in eastern areas.

Description: Dark pycnidia (flask-shaped fruiting bodies) growing from lesions exude spore tendrils in wet weather. In peas, small purplish or tan spots form on leaves, stems, and pods. On leaves, the spots enlarge, coalesce, and darken. Leaves shrivel and dry. Spots on pods are generally sunken. Depending on the species, pods may wither or deep stem lesions may form near the soil line. Ascochyta blight of okra, beans, and nightshade crops is caused by the same strain of the fungus, and the symptoms are similar. Dark spots with concentric rings are formed on leaves and stems. Dark pycnidia and spore tendrils form in concentric rings within spots. Foot rot may occur. Young okra pods develop spots and, as with peas and beans, the mycelium grows into the seed.

Life Cycle: May develop from mycelium on seeds, or spores may form on plant debris left in the garden from the preceding season. Once in contact with the host, spores require an incubation period of two to eight days. After infecting the host, spores develop within a week or two, giving rise to secondary infections on the crop.

Host Plants: Alfalfa, asparagus, beans, clover, horseradish, nightshade crops, okra, pea, and many ornamentals.

Transmission: Seed-borne and/or disseminated by wind and rain, depending on the species.

Prevention and Control: Use western-grown pea seed. Rotate crops on a three- to four-year cycle. Clean up all affected refuse. Don't plant early and late peas or beans in the same garden area.

Notes: Spores produced by pycnidia require water for dissemination, so high humidity and rainfall favor the spread of the disease.

See photograph, page 285.

Botrytis, Gray Mold

Botrytis cinerea, B. allii

FUNGUS

Range: Throughout United States and southern Canada.

Description: First symptoms are pale, water-soaked spots on flowers, leaves, or stems. These grow a soft tan or gray, almost velvety mold within a day or two. If the mold is scraped off the tissue, black sclerotia growing just beneath the skin are sometimes visible. By the time the mold appears, affected parts are rotting. *B. allii* exudes a toxin in advance of its spread. In the field, seedlings, lettuce, and berries are most often attacked. In consistently warm, damp, and cloudy weather, seedlings may succumb to botrytis before or just after emergence. Lettuce plants grown too close together show brown lesions on the stem or on leaves touching the soil before the fungus grows asexual spores and moves upward. Berries are attacked near the stem. Many post-harvest rots are botrytis fungi, particularly in the case of berries and onion neck rots.

Life Cycle: Botrytis fungi are both saprophytic and parasitic. The fungus overwinters as sclerotia on dead tissue. In the spring, spores form and spread to dying, wounded, or extremely soft plant tissues. Secondary infection is common; the obvious gray mold is made up of asexual spores ready to drift onto and infect new tissues.

Host Plants: Almost all garden plants.

Transmission: Wind- and water-borne.

Prevention and Control: Keep air circulating by spacing plants widely and pruning leaves that touch. Pick old flower petals off leaves. Remove aging leaves from plants. Maintain fast soil drainage. Minimize damage to plants. Pick off leaves that sit on the soil surface. Harvest onions in dry weather and cure well before storing.

Notes: Botrytis is a common greenhouse disease because warm temperatures, high humidity, and low air circulation encourage its growth. Succulent growth and rough treatment of plants increase the chances of a botrytis infection.

See photograph, page 285.

Cabbage Yellows

Fusarium oxysporum
f. conglutinans

FUNGUS

Range: Throughout United States and southern Canada.

Description: Dark and rotting xylem tissue in both stems and roots gives clear notice of fusarium infection. Starting at the base, leaves become dull green to yellow and drop from the stem. Plants taste bitter.

Life Cycle: *Fusarium* species invade their hosts through roots and wounds near the soil line. Spores are produced in dying tissue and released into the surrounding soil, where the soil solution carries them to new hosts. The fungus overwinters on plant refuse in the field, but also produces resting spores that are viable for at least ten years.

Host Plants: All crucifers, but most important to cabbage, kohlrabi, and collards.

Transmission: Primary infection occurs through soilborne spores, but water, wind, and tools can carry spores to new ground.

Prevention and Control: Resistant varieties should always be used in areas where fusarium is a problem. Inspect imported transplants carefully before setting out. Keep soil moisture high and maintain good nutrient balances.

Notes: Soils must be at least 65°F for germination and invasion of this disease. Deficiencies of potassium and excess levels of nitrogen favor its spread. In hot, dry seasons, more resistant crucifers such as broccoli and cauliflower become more susceptible to fusarium.

See photograph, page 285.

Clubroot

Plasmodiophora brassicae

FUNGUS

Range: Throughout United States and southern Canada, with low incidence in the Southeast.

Description: Distinguishable by the swollen, somewhat spindle-shaped galls on the roots. The first aboveground symptom is a general stunting of the plant, followed by slight yellowing and easy wilting on hot, sunny days. When left unchecked, plants often die before heading or flowering.

Life Cycle: Resting spores are released from affected roots as they decompose. In spring, they germinate, each becoming a mobile spore that moves through the soil. The spore is carried along until it comes in contact with a susceptible root hair. Once inside the root, it reproduces and stimulates abnormal growth. Resting spores are formed and the cycle repeats. Spores remain viable for ten years.

Host Plants: Crucifers.

Transmission: Soilborne.

Prevention and Control: Raise soil pH to 7.2, keep drainage excellent, and adjust nutrient balance before planting, but don't apply uncomposted manure to the area. Try to grow your own seedlings, and don't

DISEASES
Fungi

transplant any that look weak. Keep cruciferous weeds under control. Use long rotations. Dig up stunted plants to check roots; if clubroot is present, dig out and burn as much root as possible.

Notes: Clubroot is encouraged by acid soils with poor drainage. Although the optimal temperature range is 81–86°F, germination can occur at soil temperatures as low as 48°F. Excesses of potassium and both deficiencies and excesses of nitrogen favor the disease.

See photograph, page 286.

Corn Leaf Blight
Northern
Corn Leaf Blight
Trichometasphaeria turtica
(Helminthosporium turticum)

Southern
Corn Leaf Blight
Cochliobolus heterostrophus
(Helminthosporium maydis)

FUNGUS

Range: Southern corn leaf blight extends from the southern United States to areas around Illinois. Northern corn leaf blight is severe in the north central states south to Florida.

Description: Southern corn leaf blight attacks field corn most frequently, but may also invade sweet corn in corn-growing regions. The fungus first shows as small, light-colored spots on leaves which quickly coalesce or enlarge to become straw-colored, slender areas of 1½ or 2 inches long by ¼ inch wide. Lesions have parallel sides because they follow veins. Eventually, the entire leaf and then the whole plant becomes tan and dry. Northern corn leaf blight shows first as small parallel spots on lower leaves. The lesions are initially dark, grayish-green and water-soaked, becoming dry and tan as they age and enlarge. Individual lesions can be as big as 6 inches long by 2 inches wide. During humid periods, velvety, dark green to black spores are formed in the centers of lesions on both leaf surfaces.

Life Cycle: Southern corn leaf blight produces microscopic, straw-colored, vegetative spores that emerge from the pores of infected leaves. Carried by wind to new plants, these spores cause a succession of secondary infections. The fungus overwinters in plant debris, producing new spores when the weather warms in the spring. Dormant spores are viable for at least two growing seasons. Northern corn leaf blight follows a similar life cycle, overwintering in refuse and producing wind-carried spores in the spring and throughout the season.

Host Plants: Corn and other grasses.

Transmission: Wind-borne.

Prevention and Control: Varieties resistant to both leaf blights are available. Because spores can be carried so far, rotation is only minimally effective. However, to decrease local sources of infection, dispose of or plow under all plant debris, including the stubble, at the end of the season.

Notes: Both northern and southern corn leaf blight thrive in warm, humid conditions. However, southern corn leaf blight prefers hotter temperatures than northern blight. Northern blight is most prevalent during periods of heavy dews, rainfall, and warm days.

See photographs, page 286.

Damping-Off
Pythium debaryanum,
Rhizoctonia solani,
Botrytis spp.,
Phytopthora spp.,
Diplodia spp.,
Fusarium spp.,
Phoma spp.,
Aphanomyces cochlioides
FUNGUS

Range: Throughout United States and southern Canada.

Description: Occurs before the seedling emerges from the soil or soon afterwards. While pre-emergent damping-off is difficult to verify, suspect it when rows are spotty. Post-emergent damping-off shows as a water-soaked or necrotic lesion on the stem close to the soil line. Roots look small and rotted.

Life Cycle: Many damping-off organisms live on dead or dying organic matter in the soil. Their life cycles are various, but they are all able to attack soft-tissued seedlings. Only a sterile medium is free of these organisms, and no medium can remain sterile for long.

Host Plants: Almost all plant species are susceptible to one or another of the damping-off organisms.

Transmission: Soilborne.

Prevention and Control: Keep air circulating in greenhouses. Don't overcrowd seedlings. Maintain fast soil drainage. Use a sterile starting medium such as peat moss.

Notes: Stagnant, humid conditions favor damping-off organisms.

See photograph, page 286.

DISEASES
Fungi

Downy Mildew

Phytopthora spp.,
Peronospora spp.,
Bremia lactucae,
Pseudopheronospora
    cubensis

FUNGUS

Range: Throughout United States and southern Canada, with lower incidence in the Southwest.

Description: Downy mildews are grouped together because they cause the same general symptoms in affected crops: Upper leaf surfaces show pale green or yellowish areas, while corresponding lower surfaces are covered with a downy-looking mildew. The color of the mildew ranges from white or light gray to slightly purple. Leaves wilt, brown, and die. Stems, flowers, and fruits may also be affected. Secondary organisms often follow downy mildews. Cucurbits first develop the disease on older leaves. Fruits are off-color and lack flavor. Although the causal organism for cucurbits can't overwinter in the North, winds bring it in each year. On limas and soybeans, the mildew usually attacks the pods, leaving spores for next year's crop on the seed. Beets may grow in a rosette pattern. Downy mildew of spinach looks quite purple and attacks only spinach. Affected onions show a blue-gray mildew on the tops of leaves and don't store well.

Life Cycle: Downy mildew organisms enter the plant through the leaf pores or cuticle, grow between cells, and produce branched haustoria that grow within the cells to absorb nutrients. Fruiting bodies protrude through the lower leaf pores, producing the characteristic mildew. Spores produced here are responsible for secondary infections throughout the season. Secondary infections take place quickly; most species only require a week from initial infection to production of fruiting bodies. Resting spores are produced within the plant and released when it decomposes. They germinate in a film of water the following spring. Resting spores are viable for several years.

Host Plants: Beet, carrot family crops, crucifers, cucurbits, lettuce, lima bean, nightshade crops, onion, pea, soybean, spinach, and strawberry.

Transmission: Seed-, wind-, and rain-borne, and in the case of cucurbit downy mildew, beetle-vectored.

Prevention and Control: Follow a two- to three-year crop rotation. Remove and burn affected plant parts. Don't walk in the garden when plants are wet. Don't plant seed that has any fungal growth on it, and destroy weeds carrying the disease.

Notes: Most downy mildews prefer cool, humid, wet conditions. Germination can take place at temperatures as low as 45°F. Downy mildew of cucurbits is an exception: temperatures of 65–90°F are optimal for germination.

See photograph, page 287.

Early Blight

Alternaria solani

FUNGUS

Range: United States and Canada. Especially important in central and Atlantic states.

Description: Early blight of tomatoes is sometimes called collar rot because infected seedlings show lesions at the soil line. More frequently, the first warning of early blight is spotted foliage. Spots are dark brown, and often show a target pattern. They enlarge and coalesce. The leaf yellows and may drop, setting the stage for sunscald in heavily infected plants. Stems show dark, sunken lesions. On tomato fruits, the disease attacks at the stem end and moves in to form a dark rot inside the fruit. Potato plants are usually affected about the time of blossoming. Leaf spots are similar to those on tomatoes. The tubers show small, dark spots that permit entrance of other rots.

Spores are dark and velvety, and arise on fruits and tubers as well as lesions on vegetative parts.

Life Cycle: Overwinters on incompletely decomposed crop debris, forming spores when the weather warms the next spring. Several generations of spores may occur on the same lesion during the summer, allowing the disease to become widespread.

Host Plants: Nightshade crops, particularly tomato and potato.

Transmission: Wind- and rain-borne generally. Sometimes seed-borne, and flea beetles may also transmit it. Hyphae enter through cracks and wounds in tissues.

Prevention and Control: Remove all infected plants from the field or, when this is impossible, hasten their decomposition by chopping well, allowing them to dry, and finally burying them. Use a three-year rotation on all nightshade crops, and watch hedgerows for affected weeds in the same family.

Notes: Temperatures of 80°F and higher stimulate spore formation. Transmission is hastened by winds, heavy dews, and frequent rain. Poor plant nutrition encourages greater severity.

See photograph, page 286.

DISEASES
Fungi

Early Blight of Celery

Cercospora apii

FUNGUS

Range: United States and southern Canada, but most severe in warm regions.

Description: A gray cast in the center of lesions is the recognizable sign of *C. apii*. The disease first shows as tiny yellow spots on foliage when plants are about six weeks old. On petioles (leaf stems) and stems, elongated brown and sunken lesions don't appear until later in the season. Spores emerge from pores on both leaf surfaces. Plant vigor and yields are greatly diminished, and several layers of outside stems may have to be stripped from marketbound plants.

Life Cycle: Only two weeks are required from infection to production of viable spores; secondary infection in a field is almost certain. Overwintering occurs on seeds and crop debris. Temperatures of 60–70°F favor spore production. Spores remain viable for only two years.

Host Plants: Celery, celeriac.

Transmission: Seed-, wind-, and rain-borne.

Prevention and Control: Use two- to three-year-old seed, or buy from companies that treat seed with 118–122°F water for 30 minutes. Three-year rotations are generally effective.

Notes: Warm, moist weather hastens the spread of the disease. Temperatures below 40°F check it.

See photograph, page 287.

Fusarium Wilt

Fusarium spp.

FUNGUS

Range: Throughout North America, particularly in warm regions.

Description: Infects plants through roots and wounds. It secretes a toxin that decomposes cells in its path through the vascular system. The characteristic sign of all wilts is a darkening of the vascular bundles. General symptoms of each disease are wilting, yellowing, and eventual death of leaves and stems. On tomatoes, the first symptom in seedlings is a downward curling of the oldest leaves. General wilting, and sometimes death, follow soon after. Older plants may first show the disease on just one branch; lower leaves yellow and the stem droops. The disease progresses to other branches of the plant. Potatoes are infected by various strains of *F. solani* that cause fusarium wilt, dry rot, and soft rot. Dry rot is a storage disease; tuber skins show blue or white bumps over areas of internal decay. Soft rot affects seed pieces, providing access for secondary fungal and bacterial rotting organisms. Pea plants infected with fusarium may rot at the soil line, or simply show a yellowing and wilting of the leaves. Stems of infected plants become brittle. Celery hosts two forms of *F. apii*. Both diseases show up as general stunting, root rot, and darkened vascular tissue on the root, but form one usually makes outer leaves yellow, while form two attacks the heart leaves.

Life Cycle: Fusarium is a facultative saprophytic organism that overwinters on plant refuse in the soil. During the growing season, the fungus produces spores that are capable of immediate germination, but it also produces resting spores that remain viable for ten years or more.

Host Plants: Asparagus, beet, celery, crucifers, cucurbits, nightshade crops, onion, spinach, Swiss chard, and many ornamentals.

Transmission: Primarily soilborne. Secondary infection is often caused by rain or irrigation water. Transplants often bring the disease into a garden.

Prevention and Control: Strains of fusarium are crop-specific. *F. oxysporum* is a good example: *F. oxysporum* f. *conglutinans* gives rise to cabbage yellows (see page 154), f. *lycopersici* is the causal organism of fusarium wilt in tomatoes, and f. *pisi* gives peas root rot and wilt as well as

near wilt. This specificity means that gardeners can rotate fusarium-infected plants without building populations, but must remember that the viability of resting spores necessitates very long rotations of the same crop in an area to be effective. Aside from resistant varieties, soil health and plant vigor are the best defenses against this disease.

Notes: Fusarium is favored by warm soil and air temperatures. Nightshade crops are most susceptible in dry soils when light levels are low and the daylength short. Peas and chili peppers are most often attacked in poorly drained soils. Parasitic nematodes also increase susceptibility, as do low potassium and high nitrogen levels.

See photograph, page 286.

Late Blight
Phytopthora infestans,
P. capsici
FUNGUS

Range: All humid areas of United States and southern Canada.

Description: Potatoes are most often affected by late blight just after blossoming. Tomatoes may become infected shortly before blossoming. Large, water-soaked spots show first on lower leaves. If the

DISEASES
Fungi

weather is dry, the center of the spot may brown and dry. Fuzzy white spores emerge from pores on undersides of leaves. In wet weather, rotting tissue gives off an offensive odor. Stems and petioles (leaf stems) are also affected by this member of the downy mildew group. Infected potato tubers have brown or purplish shrunken spots on their skin. Beneath the skin, spots develop into a reddish-brown dry rot in cool, dry storage conditions, or a wet rot covered with white fuzz when stored in a warm, damp area. The upper halves of tomato fruit are usually affected with grayish-green, water-soaked spots that enlarge. The skin wrinkles and darkens. In moist weather, a fuzzy white growth emerges from the spot. Peppers are hosts to *P. capsici;* stems may be girdled or foliage may show dark, water-soaked spots. The spots dry and whiten. Fruits show wet spots and then shrivel.

Life Cycle: Late blight fungi produce two kinds of spores. At temperatures of 65°F and above, sporangia are predominant, while swimming spores are produced in temperatures between 56 and 65°F. Both sporangia and swimming spores are capable of infecting new tissue immediately, but swimming spores can remain viable for several weeks in the soil if conditions are not conducive to germination. The fungus invades through leaf pores or the cuticle. Mycelium grow between cells, feeding directly on cells and producing a new crop of spores about a week after infection. Mycelium overwinter in infected tubers or plant refuse, producing spores

in the spring to infect new plants. During the 1946 epidemic, pathologists tracked windblown spores for distances of 30 miles.

Host Plants: Potato, tomato, pepper.

Transmission: Wind-, rain-, and soilborne. *P. capsici* is also seed-borne.

Prevention and Control: Rogue infected plants mercilessly at the first sign of late blight. If any late blight has appeared in your potato crop, remove and burn all aboveground parts of the plant at least two weeks before harvesting. Dig tubers only in dry weather, and inspect them carefully for spots; the disease can spread in storage. Plant only certified seed potatoes.

Notes: Late blight infections are dependent on climatic factors. Spores require water for germination, and even though swimming spores are formed in low temperatures, they germinate most readily when temperatures are close to 70°F. Watch for the disease when cool, moist nights are followed by warm, muggy days, or a succession of cool, rainy days are followed by warming and high humidity. Little infection occurs when temperatures are higher than 80°F and humidity is lower than 90%.

See photograph, page 287.

Powdery Mildew

Erysiphe spp.

FUNGUS

Range: Throughout North America, particularly in southern United States.

Description: White mycelium growing on the surface of the plant is the dominant characteristic of powdery mildew. The powdery appearance is given by spores growing from the mycelium. Round white spots usually show first on the undersides of older leaves. The spots enlarge, coalesce and finally cover both leaf surfaces with a white powdery growth. Leaves become pale, then brown and shrivel. Cucurbit fruits ripen prematurely, and because they lack their customary sugar content, have poor texture and flavor. Pods of peas and beans may be covered with the fungus.

Life Cycle: Windblown spores land on leaves or stems, where they germinate into tangled masses of branched mycelium. Hyphae send penetration pegs into the plant, and haustoria feed directly on the cell sap. *Erysiphe* species are obligate parasites: They feed only on living cells. The fungus feeds for several days before becoming apparent. Secondary cycles begin about a week after the first infection. The fungus overwinters as sexual fruiting bodies living on plant refuse, or as mycelium in buds or ornamental hosts and weeds. The fruiting bodies that form late in the season are sometimes dark. In extreme northern areas, most primary infection is due to windblown spores from the south.

Host Plants: Crucifers, cucurbits, legumes, pepper, many ornamentals, and, in the Southwest, lettuce.

Transmission: Wind-borne. Seed-borne in peas and beans.

Prevention and Control: Rotation is effective as long as hosts of the same species are also controlled. Watch for powdery mildew of composites, particularly sunflowers, as well as mildewed phlox and hollyhocks, near cucurbits. A different species attacks both crucifers and legumes. Rogue and destroy infected plants before spores form; remove plant refuse from the garden in fall.

Notes: Powdery mildews do not need to germinate in water films; relative humidity levels of only 20% are adequate. At ambient temperatures of 80°F and higher, spores lose viability within only a few hours. They can't germinate at temperatures lower than 30°F, but do well at 40°F.

See photograph, page 288.

DISEASES
Fungi

Red Stele

Phytopthora fragaiae

FUNGUS

Range: Throughout United States and southern Canada. Particularly important in the North.

Description: This member of the downy mildew family attacks only roots of the strawberry and loganberry plants. In the spring, plants look stunted, and leaves may take on a gray or purplish cast; yields are greatly diminished. Roots sliced longitudinally to show the central vascular system, or stele, look red and rotted.

Life Cycle: Red stele infects small feeder roots first, moving through the plant to the central roots. Swimming spores are released into the soil solution, where they swim to new roots, and resting spores carry the disease through the months when the soil is too warm for disease initiation. Resting spores remain viable for ten years.

Host Plants: Strawberry, loganberry.

Transmission: Soilborne. Carried with transplants, tools, and the soil solution.

Prevention and Control: Plant only certified stock. Strawberry beds should be located on well-drained soil that warms early in the season. If red stele invades, destroy the crop and replant in other locations for a minimum of ten years. This disease spreads quickly, and is nearly impossible to eradicate except by starvation.

Notes: Cool, wet soils encourage the spread of this fungus.

See photograph, page 288.

Root Rot

Pythium spp.,
Rhizoctonia solani,
Pellicularia filamentosa,
Fusarium solani,
F. cucurbitae,
Phoma apiicola,
Aphanomyces spp.

FUNGUS

Range: Throughout United States and southern Canada.

Description: The first signal of root rot is that leaves yellow or discolor, and the plant grows more slowly than normal. If plants are infected early in their lives, they generally die. Fibrous roots are affected first; they rot off as the disease progresses to the main or taproots. Pull up plants to inspect the root system.

Life Cycle: Most species causing root rot live on both dead and live tissue. Some, such as the *Aphanomyces* species, which are the major cause of pea root rot, release swimming spores that can travel quickly in the soil solution. Long-term viability of most root-rotting fungi is guaranteed by resting spores or by their ability to inhabit dead organic matter.

Host Plants: Almost all plant species are susceptible to one or another of the root rot organisms.

Transmission: Usually soilborne.

Prevention and Control: Identifying the exact organism causing the root rot is nearly impossible for anyone but a pathologist, so rotations can sometimes give more trouble than help; for example, peas, spinach, and cucurbits are all attacked by the same *Pythium* species, even though they are in different families. The best prevention is good soil aeration and drainage. Plants should not be set out when the weather is too cool for rapid growth. Good nutrition protects plants to some extent.

Notes: Cool, wet soils favor these organisms. Generally, attacks come in the spring when the soil is warming, or in the fall during a period of wet weather.

See photograph, page 288.

Rots
Sclerotinia spp.
FUNGI

Range: Throughout United States and southern Canada.

Description: Attacks both growing and stored crops. While this rot can look like many other diseases in the early stages, large, black sclerotia embedded in a white cottony growth give it away. Lower leaves and stems are attacked first. Plants develop a soft, watery rot. Affected leaves brown, dry, and drop to the ground. Stems may be girdled, and flowers and buds are often attacked with a wet rot. Often, the white mycelium and black sclerotia are not visible until the leaf, bud, or stem is on the ground. Depending upon species, the tough, black sclerotia range from about 1/8 inch long to almost 1 inch. Look for them inside the stems of woody ornamentals and on the rotted tissue of herbaceous plants.

Life Cycle: Sclerotia are resting bodies which the fungus produces to carry it over the winter and through up to ten years of dormancy. In the spring, spore-producing stalked cups grow from the sclerotia. These cups are also large, growing up to 1 inch in diameter, and could be overlooked as wild mushrooms. It takes

DISEASES
Fungi

three to six weeks for spores to be produced. Like many other fungi, the hyphae are so sticky that they can hold tight to the leaf or stem while the penetration peg bores through the cuticle. The fungus excretes an enzyme that digests the walls between plant cells.

Host Plants: Most garden plants. In general, affected plants and diseases include: stem rot—carrot, celery, lettuce, nightshade crops, and salsify; lettuce drop—endive, lettuce; pink rot—celery; cottony rot—bean, carrot, crucifers, cucurbits, parsnip, and pea. Many ornamentals are also susceptible.

Transmission: Wind- and water-borne; mechanically transmitted on soil or tools.

Prevention and Control: Do not rotate susceptible crops; most species are indiscriminate about their hosts. However, grasses are not susceptible; rotate with sod if the problem seems to be out of control. Good drainage and soil aeration are essential. Remove all infected plant debris, being particularly careful not to scatter the sclerotia.

Notes: Moisture and temperatures in the 70–80°F range favor the development of spores, and germination occurs readily at 55–85°F. Storage vegetables are most susceptible when temperatures are above the optimum range.

See photograph, page 288.

Rust
Puccinia spp., *Uromyces* spp.
FUNGUS

Range: Throughout United States and southern Canada.

Description: Rusts of garden crops are generally characterized by reddish-brown spores during midsummer. Affected plants are stunted and, in severe cases, die prematurely. In asparagus, small cavities on the stems are the first symptoms of rust. By July and August, reddish-brown spores are apparent on ferns and stems, giving way in the fall to black spores that arise from the same areas or from new fruiting bodies on the plant. These spores overwinter on the stalks, and germinate the following year on emerging shoots. On beans, reddish-brown spores form in pustules on the undersides of the leaves during the summer. The black spores appear most frequently on the undersides of leaves, but sometimes on the upper sides as well, in which case they are often surrounded by a yellow border. Bean rust's life cycle is fast: It takes only ten days between infection from a summer spore to production of more spores. Common corn rust shows in summer as reddish-brown pustules on both sides of the leaf; the black fall spores are also on both leaf surfaces. Spores overwinter on refuse, and germinate in the spring to infect sheep sorrel, where blisters containing male and female spermatia form on both leaf surfaces. After opposite types of spermatia fuse, pale yellow spores grow on the undersides of the leaves; these spores blow away to infect corn plants. Corn rust can also reproduce without sheep sorrel, particularly in warm areas where it overwinters in the summer-spore stage. Winds carry these spores north each year. The rust species known as southern corn rust has yellow spores.

Life Cycle: Rusts have the most complicated life cycle of all obligate parasitic fungi. Many species have five different spore forms in one life cycle. Monoecious rusts complete a life cycle on only one host, but heteroecious species, such as the well-known cedar-apple rust, require two different hosts to complete a cycle.

Host Plants: Alfalfa, apple, asparagus, beans, beet, bramble fruits, carrot, clover, corn, currant, eggplant, gooseberry, Jerusalem artichoke, lettuce, okra, onion, pea, peanut, salsify, spinach, and sweet potato.

Transmission: Wind-borne.

Prevention and Control: Keep plants spaced widely enough to promote good air circulation within the row or bed. Plant only those varieties of asparagus which are resistant to rust. Keep soil moist. Rogue infected plants. Remove old stalks after they've dried in fall. Keep humus levels high to encourage *Darluca filum,* a

fungus that parisitizes asparagus rust fungi. Rogue infected weeds and annual crops during the season, and remove and burn crop refuse after harvest. Destroy infected brambles in fall or early spring.

Notes: High humidity and soils with excessively high nitrogen levels that promote sappy crop growth encourage rusts.

See photograph, page 289.

Smuts
Corn Smut
Ustilago maydis
Onion Smut
Urocystis cepulae
FUNGI

Range: Throughout United States and southern Canada. Corn smut is most destructive in southern areas, while onion smut is primarily a disease of the North.

Description: Although ears are most often affected by corn smut, the white galls characteristic of the disease can form on any actively growing portion of the plant. Galls range in size from ¼ inch to 8 inches. The interior of the gall is white at first, but as the fungus grows, the white

DISEASES
Fungi

membrane covering it bursts to release masses of black spores. Look for onion smut when plants are young; blisters form just under the epidermis on first leaves and near the surface of bulbs and roots. As galls mature, a mass of dark spores is visible through the skin. Secondary rots often attack smut-infected plants.

Life Cycle: Spores of corn smut are blown onto plants, where they cause local infections; the disease does not travel through the plant. The spores released from mature galls grow sporidia that release sexually differentiated spores. Spores are carried to new plants, where hyphae of opposite types fuse and cause immediate secondary infections. Spores also overwinter in soil, crop debris, and manure, producing sporidia the following spring or, if circumstances warrant, remaining dormant for as long as seven years. Onion smut attacks seedlings from the day after germination to the time when the first leaf is mature; spores can penetrate only young roots and seed leaves. But after penetration, the fungus grows through the plant until reaching the leaves where it forms blisters just under the skin. Young bulbs also show dark pustules. When pustules rupture the skin, dark spores are released into the soil, where they infect new plants or lie dormant for many years.

Host Plants: Corn, grasses, and grains are susceptible to *Ustilago*; members of the onion family, wheat, and grasses are susceptible to *Urocystis*.

Transmission: Corn smut is wind-borne. Onion smut is soilborne, and may be transported on tools, shoes, and in the soil solution.

Prevention and Control: For corn smut, resistant varieties are available. Galls should be picked off plants and burned before spores are formed. Three- to four-year rotations are generally effective. Check onion family seedlings for smut pustules; destroy infected plants. If a seedling in a flat displays the disease, throw the entire flat away. Rapid growth in warm soil conditions minimizes infection.

Notes: Corn smut can germinate at temperatures of 46–98°F, although optimum temperatures for germination are 80–90°F. Dry weather early in the season followed by a period of moderately rainy weather encourages infection. Plant succulence as the result of excessively high nitrogen levels encourages invasion, as do wounds. Onion smut is inactivated at soil temperatures of 80°F or above.

See photograph, page 289.

Southern Blight
Sclerotium rolfsii
FUNGUS

Range: Southern United States.

Description: Attacks plants first at the soil line, producing a soft rot. If stems resist girdling, the fungus continues to grow up and out from the initial point of infection. Within a few days of infection, a thick white mycelial growth covers infected areas, and often spreads along the soil surface around the plant. Sclerotia form within the mycelium. Their initial white coloring makes them difficult to see, but they darken to yellow and then a reddish or golden-tan color as they mature, finally resembling mustard seeds.

Life Cycle: Southern blight excretes oxalic acid in concentrations strong enough to kill cells in its path of growth. This action accounts for both its ability to prey on so many different kinds of plants and its growth on plant surfaces; it doesn't need to penetrate far to find nutrition. The fungus overwinters either as sclerotia or mycelium living within plant debris on the field. Sclerotia germinate in the spring in warm, wet conditions. When dormant, they are viable for many years.

Host Plants: Almost all plants except grasses. Economically significant for peanuts and nightshade crops.

Transmission: Soilborne primarily. Sometimes seed-borne. Water, tools, and shoes can transport the heavy sclerotia.

Prevention and Control: Keep soil organic matter high; nitrogen levels and aeration are increased, and predators and parasites keep southern blight in check. Deep-plow all plant debris by covering it with a minimum of 4 inches of soil, burying the topsoil as well. Researchers recommend "non-dirting" cultivation systems, which prevent soil from being thrown against plants, as well as the use of weed-free raised beds. When roguing plants, carefully scrape up the top inch of soil for a diameter of about 8 inches around every infected plant, taking care not to drop the sclerotia. Use corn or another grass in rotations.

Notes: Sandy soils without adequate aeration favor this disease. Nitrogen deficiencies increase plant susceptibility.

Verticillium Wilt
Verticillium albo-atrum
FUNGUS

Range: Throughout United States and southern Canada.

Description: The first symptom of verticillium is a wilting of leaves and stems on one or more branches. Margins of leaves may curl upward before yellowing and dropping off. The whole plant may die. Fruit is generally small. Like all wilts, verticillium travels through the vascular

DISEASES
Nematodes

system, giving it a characteristic dark look and plugging vessels.

Life Cycle: Verticillium is very long-lived. Spores can persist on dead organic matter in the soil for as long as 15 years. The fungus enters through roots and wounds near the soil line, infects the vascular system, and overwinters in crop debris.

Host Plants: Most food crops, as well as many ornamentals and trees. Tomato, potato, eggplant, cucurbits, and beans are most severely affected.

Transmission: Soilborne. Can be carried by water, tools, and shoes.

Prevention and Control: Despite the long-term persistence of verticillium, four-year rotations of highly susceptible crops minimize infection. Remove all infected crop debris at the end of the year, and burn it unless you can make a hot compost pile (one that reaches 160°F for three or four days). In the North, raising temperatures around plants with cloches or plastic tunnels may inhibit the disease.

Notes: Verticillium is favored by slightly cooler temperatures than fusarium, and thus is more common in the North or during cool periods. The optimum temperature for infection is 70°F, although it grows at both higher and lower temperatures.

See photograph, page 289.

Root-Knot Nematode
Meloidogyne spp.
NEMATODE

Range: Throughout United States, though more common in the South.

Description: The first sign of root-knot nematodes is usually stunting. This is often followed by wilting and yellowing, and sometimes by death. Digging up infected plants reveals galls or swellings of various sizes on the roots or tubers. Secondary infections of fusarium and bacterial wilts may occur.

Life Cycle: Newly hatched larvae move through the upper 2 feet of soil until each finds a root, which it penetrates. Once inside, it becomes sedentary. Glandular secretions injected by the larva into the root cause surrounding cells to enlarge and form a gall, or root knot, on which the nematode feeds. Adult females are pear-shaped and whitish; males are threadlike. The female deposits 300 to 3,000 eggs in a yellow-brown gelatinous mass. Larvae escape into the soil when the infected root cracks or decays, and the cycle begins again. Several generations are born each season; fewer in the North. Nematodes overwinter in the soil.

Host Plants: Over 2,000 plants are susceptible to root-knot nematodes, including fruit trees, most crops, and ornamentals. Greenhouse crops are also frequently infected. Grains and grasses are resistant or immune.

Transmission: Soilborne. Also carried in galls on infected roots.

Prevention and Control: Some root-knot species are more host-specific than others; your local Extension office should be able to identify the nematodes attacking your crops and recommend a rotation. All respond to rotations with marigold mixtures such as 'Nemagold'. Tomato varieties resistant to root-knot nematodes carry the letter "N" after the variety name in seed catalogs; planting these varieties helps insure a good harvest.

Notes: Root-knot nematodes generally prefer sandy or peaty soils and tropical conditions, and therefore are more prevalent in the South and in greenhouses than in Northern areas.

See photograph, page 290.

Aster Yellows

Chlorogenus callistephi var. californicus

VIRUS

Range: Throughout United States and southern Canada.

Description: Symptoms vary according to the crop affected. Carrots are stunted and develop too many root hairs, usually slightly thickened or growing in bushy groups, as well as yellowed, bronzed, and distorted foliage. In lettuce, the disease is known as white heart because the interior is unnaturally pale. Potatoes and tomatoes show leaf rolling and stem distortion. Celery shows stalk twisting and stunting, particularly toward the center. Cracking and yellowing is also common. Cleared veins are common on most plants with aster yellows. Other characteristic symptoms include too erect a habit, excessive adventitious root growth, and petiole (leaf stem) and stem distortions. Soft rot organisms often infect the plant's crown late in the season.

Life Cycle: Aster yellows are transmitted when an infected leafhopper feeds. Reproducing rapidly within the plant, the virus is easily transmitted to new leafhoppers. This organism is dependent for part of its life cycle on the insect; it must live within the leafhopper for about ten days to two weeks before it can infect a new plant. The virus lives only about 100 days inside insects unless they become reinfected. Perennial crops and weeds harbor the virus from one season to the next and can infect a new crop of insects.

Host Plants: Many. Particularly carrot, celery, cucurbits, endive, New Zealand spinach, potato, onion, strawberry, and tomato. Many ornamentals, both annual and perennial.

Transmission: Leafhoppers.

Prevention and Control: Eliminating leaf-hoppers is more easily said than done since they are so small and fast. However, if aster yellows have been a problem in the past with a particular crop, screening, covering plants with floating row covers such as Reemay, or placing the crop under protective tunnels may be practical. Check weeds around the garden for signs of the disease, and pull and burn any that are infected.

See photograph, page 290.

Bean Mosaic

Marmor spp.

VIRUS

Range: Throughout United States and southern Canada.

Description: Mottled leaves are the first symptom of bean mosaic. If seed-borne, the first leaves show chlorotic (yellowed) areas and signs of distortion. Leaf margins often roll downward, and generalized blistering or puckering along the veins may also be displayed. Plants are stunted and internodes (stem segments between leaves) too short. If pods form, they are often small. One strain produces "greasy pod" in western areas, a condition in which the pods form but look greasy.

Life Cycle: This virus is most often insect-vectored to new plants, although mechan-ical transmission is also a threat. Depending upon plant age at the time of infection, symptoms and severity vary. Once within the host, the virus reproduces rapidly. It can overwinter in crop debris or weeds, and remains viable for many years.

Host Plants: Beans. Some bean mosaic species affect clovers, pea, and ornamentals such as gladiolus and freesia.

Transmission: Aphids and other insects, gardeners, and occasionally, infected seed.

Prevention and Control: Use resistant varieties when possible, and buy western-grown seed that is certified disease-free. Pull and burn any plants that display signs of the disease, and do not let crop debris stand in the field after harvest. Wash and change clothes after touching plants that look as if they have a mosaic.

Notes: Disease symptoms are more obvious and severe at high temperatures.

See photograph, page 290.

Beet Curly Top

Ruga varrucosans

VIRUS

Range: Western United States and southern Canada.

Description: Symptoms of this disease vary according to the crop. On beets, veins in foliage clear and leaves curl upward before yellowing, wilting, and dying. Sometimes, pointed tissue protrudes from veins on the undersides of leaves. There may also be an abnormal increase in the number of roots growing from the main root. In tomatoes, the disease is characteristically called yellows because the plant yellows and dies if infected at a young age. If infected near maturity, leaves curl and become thick and leathery, and the plant habit is abnormally upright. The plant may become pale, and few fruits are formed or come to maturity. Cucurbits show the disease by dark coloration and a turning up of the growing tips in combination with yellowing of old leaves. New leaves are unusually small and internodes (stem segments between leaves) very short. Beans show clearing of veins or puckering and downward curling of leaves.

Life Cycle: The virus infects plants as the beet leafhopper feeds and deposits it in plant tissue. It travels to the phloem tissues of the plant, causing distortion of new tissues, an off-color, and general stunting. Uninfected beet leafhoppers pick up the disease from infected plants and transmit it to new tissues the same or the following year. Leafhopper eggs may be laid on perennial hosts for overwintering. If so, they hatch and feed on the host during the early spring and fly to infect garden annuals later in the summer.

Host Plants: Beans, beet, carrot, celery, crucifers, cucurbits, New Zealand spinach, Swiss chard, and many ornamentals.

Transmission: Beet leafhopper.

Prevention and Control: Plant vigor is the best preventive. Because this disease is vectored by the beet leafhopper and is most injurious to young plants, floating row covers, or plastic or screen tunnels, covering seedlings or transplants can often inhibit the spread of beet curly top. Protective devices are most necessary in those gardens within the regions where sugar beets are grown. (But remember that leafhoppers will fly hundreds of miles to find new hosts if necessary.) If the disease is noted in the garden, the sickly plant should be pulled, roots and all, and burned. Rotation is of no use in the control of this disease.

Notes: This disease is most severe when both temperatures and light intensity are high and relative humidity is low.

See photograph, page 290.

Cucumber Mosaic

Marmor cucumeris

VIRUS

Range: Throughout United States and Canada.

Description: Mottled green-and-yellow leaves are the first noticeable symptoms

DISEASES
Viruses

of this disease. Leaves are usually stunted and distorted, and internodes (stem segments between leaves) are shorter than normal. In tomatoes, this organism causes "shoestring," a condition in which leaves are extremely narrow. Fruit set is reduced and, in the case of cucumbers, nearly mature fruit is often distorted with a mottled or very pale color. Spinach displays a rosetted pattern and leaves are usually extremely chlorotic (yellowed). Celery displays cleared veins, stunting and mottling of inner leaves.

Life Cycle: Cucumber mosaic enters the plant through natural openings or wounds, and once there reproduces rapidly. Subsequently, pests and people pick up the disease through feeding or contact and move it through the planting. Insects often carry the virus to its winter host plants—milkweed, pokeweed, and some mints—as well. This virus has a long viability without a host and, once present, is difficult to eradicate.

Host Plants: Many, including celery, curcurbits, nightshades, and spinach. Ornamentals affected include geranium, myrtle, delphinium, and petunia.

Transmission: Primarily vectored by aphids and cucumber beetles, mechanically transmitted by gardeners. Occasionally seed-borne.

Prevention and Control: Use resistant varieties when possible. Check all surrounding weeds for signs of mosaic, and pull and burn any suspects. Wash hands thoroughly and change clothes after touching infected plants.

Notes: Temperatures between 70° and 80°F favor the increase of this disease.

See photograph, page 290.

Potato Leaf Roll
Corium solani
VIRUS

Range: Throughout United States and Canada.

Description: Leaf roll is characterized by an upward rolling of the leaf margins, usually toward the top of the plant if the disease is acquired in the present season. Oldest leaves are first affected if disease comes from infected stock. Leaves may also be unnaturally purplish or reddish on the undersides and very thick and leathery. Plants are stunted and abnormally erect, and tuber production is greatly reduced. Some potato varieties show brown tissue within the phloem vessels of stems or tubers. Even if seed-borne, disease symptoms do not show until plants are at least a month old.

Life Cycle: Overwinters either in infected seed stock or on perennial weeds and crops. If infected seed is planted, the disease is evident early enough in the season so that a careful gardener can destroy the plant, but by that time the virus may have been carried to healthy plants. The virus reproduces rapidly and is carried by insects to nearby plants and weeds.

Host Plants: Potato and other nightshade family weeds and crops.

Transmission: Aphids and other insects. Sometimes seed-borne.

Prevention and Control: Plant only certified disease-free seed potatoes. Rogue all infected plants and burn them. Check nearby solanaceous weeds for signs of the disease, and destroy any that show them.

See photograph, page 291.

Tobacco Mosaic Virus (TMV)

Marmor tabaci

VIRUS

Range: Throughout United States and southern Canada.

Description: Mottled leaves are the most characteristic symptom of the disease, but sharp definitions between green and yellow areas are less distinct than in many other mosaic diseases. Some leaf puckering may occur, especially near the veins. Plants are stunted and often malformed. Fruit sometimes shows a darkening of the vascular elements or yellow, sunken areas on the skin.

Life Cycle: This virus is able to remain viable without a host for many years. Like all viruses, this organism is very small and can enter a plant through a wound as insignificant as a broken hair on a leaf or a damaged root hair. It spreads rapidly once inside the host, causing significant decrease in chlorophyll production and thus in growth and yield. It can remain viable for many years in dried crop residue and tolerates very high temperatures.

Host Plants: All nightshades, including ornamentals in the family such as nicotiana, as well as beet, buckwheat, pinto bean, spinach, and some crucifers.

Transmission: Primarily mechanical: gardeners carry the disease from handling cigarettes or other tobacco products or from touching a diseased plant and then uninfected tissue. Can be seed-borne in petunia and tomato.

Prevention and Control: Use resistant varieties when available. Should any crop display signs of mosaic, pull it immediately and remove it from the garden before burning. (Burning does not always destroy this virus.) Wash before touching healthy crops after touching one with a

DISEASES
Viruses

viral disease. Smokers should wash with soap and water and, to be sure, dip into skim milk and then fresh water before working with susceptible plants. Watch all hedgerows and borders for signs of mosaic on weeds in the nightshade family, and pay attention to plantings of petunias.

See photograph, page 291.

Tobacco Ring Spot
Annulus tabaci
VIRUS

Range: Throughout United States and Canada.

Description: Symptoms vary according to the plant affected. In general, necrotic (dead) spots on leaves are the first symptoms, although the area covered and pattern varies. Sometimes, chlorotic (yellowed) areas form in concentric rings. On spinach, large, irregular areas are chlorotic, while cucurbits display tiny necrotic dots on leaves and small pits on fruit. The disease is known as bouquet disease in potatoes because plants have shortened stems and internodes (stem segments between leaves), giving a rosetted appearance. Dark lesions are also common on the undersides of potato leaves. Eggplants are stunted and yellow. Petunia plants are stunted and distorted, with mottled leaves. Petioles (leaf stems) and stems may have dark streaks or rings, and growing tips may look blighted.

Life Cycle: This virus is usually transmitted by feeding insects. Once within the plant, it reproduces, affecting chlorophyll production and formation of plant tissues. It overwinters in susceptible weeds, perennial crops, and petunia seed. Insects reinfect garden plants each spring.

Host Plants: Many, including beet, celery, cucurbits, nightshades, soybean, and spinach.

Transmission: Grasshoppers, thrips, and other insects. Sometimes vectored by nematodes, particularly *Xiphinema americana*. Can be seed-borne in petunia.

Prevention and Control: Eradicate any crop or weed displaying symptoms of viral disease, burning to destroy. Try to keep grasshopper populations low.

See photograph, page 291.

Weeds

An Overview

What makes a weed? Various garden writers give various definitions: A weed is a plant out of place; a weed is a plant that grows well in disturbed areas; a weed is a plant that competes well with cultivated crops; a weed is a nuisance.

Additionally, some weeds are poisonous or allergenic to livestock, people, or even other plants. They may harbor insect pests and plant diseases, and they cause the largest economic loss of any factor, including drought, pests, and diseases.

But weeds can also be beneficial. As indicator plants, they can tell you things about your soil and growing conditions more surely than most cultivated crops. (See the table, Weeds as Indicator Plants, on pages 180–81.) They form a valuable bank of genetic stock from which we can breed stronger, healthier food crops. Handled correctly, they can make good green-manure crops. Some enlarge the feeding zone for cultivated crops, and deep-feeding weeds bring up nutrients from the subsoil. Wildlife often depends on weedy areas for food and shelter. Some weeds are good medicine, some are beautiful, some protect and heal unhealthy soils, and some are very good food.

For the gardener with only a small piece of cultivated land, weed control is a relatively simple matter. If a plant is a weed—if it is interfering with the crops you want to grow—you can pull it, dig it, till it, or smother it with a deep mulch. For growers working on larger pieces of land, weed control becomes more sophisticated. Farmers must rely on good timing and appropriate cultural and control techniques to keep weed populations from interfering with crop production.

This section includes only those weeds considered to cause the most serious threat by agronomists across the United States and southern Canada. A weed in your garden may not be included; it could be a real problem in your area, but because its range is limited, might not qualify for inclusion. However, as you leaf through these entries, you're certain to see old friends and adversaries.

Weed Seeds

Soils contain millions of weed seeds. Researchers in England once dug up and sifted through the top few inches of soil on a hectare (2.47 acres) of land. They counted 1.33 million seeds of prostrate knotweed, 1.73 million shepherd's purse seeds, 3.21 million chickweed seeds, and an alarming 16.6 million seeds of annual bluegrass. This is not surprising when you consider the number of seeds a single weed plant can produce. For example, curly dock sets an average of 29,500 seeds per plant, purslane sets 52,300, redroot pigweed sets 117,400 seeds, and mullein sets 223,200 seeds *per plant*.

Even though it may seem so, not all weed seeds germinate at one time. Very often, sprouting and growth are inhibited by environmental conditions. The seed may be buried so deeply that the percentage of oxygen in surrounding soil is too low, or the percentage of carbon dioxide too high. Temperature, daylength, and moisture conditions may not be correct. In these cases, many seeds go through an "enforced" or "induced" period of *dormancy.*

When dormancy is *enforced,* the seed is capable of germinating almost immediately after the limitation is removed. For example, the weeds that sprout in your early garden soils may have formed late in the last season and become dormant in response to low photoperiods and/or temperatures. When spring daylengths, as well as other factors such as temperature and oxygen levels, signal good growing conditions, they sprout.

Induced dormancy is also a consequence of exposure to less than ideal conditions. However, seeds with an induced dormancy differ from those with an enforced

WEEDS

An Overview

WEEDS AS INDICATOR PLANTS

Condition	Weed
Hardpan or crust; compacted	Cruciferous weeds (except Shepherd's Purse) Horse Nettle Morning-Glory Plantain Quackgrass
Compacted, but with good nutrition	Chickweed Lamb's-Quarters
Often come with cultivation	Carpetweed Dandelion Mallow Pigweed Plantain Prickly Lettuce Prostrate Knotweed Stinging Nettle Thistle
Rich soils	Burdock Ground Ivy Lamb's-Quarters Pigweed Purslane
Sandy soils with low humus	Pinks Ragweed Rose White Cockle Wild Garlic Wild Lettuce
Acid soils	Chickweed Daisy Dock Oxeye Daisies Plantain Sorrel

WEEDS
An Overview

Condition	Weed
	Sowthistle Yarrow
Alkaline soils	Lamb's-Quarters Mustards
Saline soils	Shepherd's Purse
Poorly drained soils	Beggarticks Canada Goldenrod Curly Dock Hedge Bindweed Joe-Pye Weed Sheep Sorrel Smartweed
Dry soils with low humus	Mustards

dormancy in that they began life as a nondormant seed, and only became dormant in response to poor conditions. For example, a winter cress seed, which drops to the ground in early June, ready to begin the germination process almost immediately, can become dormant if it is buried too deeply or if moisture levels are too low.

Some seeds are "innately" dormant; they must go through one or another process before they can germinate. Some of these seeds must go through a period of alternate freezing and thawing. Others, such as lamb's-quarters seeds, are coated with a chemical that inhibits germination; leaching (washing away) of the chemical is necessary for growth to occur.

Some weeds produce both immediately dormant and nondormant seeds on the same plant at the same time,

WEEDS
An Overview

just as some produce both seeds from self-fertilizing flowers and those formed from the union of pollen and ovule produced on differently sexed flowers.

Annual, Biennial, or Perennial?

Annual weeds live only one season from germination to maturity, seed production, and death. They guarantee their survival by making seeds rather than bulbs, corms, or reproductive rootstocks—tactics often used by perennials. And seed production is often prodigious. At least 80 percent of the weeds in your garden are annuals. Well-known annuals include the ragweeds, pigweeds, smartweeds, purslane, chickweed, knotweed, and lamb's-quarters.

Winter annuals act almost like biennials. They often germinate in mid- to late season, making a small rosette of leaves on the soil surface. Come fall and frost, they seem to die back, but the next spring, the rosette reappears, and in its midst tall flowering stalks grow. Flowering, seed production, and death occur in spring or early summer. Shepherd's purse is a winter annual.

Biennials live for two seasons, producing vegetative growth the first year—often in the form of a low-lying rosette of leaves—and flowering and setting seed the second. Common biennials are Queen Anne's lace, mullein, burdock, and teasel.

Perennials live for at least three and often for many years, usually reproducing by seed and vegetative means every season. Many grow long, tenacious taproots that make them almost impossible to pull. This means that the frustrated gardener must cope with the continuous regrowth of the parent weed as well as its seeds and offsets. Because of their reproductive rootstocks and stems, some perennials can send up new plants as far as 20 feet from the parent plant. Familiar perennials are the golden-rods, dandelion, chicory, bindweed, and the plantains.

WEEDS
An Overview

Some of our most feared and hated weeds are woody perennials. These include poison ivy, kudzu, Japanese honeysuckle, and the multiflora rose. Birds enjoy the nutrient-rich seeds of woody perennials and are one of the main causes of their rapid spread. Some of these plants are also adept at vegetative propagation, with new plants springing up wherever their creeping stems touch the soil.

Grasses often seem like the worst of weeds, the most difficult to see and, once you've seen them, the hardest to uproot or keep from seeding. Some perennial grasses, such as quackgrass, can produce new plants from underground stems fully 6 yards from the original plant. Most perennial grasses reproduce from rhizomes or rootstocks as well as from seed, and even some annuals, like crabgrass, can root and send up new plants from stem nodes.

Because the growth habits and reproductive strategies of weeds vary depending on their life cycles, organic control is geared to the annual, biennial, or perennial nature of each weed. Learning which weeds fall in which category is the first step in a sensible control program. Weeds in this section are listed alphabetically by common name according to their growth habit; there are chapters for annual, biennial, perennial, woody perennial, and grass weeds. Latin names are also given.

Controlling Weeds
Control methods for weeds differ in response to several factors. In addition to the growth and reproductive regimens of each, the environment, the plant community, and your own capabilities and constraints all influence the effectiveness of any control measure you might plan.

Understanding is the first tool of the gardener. Without a basic knowledge of the characteristics of the plant that you are trying to eradicate, you can make very

WEEDS
An Overview

serious mistakes. For example, more than one person has discovered that tilling up comfrey roots or quackgrass rhizomes only spreads and multiplies these hardy creatures. Letting small, late lamb's-quarters flower is equally disastrous; viable seeds can form on plants only a few inches tall. Whether trying to grow or eliminate a plant, the first defense is always observation and self-education.

Gardeners who stand over a patch of ground which supports both cultivated crops and weeds are often unsure of which is which. Plant communities are complex; not only do members of the same species differ, species formation, as well as domination, changes as the environment changes, and the environment changes as the species change. For example, seed production of many weeds increases with distance between like plants.

To make matters more complex, weeds sometimes mimic the crop they grow in. Years of survival of the weeds that were hardest to distinguish from the crop—and thus most likely to be overlooked—have resulted in some weeds, such as a weed corn in Central America and a barnyard grass of rice fields in California and the Orient, which, in their pre-flowering stages, are virtually indistinguishable from the crop itself. If you suddenly notice a flowering lamb's-quarters in your mint patch or a grass in the daylilies that you'd swear wasn't there the day before, you've probably been tricked by a mimic. Was the lamb's-quarters plant the same height as the mint, and growing on a single thin stem, rather than its usual bushy habit? Were the leaves of this particular grass unusually broad and thick like the daylily's? Even a careful inspection often fails to reveal these most insidious weeds until they flower.

Gardeners who wish to decrease weed populations—and their own control efforts—are wise to adapt control measures to the situation at hand rather than simply following the same procedures year after year and weed after weed.

General control guidelines include preventing annuals from setting seed and uprooting perennials as soon as you see them. Biennials fall between: The first year, treat them as perennials, but if you don't notice them until the second (or seed-producing) year, control as for annuals. A 2- to 4-inch layer of mulch will smother most annual weeds if applied early in the season. Make sure the mulch you use is free of weed seeds, however; a weedy hay mulch will cause more of a problem than it cures. Cover cropping is also a good weed-smothering technique if you can spare a bed or field for a season, and it enriches the soil. Closely planted beds will also shade out many weeds.

Mulching, cover-cropping, and close planting also weaken perennial weeds significantly, making them easier to eradicate. There are some excellent hand-weeders on the market for those hateful perennial taproots, including long-handled pincers that pull weeds out like tweezers. Check garden and tool supply catalogs if perennial weeds are getting the better of you. Mowing a perennial-infested field at weekly or biweekly intervals from first flowering, when perennials are most vulnerable, until heavy frost will weaken the plants and eventually kill them.

Consider control of woody perennials as a worthwhile three-year project. Try to spot woody perennials early and remove them before they become well established. Dig up all plant parts as often as you see them and remove them from the garden, yard, or field. Wear protective clothing when handling poison oak or ivy, and do not burn these plants. Mulch areas that have hosted woody perennial weeds heavily, using heavy layers of newspaper or hay covered with weighted black plastic.

To combat weed grasses, pull up new plants when-

FLOWER TYPES

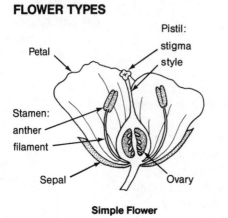

Petal

Pistil:
stigma
style

Stamen:
anther
filament

Sepal

Ovary

Simple Flower

Ray flower

Disk flower

Sepal

Compound Flower

LEAF SHAPES

Simple, Entire

Simple, Lobed

Compound, Entire

LEAF ARRANGEMENTS

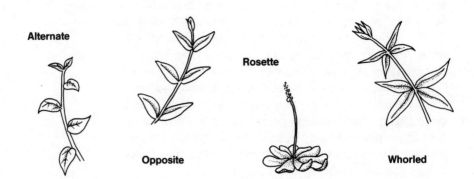

Alternate

Rosette

Opposite

Whorled

ever you see them; they'll set seed sooner than you think, and it's imperative to prevent seeding. Don't leave uprooted plants in the garden; they'll just reroot and start over. Compost them in a hot pile. Dig out as much of established plants as you can; every piece you leave behind could be a new plant in the making. Once you've dug up the plants, mulch the area heavily to prevent regrowth. In lawns, dig out undesirable grasses, and mow frequently enough to prevent weed grasses from setting seed. Like woody perennials, these weeds will take several seasons to control.

If perpetual vigilance doesn't sound like your idea of summer fun, and you don't mind if your beds aren't pretty as pictures, you'll like Canadian research findings for reducing weed control. The researchers found that vegetable crops had critical control times, when weeds absolutely *had* to be controlled if yields weren't to suffer, but that not controlling weeds the rest of the time didn't really have a detrimental effect on yields. Put generally, if you control

ROOT TYPES

Taproot

Fibrous

CREEPING STEMS

Runner (aboveground)

Rhizome (underground)

WEEDS

An Overview

weeds for several weeks after transplanting or seeding, until the crop plants are well established, then weed every three to five weeks until harvest, your crop will produce without significant yield reductions.

Biological Control: The Future?
How handy it would be to have a magic fungus or hungry insect that ate only weeds. True, some biological controls exist, but they do not yet offer growers a ready solution to most weed problems in the garden.

Biological control is tricky; a fungus or insect that attacks a weed may attack a cultivated crop in the same family once its preferred host is eliminated. After all, Colorado potato beetles once dined most happily on buffalo bur, a weed in the nightshade family, and only switched to potatoes, eggplant, and petunias after these crops were introduced into their habitats. Additionally, if a weed that is the preferred host of an insect or disease is eliminated by a biological control organism, the disease or insect will more than likely adapt to live on related cultivated crops.

Nonetheless, some startling successes have been achieved. In 1945, a beetle was released that brought good control of St.-John's-wort in only three years. Russian thistle can be controlled by a species of moth, and two kinds of weevil will attack puncture vine. Smartweed carries a smut that is host-specific, and geese prefer weed grasses even to strawberry leaves, making them good natural controls. As time and research go on, we are likely to see more weeds controlled by the intelligent release of parasites and predators that destroy or inhibit them without interfering with the plants we choose to cultivate. Until then, good gardeners have no choice but to pull, hoe, till judiciously, mulch, covercrop, and remember that weeds are both enemies and allies.

Annual Sowthistle

Sonchus oleraceus

COMPOSITAE

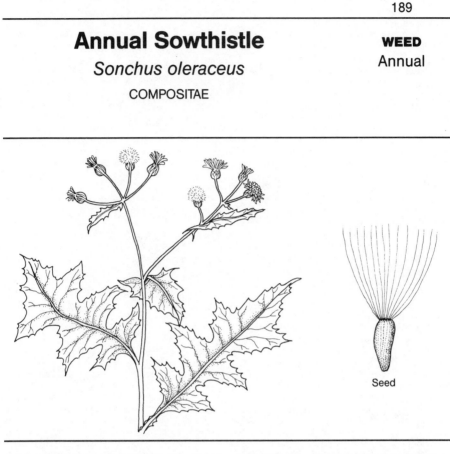

Seed

Range: Throughout United States and southern Canada; particularly troublesome in coastal regions.

Description: Plants are 1 to 6½ feet tall. An erect, branched plant with stems that contain a milky juice. Leaves are alternate and more numerous toward the base than the top. The major leaves on the plant are deeply cut into one to three lobes along each side and have an arrow-shaped terminal lobe. Leaf margins are prickly. The pale yellow flower heads are rounded and dense. Seeds are carried to new ground by hairy pappuses. Blooms June to October.

Life Cycle: Annual, reproducing by seeds.

Prevention and Control: Hoe and pull. Watch waste places for blooming sowthistles and mow them prior to seed formation.

Notes: Sowthistles are common in both cultivated and uncultivated areas with good light conditions. Perennial sowthistle, a troublesome weed in northern grain-growing areas, looks like the annuals in the family, although the leaf is less prickly and the flower a more vivid yellow. The perennial species reproduces from the rootstock as well as from seeds and must be dug to be eradicated.

WEED
Annual

WEED
Annual

Black Nightshade, Deadly Nightshade
Solanum nigrum
SOLANACEAE

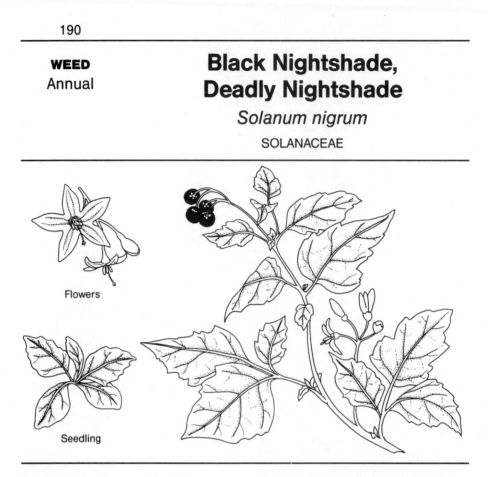

Flowers

Seedling

Range: Eastern half of United States and southeastern Canada.

Description: Plants are 1 to 2 feet tall. A low, spreading plant that branches prolifically. Slightly toothed leaves are alternate, ovate, and simple. The five-petaled blooms are white and look a great deal like tomato flowers, especially since they droop in clusters. Small green berries turn black upon maturity and contain numerous seeds. Yellow to brown seeds are small, wrinkled, dull, and flattened. Blooms July to September.

Life Cycle: Annual, reproducing by seeds.

Prevention and Control: Nightshade is rarely present in epidemic proportions, so it's effective to pull the stray plant that takes root in your garden.

Notes: Prone to pests and diseases common to other solanaceous crops. Nightshade is especially prevalent in disturbed soils. Occasionally found in shaded areas. Some observers think nightshade in the garden indicates that the soil is tired of root crops.

Carpetweed
Mollugo verticillata
AIZOACEAE

WEED
Annual

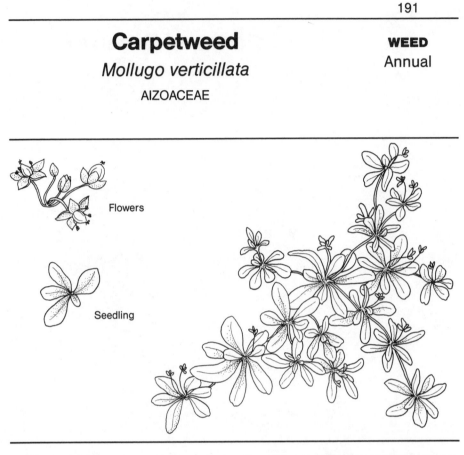

Flowers

Seedling

Range: Throughout United States, except north central areas, and southern Canada.

Description: Stems grow to 1 foot long. A bright green, prostrate plant that spreads outward in all directions from its central taproot. It branches copiously at the base, making a flat carpetlike mat. Three to six whorled leaves grow from each stem node. Leaves are simple, smooth and taper to a very small petiole. Two to five small white flowers with five petals grow from each node. Tiny capsules are three-lobed and hold numerous orange-red, ridged seeds. Blooms June to September.

Life Cycle: Annual, reproducing by seeds.

Prevention and Control: Pull carpetweed immediately. This plant grows, flowers, and sets seeds rapidly. In cases of serious infestation, hoeing just below the soil line is effective.

Notes: Carpetweed likes good drainage and moderate to excellent fertility. Especially prevalent on sandy soils.

WEED
Annual

Catchweed Bedstraw

Galium aparine

RUBIACEAE

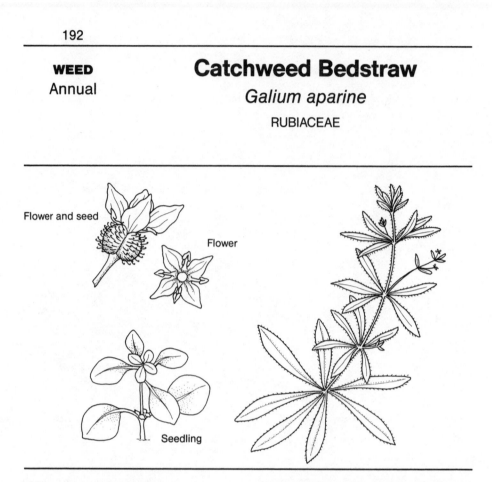

Flower and seed

Flower

Seedling

Range: Throughout United States and southern Canada.

Description: Stems are 8 inches to 5 feet long and are prostrate except at their tips. They are jointed, slender, and tough, with four ridges. Short, bristly hooks grow along the ridges. Six to eight lanceolate leaves with a single, central vein form a whorl at each joint. Leaves have sharp bristles at margins, tips, and upper surfaces. Groups of one to three small white flowers with four lobes joined into a corolla grow on stalks from leaf axils. A two-chambered, spherical, bristly seedpod develops from the base of the flower. Blooms May to July.

Life Cycle: Annual, reproducing by seeds.

Prevention and Control: Hoeing and pulling will eradicate catchweed bedstraw from the garden. It is more frequently a weed on the edges of pastures than in garden areas, and should be mowed before flowering and setting seed.

Notes: Catchweed bedstraw prefers moist, rich soils with moderately good drainage. It is often found in soils that once formed creek or river beds, on the edges of woodlands, and in slightly shaded areas formed by hedgerows and fences. Flowering occurs fairly early in the season, so plants should be removed as soon as they are noticed.

Common Chickweed
Stellaria media
CARYOPHYLLACEAE

WEED
Annual

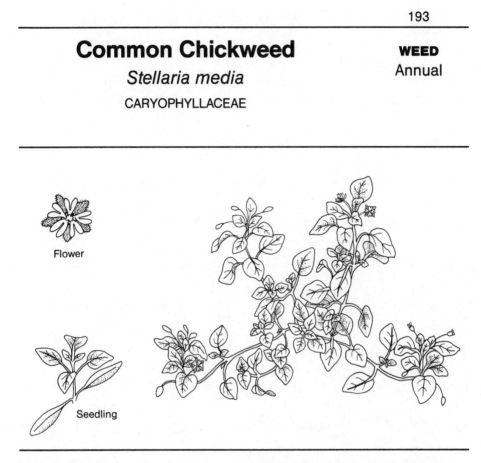

Flower

Seedling

Range: Throughout United States and southern Canada.

Description: Stems may reach 3 feet, but usually grow to 1½ feet long. Bright green, often forming a loose mat on the soil surface with stems that are usually erect toward the tips. Stems branch copiously from each other as well as the central crown arising from a fibrous, shallow root system. Leaves are simple, oval, and pointed at the tip, opposite, and sometimes hairy toward the petioles. The five white petals are usually split, giving the appearance of ten petals. Five green and hairy sepals extend beyond the petals. An ovoid capsule holds many red-brown seeds with obvious bumpy ridges. Blooms February to December.

Life Cycle: Annual or winter annual, reproducing both by seeds and creeping, rooting stems. Often sets seed in fall and/or winter in mild climates.

Prevention and Control: Pulling is the best remedy. Because stems root easily from the nodes, weed into buckets. Dump plants into a compost pile.

Notes: A dense growth of chickweed can impede exchange of air between soil and atmosphere and contribute to excess soil moisture. Though this plant likes rich soil, it tolerates high acidity. It makes the most vigorous growth during cool weather when soil moisture and humidity are high. Edible.

WEED
Annual

Common Cocklebur

Xanthium pensylvanicum

COMPOSITAE

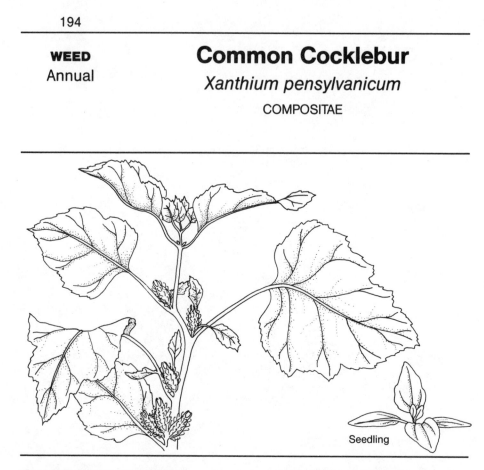

Seedling

Range: Throughout United States and southern Canada, with the exceptions of Quebec and northern New England.

Description: Plants can grow to 4 feet, but are usually between 1 and 2½ feet tall. Erect, ridged, hairy, and sometimes red-spotted stems are so branched that cocklebur soon looks like a bush. Leaves are alternate, simple, long-petioled, and rough on both sides. The overall leaf shape is almost triangular to heart-shaped with deep teeth and a serrated margin. Male, or staminate, flowers grow in short terminal spikes and drop soon after the pollen has been shed. The female, or pistillate, flowers grow in clusters in axils. Light brown burs develop from the female flowers. These burs have two sharp, incurved beaks at the top and are covered with prickles, each with a sharp hook at the end. The hooks attach to passing people or animals. Blooms August and September.

Life Cycle: Annual, reproducing by seeds.

Prevention and Control: Hoeing and pulling are effective controls for cockleburs in gardens. On fields, mow before the plants flower.

Notes: Cocklebur seedlings are poisonous to livestock. Cocklebur grows well in wet soils.

Common Mallow
Malva neglecta
MALVACEAE

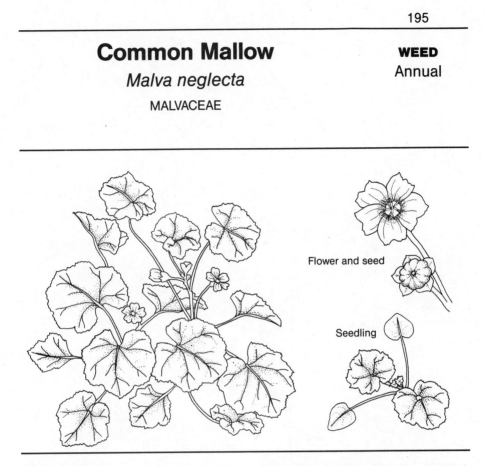

Flower and seed

Seedling

Range: Throughout United States and southern Canada.

Description: Stems are 4 inches to 1 foot long. They branch at the base, and may be nearly erect or spreading close to the ground. Even on procumbent stems, tips are erect. Alternate leaves are rounded with a cordate base, meaning that the base looks like the top of a valentine heart. Leaves are slightly hairy and have long petioles. Margins are slightly toothed and have rounded lobes. Flowers are single or clustered and grow from leaf axils. Flowers are small relative to the size of the leaves, and have five white to pale lavender or pink petals. Stamens are numerous and fused into a column around the pistil. The seedpod is composed of 10 to 20 segments. When seeds have matured, the seedpods resemble those of its close relative, the hollyhock. Blooms April to October.

Life Cycle: Annual or biennial, reproducing by seeds.

Prevention and Control: Pulling and hoeing are effective controls in the garden. Do not let plants flower or set seed on nearby waste areas or along roadsides.

Notes: Common mallow will grow in many environments, but prefers sunny areas with moderately good moisture levels.

WEED
Annual

Common Ragweed
Ambrosia artemisiifolia
COMPOSITAE

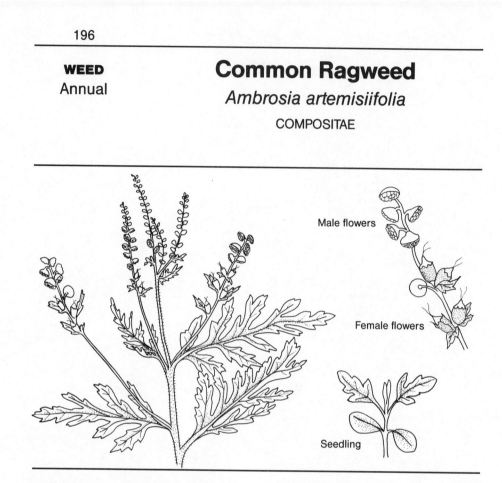

Male flowers

Female flowers

Seedling

Range: Throughout United States and southern Canada. Particularly serious in eastern and north central United States.

Description: Plants are from 1 to 5 feet tall. Erect stems are either simple or branched toward the top and carry smooth, deeply lobed leaves. Leaves are sometimes opposite at the base of the plant, but are more commonly alternate for the entire length of the stem. Single plants carry both male and female flowers. The male flowers are at the tips of the branches and the female blooms grow from the bases of leaves lower on the same terminal branch or, less frequently, from leaf axils. The cup-shaped male blooms point downward. Blooms July to September.

Life Cycle: Annual, reproducing by seeds.

Prevention and Control: Because ragweed is so shallow-rooted and reproduces only by seed, hoeing and pulling are effective. Mow nearby roadsides and other weedy spots before the plants bloom to prevent seed formation.

Notes: Ragweed can become a serious pest, particularly for people with allergies. This plant is adaptable, growing equally well on cultivated ground, neglected fields, along roadsides, and even in sandy soils near the ocean. It is able to grow in fairly moist to fairly dry conditions, but prefers good light to shade.

See photograph, page 294.

Corn Cockle
Agrostemma githago
CARYOPHYLLACEAE

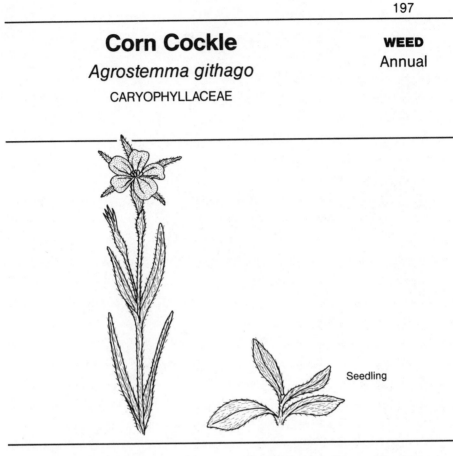

Seedling

Range: Throughout United States and southern Canada.

Description: Plants are 1 to 3 feet tall. The erect stem is covered with soft hairs, bulges slightly at the nodes, and is simple or branched toward the top. Lanceolate, opposite leaves are also hairy. Purplish-pink flowers arise from long peduncles growing from nodes. The five petals are encircled by narrow green sepals which are longer than the petals themselves. The calyx is quite prominent and encloses the capsule which holds small, black, spiny seeds. Blooms May to September.

Life Cycle: Winter annual, reproducing by seeds. Germinates most commonly in the fall and sends up flower stalks the next spring.

Prevention and Control: Seed is rarely viable for more than a year if it is buried to a depth of 6 to 8 inches. Pull the occasional plant in your garden as soon as you see it. On fields, do not use wheat or grow rye to maturity more than once in four years.

Notes: Seeds are poisonous. Stock and poultry must be kept off fields with corn cockle. As a companion to both winter rye and wheat, it prefers the same soil types and growing conditions. A pretty plant.

Devil's Beggarticks
Bidens frondosa
COMPOSITAE

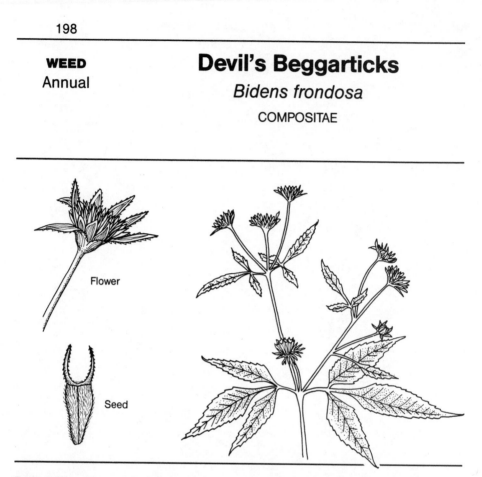

Flower

Seed

Range: Throughout United States and southern Canada.

Description: Plants grow from 2 to 5 feet tall. A group of four-ridged and almost square spreading stems arises from a shallow, multi-branched taproot. Stems are generally hairless. Leaves are opposite and compound with three and, less frequently, four or five divisions. Toothed leaves sometimes have short, soft hairs on the undersides but are always smooth on the top surfaces. Veins from the central rib to the margins are quite visible. Flowers at the ends of branches can be solitary or grouped. Two rows of bracts surround the base of the rounded bloom; the outer bract is leaflike and longer than the yellow ray flowers. Ray flowers are sometimes absent and do not produce seed. Disk flowers are orange, five-toothed, and perfect. The seed is long and wedge-shaped with two barbed awns at the top. Blooms July to October.

Life Cycle: Annual, reproducing by seeds.

Prevention and Control: Hoeing or pulling is effective for devil's beggarticks. Do not let plants in adjacent areas flower.

Notes: Devil's beggarticks prefer rich, moist soil but will live under less ideal conditions. Look for it along roadsides, in waste places, and in damp areas. Animals may bring seeds into your garden.

Field Dodder

Cuscuta pentagona

CONVOLVULACEAE

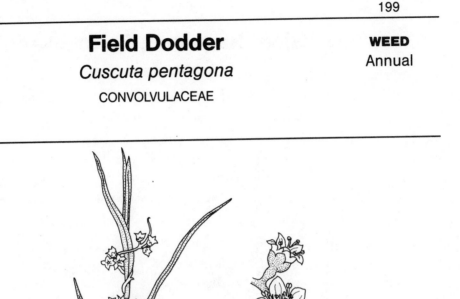

Flowers

Range: Throughout United States below Vermont and Great Lakes, with the exception of the Pacific Coast. Prairie provinces in southern Canada.

Description: Stems may reach 7 feet long. Almost clear to slightly pink, threadlike stems emerge from the ground. Dodders lack leaves because they are not chlorophyll-producers. Instead, they have tiny suckers that attach to host plants. Once attached, the stem breaks from the root. The pale, whitish flowers are prolific and are produced in loose, rounded clusters. The calyx is large relative to the petals that make up the five-pointed corolla. Seeds are numerous, fairly small, and yellow to reddish-brown. Blooms July to September.

Life Cycle: Annual, reproducing by seeds.

Prevention and Control: Dodder is likely to migrate into fields and gardens with small-seeded grains and cover crops or on mulch hay. At the first sign of the plant, pull both dodder and host and compost at 160°F if flowers have not yet formed. If flowers have formed, pull up the dodder and host plant and put them into a plastic bag to put out with the trash. If dodder is mixed in with a cover crop, keep the area mowed.

Notes: Field dodder is a parasite. It prefers areas with dry soils.

WEED
Annual

Giant Ragweed, Buffaloweed
Ambrosia trifida
COMPOSITAE

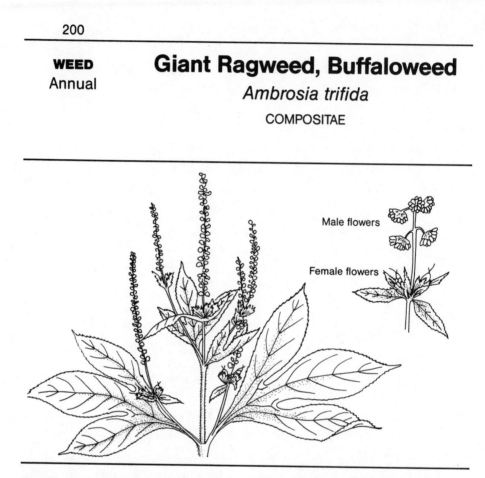

Male flowers

Female flowers

Range: Throughout United States, with the exception of Pacific Coast areas, and into southern Canada from southwest Quebec to British Columbia.

Description: Plants can grow to 15 feet tall, but are usually 2½ to 6 feet tall. Stems are coarse-haired and rough to the touch. The plant is erect and branches toward the top. Hairy leaves are opposite with margined petioles, meaning that there is a border of leaf tissue along each side of the petiole. Leaves at the top of the plant are occasionally entire, but the characteristic leaf is divided into three deep lobes. Male flowers are formed on spike-shaped racemes on stem tips, while the petal-less female flowers nestle into leaf axils at the top of the plant. Male flowers point downward so that the abundant pollen can drop to fertilize the female flowers below. Blooms July to September.

Life Cycle: Annual, reproducing by seeds.

Prevention and Control: Mow all waste places frequently to prevent the formation of flowers and seeds. Hoe or pull ragweeds that appear in the garden.

Notes: Giant ragweed prefers good soils with moderately high moisture levels and bright light, but will grow in less ideal conditions. It is common in hedgerows and along the edges of fields and roadsides. Pollen is extremely irritating to hayfever victims.

Jimsonweed

Datura stramonium

SOLANACEAE

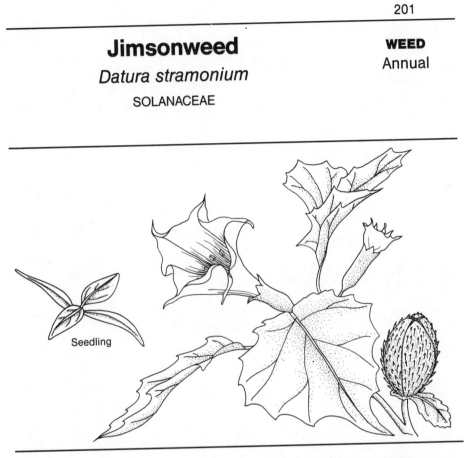

Seedling

Range: Eastern, Southwestern, and North-western United States. Northeastern Canada.

Description: Plants may grow to 5 feet tall. Bushy with spreading, unevenly toothed, simple, ovate leaves. Stems are some-times slightly purple. White to pink flow-ers have a deep, funnel-shaped corolla arising from a short stalk in branch axils. Once open, the five-pointed corolla looks something like a small morning-glory flower. Seed capsules are four-lobed and distinctly spiny. Blooms June to September.

Life Cycle: Annual, reproducing by kidney-shaped, flattened, and slightly pitted seeds.

Prevention and Control: Cautious grow-ers pull and compost jimsonweed prior to capsule formation.

Notes: In habit and coloration, jimson-weed resembles eggplant. It harbors most of the diseases and pests common to other solanaceous crops. A narcotic poison. Likes full sun. A beautiful plant.

WEED
Annual

Knotweed

Polygonum aviculare

POLYGONACEAE

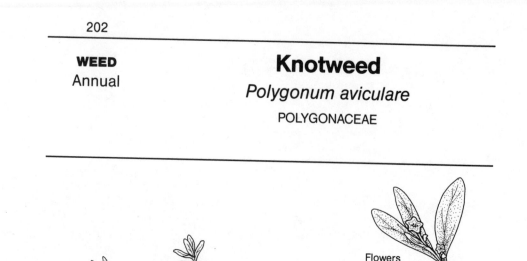

Flowers

Seedling

Range: Throughout United States and southern Canada.

Description: Stems are 4 inches to 2 feet long. Forms mats on the soil surface. Slender, ridged stems arise from thin taproots and branch in all directions. They lie prostrate, but may ascend slightly at the flowering tips. Slightly blue-green leaves are alternate, entire, and elliptical, with somewhat pointed tips. At the base of the leaf, the short petioles are attached to a short sheath formed by the stipules. Flowers are small and grow in clusters from the axils formed by the sheath and petiole. Blooms June to October.

Life Cycle: Annual, reproducing by seeds.

Prevention and Control: Pulling when the plant is young is the best control. Hoeing is effective on older plants, as long as the crown of the plant just at or slightly below the soil surface is severed from the roots. If it infests garden areas badly, add compost or aged manure and covercrop the area with a deep-rooted plant for two to three years.

Notes: Knotweed indicates a compacted soil. It is more likely to reside in permanent pathways than in your beds. Eliminate it from these areas by aerating with a spading fork and then covering with a deep mulch.

Lamb's-Quarters

Chenopodium album

CHENOPODIACEAE

WEED
Annual

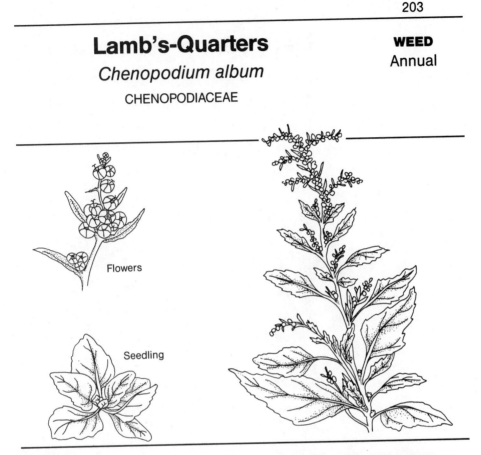

Flowers

Seedling

Range: Throughout United States and southern Canada.

Description: Plants grow to 6 feet tall. When young, the top surfaces of the leaves look dusted with silvery sparkles, while the undersides look white and mealy. Stems are upright and branched, sometimes a great deal, sometimes sparsely. They may have streaks of lighter green or red. Leaves are alternate, simple, toothed, and generally wider on the bottom than the top of the plant. Green or reddish-green, petal-less flowers grow in irregularly shaped spikes at the tops of branches and upper axils. Blooms June to October.

Life Cycle: Annual, reproducing by seeds. In the fall, very young plants can flower and set seed before frost.

Prevention and Control: Pull or hoe lamb's-quarters as young as possible in serious infestations; they grow rapidly and become a chore once they are taller than 6 to 8 inches. In hot, dry weather, pulled seedlings can be left in the garden. Otherwise, compost them.

Notes: Lamb's-quarters are aphid traps. Lamb's-quarters are good indicators. Nitrogen-deficient plants have a red-purple sheen, dry plants become limp, and plants struggling with adverse soil conditions are more stiff than normal. Edible.

See photograph, page 295.

WEED
Annual

Marshpepper Smartweed
Polygonum hydropiper
POLYGONACEAE

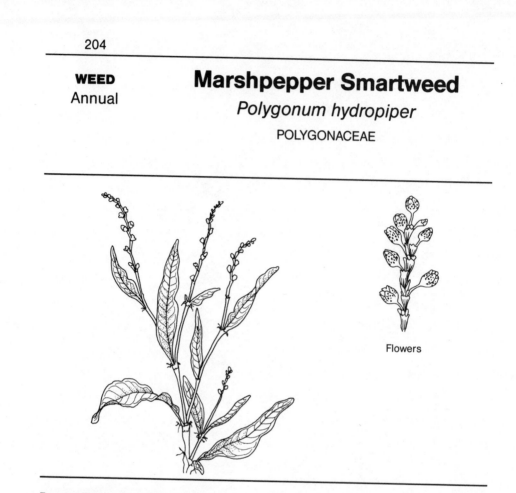

Flowers

Range: Throughout United States, with the exceptions of southern Georgia and Florida, and southern Canada.

Description: Plants are 1 to 2 feet tall. Stems are prominently jointed. They are erect, smooth, and sometimes reddish. Leaves are alternate, narrow and pointed at the tips, and have smooth to slightly wavy margins. Petioles are small or absent, and the leaf may be attached by a sheathlike structure from which stipules with bristly margins extend. Small, green flowers form on terminal spikes that droop in lax arches. The calyx, which sometimes has slightly reddish margins, protects the dry, lens-shaped or triangular fruit that contains a single seed. Blooms June to November.

Life Cycle: Annual, reproducing by seeds.

Prevention and Control: Hoeing or pulling this plant is effective. Improve drainage, or if that is impossible because of a high water table, build raised beds that contain large volumes of compost and organic matter.

Notes: Marshpepper smartweed prefers marshy, boggy areas, and is most often found on low soils without adequate drainage. It collects calcium, and will return it to the compost pile. Birds like the fruit and spread it to new ground. Peppery stems and leaves are edible.

Mayweed

Anthemis cotula

COMPOSITAE

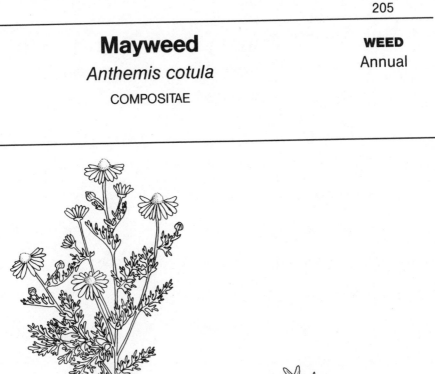

Seedling

Range: Throughout United States and southern Canada.

Description: Plants can reach 2 feet tall. The multi-branched stem is erect and either smooth or covered with soft hairs. Leaves are alternate and light yellowish-green. Arising directly from the stem, they are finely divided into narrow segments. They may be covered with tiny hairs. Small, white ray flowers surround a center of yellow disk flowers. Blooms May to September.

Life Cycle: Annual, reproducing by seeds. In some climates, mayweed is a winter annual, germinating in the late fall, over-wintering, and sending up flower stalks the following spring.

Prevention and Control: Hoeing and pulling is effective for plants in the garden. Mow all waste areas to prevent formation of new seeds.

Notes: Common names for this plant include stinkweed, fetid chamomile, dog fennel, and stinking daisy, all referring to the highly unpleasant odor given off by the leaves. Suspect compacted soil conditions if mayweed becomes a serious pest; aerate and add compost or aged manure.

WEED
Annual

Pennsylvania Smartweed
Polygonum pensylvanicum
POLYGONACEAE

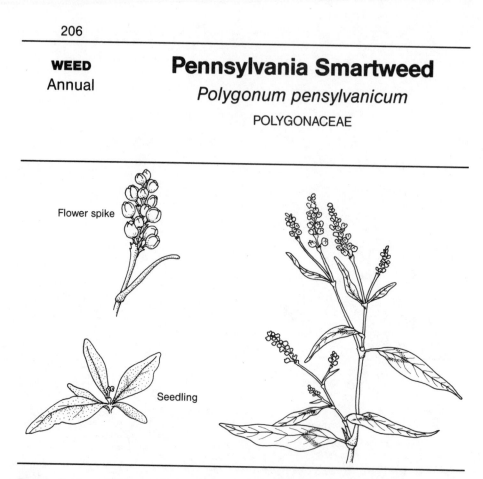

Flower spike

Seedling

Range: Eastern and Central United States as far west as Wyoming. Southeastern Canada.

Description: Plants grow to 4 feet tall. Erect, somewhat tough stems with swollen joints. A slight reddish cast may be apparent under the dull green color. Leaves are alternate and elliptical with pointed tips. Stiff little hairs, which point toward the tip, may lie close to the margin. The leaf has a short petiole extending from a sheath that encircles the stem. As the plant matures, lower sheaths dry and fall off. Stiff flower spikes are rose-colored and densely packed on a stalk with tiny glandular hairs. Fruits are reddish-brown or dark brown. Blooms late May to October.

Life Cycle: Annual, reproducing by seeds.

Prevention and Control: Pulling or hoeing are effective controls for this annual plant. Do not let seed set on plants growing in ditches or roadsides near your garden.

Notes: Pennsylvania smartweed can tolerate wet or compacted soils, filtered shade, acidity, and poor nutrition. If it becomes a serious pest in the garden, suspect one or another of these conditions, but most particularly poor drainage. As the soil improves, Pennsylvania smartweed populations will decrease.

Prickly Lettuce
Lactuca serriola
COMPOSITAE

WEED
Annual

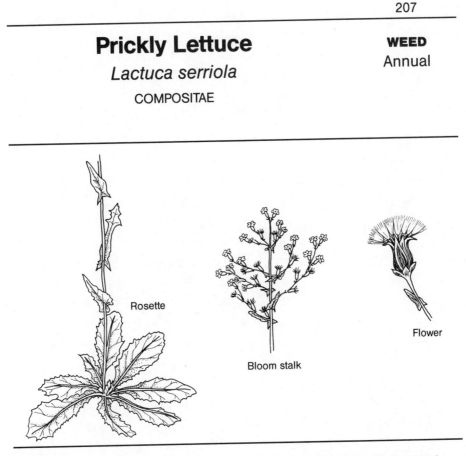

Rosette

Bloom stalk

Flower

Range: Throughout United States and southern Canada.

Description: Plants may grow to 5 feet tall. Stems are pale green and may be prickly toward the bottom. When broken or cut, they release a very bitter, milky fluid. Leaves are alternate, sometimes blue-green, and sport prickles from the wavy or toothed margins. They clasp the stem tightly and have two lobes that project beyond the attachment point. The taproot is thick and long. Flowers are numerous, small, and pale yellow. Seeds are tufted. Blooms July to September.

Life Cycle: Annual, winter annual, or biennial, reproducing by seeds. Seeds are carried by the wind. Can resprout from the crown if it is left standing.

Prevention and Control: Hoe or pull prickly lettuce plants as you see them, cutting below the crown. Do not let them set seed. Rarely present in epidemic proportions on cultivated land, but can be a problem in old pastures or neglected fields. Mow or cut prior to blossoming and again every two to three weeks thereafter to take down new sprouts and deplete the plant's reserves.

Notes: Most commonly found on light soils with good drainage. Wild lettuce carries many of the same diseases as cultivated lettuce, so it should be eliminated.

WEED
Annual

Prickly Sida

Sida spinosa

MALVACEAE

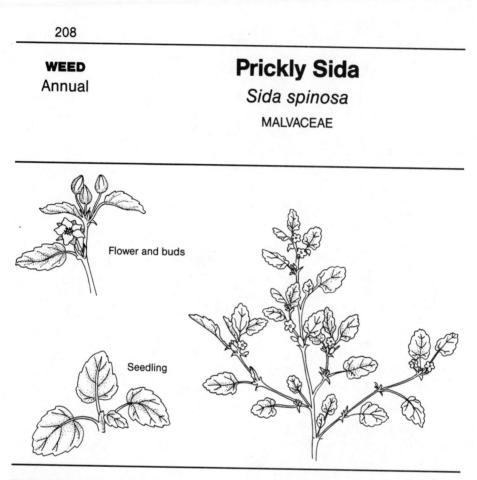

Flower and buds

Seedling

Range: Throughout eastern two-thirds of United States.

Description: Plants are 8 inches to 3⅓ feet tall. Stems are erect, hairy, and many-branched. Leaves are alternate and lanceolate with toothed margins. Two spiny projections grow from the base of each node below the leaf petiole. Flowers also grow on short stalks from the nodes. Light yellow flowers are five-petaled. Numerous stamens are fused toward the bottom to form a column surrounding the pistil. The five-sepaled calyx encloses the bottom of the seedpod. This also has five sections, each topped by two sharp beaks that separate to release a single seed when the pod is mature. Blooms June to October.

Life Cycle: Annual, reproducing by seeds.

Prevention and Control: Prickly sida is easy to pull when it is young and small. It grows a long, tenacious taproot fairly early in the season, so the most effective control is cutting stems from the root with a very sharp hoe. Do not let plants in waste areas, fencerows, or roadsides flower and set seed.

Notes: Prickly sida is ideally suited to the climates and soils of the southern states, and should be controlled in areas close to your garden. Even though only five seeds are produced per flower, the number of flowers on a plant guarantee a strong survival rate.

Prostrate Pigweed
Amaranthus blitoides
AMARANTHACEAE

WEED
Annual

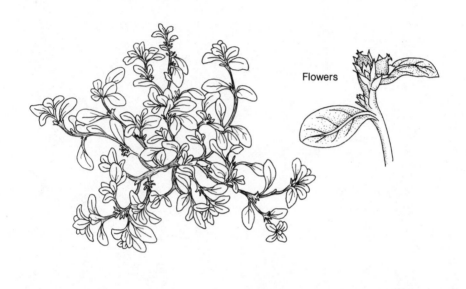

Flowers

Range: Throughout southern Canada and United States, except southernmost areas of Texas, Florida, and California.

Description: Stems are 8 inches to 2 feet long. Pigweed branches from the base and at nodes along each stem, spreading over the ground in a low mat. The reddish stems are smooth and often erect at the growing tips. Leaves are numerous, small, simple, and oval or obovate. At the base, they narrow to a long petiole. Inconspicuous flower clusters in the axils lack petals. The bracts are equal in size to the sepals, tapering to points that feel prickly to the touch. Lens-shaped seeds are shiny black. Blooms July to October.

Life Cycle: Annual, reproducing by seeds.

Prevention and Control: Vigorous hoeing and pulling are the most effective controls. Because seeds are so plentiful and flowers so inconspicuous, be careful to remove plants early in the season. This weed should be carried out of the garden rather than left in the walkways.

Notes: Dry, sandy soils are the chosen habitat of prostrate pigweed. However, it can and will adapt to any garden soil that has good drainage.

WEED
Annual

Purslane

Portulaca oleracea

PORTULACACEAE

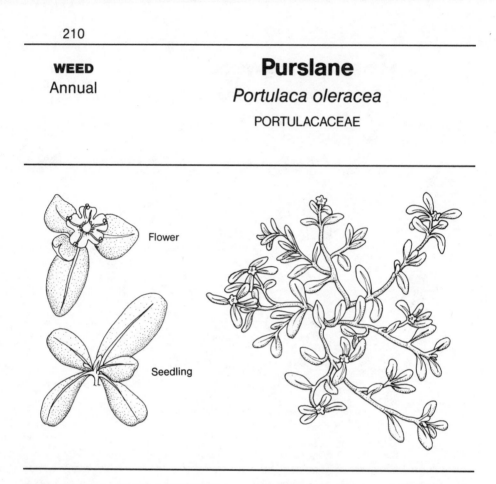

Flower

Seedling

Range: Throughout United States and southern Canada.

Description: Stems grow to 1½ feet long. Stems are smooth, succulent, prostrate, and branch to form dense mats on the soil surface. Very often, they have a reddish cast, as do the fleshy leaves. Alternate or almost opposite leaves attach directly to the stems and are rounded to oval in shape with smooth margins. Leaves may grow in clusters at the stem tips. Flowers are pale yellow and small. They open only in the morning on sunny days, and grow singly in axils or in groups within the terminal leaf clusters. The calyxes are green and enclose the petals, forming seed capsules that contain numerous tiny seeds. Blooms July to September.

Life Cycle: Annual, reproducing by seeds and stem pieces.

Prevention and Control: Purslane does not germinate until soils have warmed and may be missed in early cultivations of the garden. Pulling and hoeing are effective controls. Stems, which can reroot, should not be left in the garden, particularly after they have flowered.

Notes: Purslane leaves, stems, and plant habit look a great deal like its ornamental relative, portulaca (moss rose). Crisp and succulent, the stems and leaves of purslane are excellent additions to the salad bowl.

See photograph, page 293.

Redroot Pigweed
Amaranthus retroflexus
AMARANTHACEAE

WEED
Annual

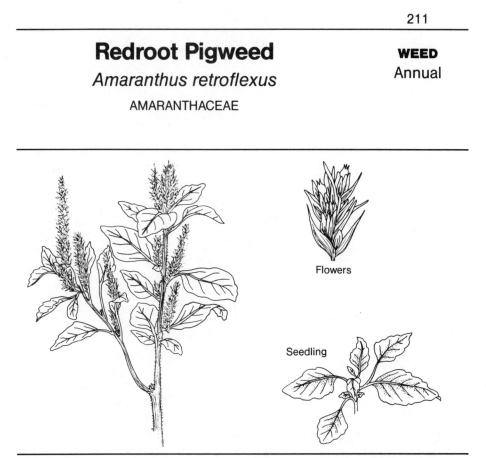

Flowers

Seedling

Range: Throughout United States and southern Canada.

Description: Plants grow to 10 feet tall. Stems are slightly reddish and upright. Alternate, simple leaves are dull green and rough-looking with a shape described as rhombic. Leaf margins are slightly wavy and petioles are long. Flower clusters look more like green bottle brushes than blooms; they grow in terminal spikes. Seeds are shiny black or red-brown. The tough, grasping taproot is distinctly red. Blooms July to October.

Life Cycle: Annual, reproducing by seeds. Plants with a two-month season grow 1 to 3 feet tall before blooming and setting seed, but plants that germinate and grow in the late summer and early fall will produce seed when only a few inches tall. A single plant produces up to 200,000 seeds, which can remain viable as long as 40 years.

Prevention and Control: Pull or hoe every single seedling. Remove pulled plants from the garden; they reroot easily. In serious cases, fallow the soil, shallowly harrowing or raking it at seven- to ten-day intervals to uproot each succeeding flush. After midseason, plant a quick smother crop such as buckwheat and till in this green manure a week before seeding the area to winter rye.

Notes: Redroot pigweed prefers the rich soil and bright light in your garden, but can adapt to grow almost anywhere.

Shepherd's Purse

Capsella bursa-pastoris

CRUCIFERAE

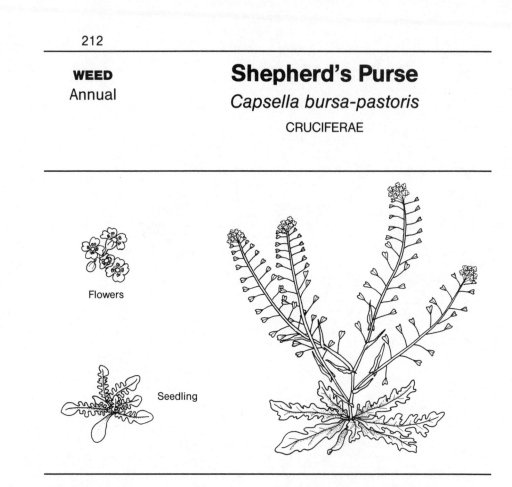

Flowers

Seedling

Range: Throughout United States and southern Canada.

Description: Plants reach 8 inches to 1½ feet tall. A basal rosette of lobed leaves often appears in the late summer or fall, but can also grow in the spring or summer. After the rosette has overwintered or is well established in the spring or summer, erect stems grow from the crown. Stems are branched and often covered with tiny grayish hairs. Leaves growing from the stems are smaller and more narrow than those forming the basal rosette. They clasp the stem and are serrate to slightly toothed with an overall arrow shape. Four-petaled white flowers grow in long racemes at the ends of branches. Seedpods develop at the ends of long stalks and are triangu-lar in shape with two distinct valves that are thicker at the partition that separates them than at their edges. Blooms March to November.

Life Cycle: Annual or winter annual, reproducing by seeds.

Prevention and Control: Hoeing and pulling are effective. Do not let this plant flower or set seed. It will disrupt neighboring plants if pulled after its seedling stage. It reroots easily; remove pulled plants from the garden and compost.

Notes: Shepherd's purse is present in almost all gardens, fields, and roadways.

Spanish Needles
Bidens bipinnata
COMPOSITAE

Seed

Seedling

Range: Throughout eastern part of United States south of upper New York state, and west to Kansas.

Description: Plants grow to 5 feet tall. Erect, branching stems are angular and ridged. Opposite leaves arise from long petioles and are divided into opposite leaflets along the central vein and a centered section at the apex. Leaflet margins are toothed. Flower heads are carried singly on long, leafless peduncles, or branches, toward the top of the plant. Two rows of bracts surround flower heads, the outer set looking almost like tiny green leaves. Pale yellow ray flowers surround darker yellow disk flowers in the center of the head. The long, slender seeds that form from the central disk flowers have three to four stiff barbed pappuses at the top. Blooms August to October.

Life Cycle: Annual, reproducing by seeds.

Prevention and Control: Hoe or pull this plant. Watch waste places and areas along woods, walls, fences, and hedgerows for Spanish needles and mow before flowers form.

Notes: Although its favorite habitat is moist and sunny, Spanish needles will grow in sandy or rocky soils, open fields to slightly wooded areas. Barbs stick to passing animals or woven clothing, assuring seed dispersal over a wide area.

WEED
Annual

Spotted Spurge

Euphorbia maculata

EUPHORBIACEAE

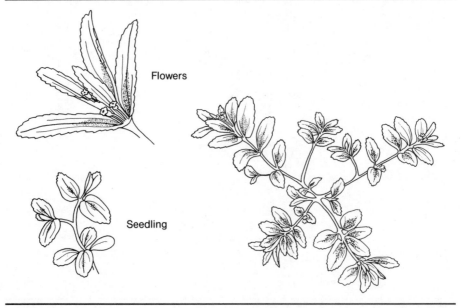

Flowers

Seedling

Range: Eastern two-thirds of United States, Pacific Coast region south to central California. Areas in eastern half of southern Canada.

Description: Plants are 1⅔ to 3⅓ feet tall. Rigidly erect or slightly spreading; it can have a multi-branched stem or one that branches only toward the top. Stems have milky sap. Opposite leaves are oval or ovate-lanceolate and have a serrated margin. A reddish area near the base of the leaf gives the plant its name. Tiny male and female flowers form at the tops of branches on long stalks. The seed capsule, which develops from the female flower, is usually three-lobed but sometimes four-lobed. Seeds are three-sided, small, and pitted. Blooms June to October.

Life Cycle: Annual, reproducing by seeds.

Prevention and Control: Hoeing or pulling are effective in the garden. Spotted spurge germinates only in warm soils; look for seedling plants in late spring and early summer.

Notes: Spotted spurge can grow well in slightly dry soils with a high percentage of sand or gravel. The most important requirement for this plant is good light; you won't find it in wooded areas. A heavy plant canopy in an intensive bed area will inhibit plants that germinate late in the season.

Tall Morning-Glory

Ipomoea purpurea

CONVOLVULACEAE

WEED
Annual

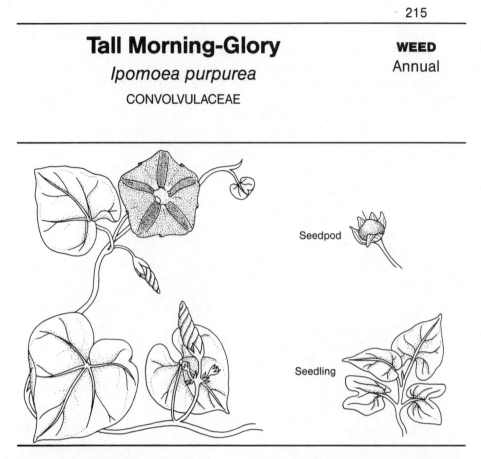

Seedpod

Seedling

Range: Throughout the eastern half of United States and Pacific Coast areas.

Description: Stems are 3 to 10 feet long. Stems may be slightly hairy and twine around plants and objects in their path. Alternate leaves are distinctly heart-shaped, with smooth margins and obvious veins arising from the midrib. Like the flowers, they are borne on long petioles. Flowers are blue, purple, red, white, or variegated, with long corollas. They normally grow in groups of three to five from each flower stalk. The five-pointed calyx is hairy and prominent. Blooms July to September.

Life Cycle: Annual, reproducing by seeds.

Prevention and Control: Morning-glories can become so troublesome in warm climates that each and every shoot near the garden should be hoed or hand pulled.

Notes: Tall morning-glory is not particular about soil, but it does like good light and warm temperatures. Watch for bird-sown vines growing from the sides and tops of hedges and along fencerows. In southern areas, volunteer plants in nearby waste places should not be allowed to flower.

WEED
Annual

Velvetleaf
Abutilon theophrasti
MALVACEAE

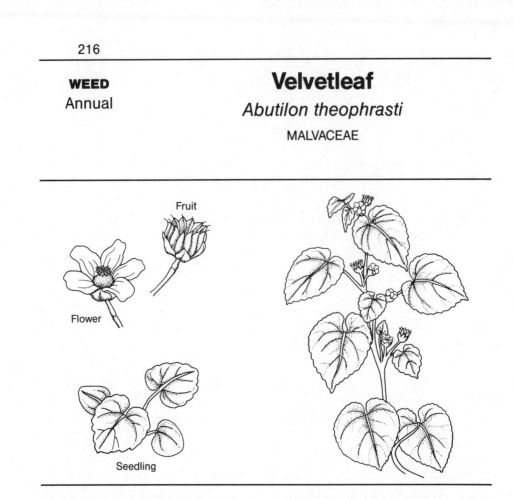

Fruit

Flower

Seedling

Range: Throughout United States except Far North and Deep South.

Description: Plants reach 2 to 6 feet tall. Stems are erect and covered with velvety hairs. Leaves are alternate and heart-shaped with tapering, very pointed tips. Leaves are also coated with short, velvety hairs. Flowers each have a small stalk growing from the top of a long petiole arising from a leaf axil. The corolla has five yellow petals and numerous visible stamens encircling the taller pistils. Large, cup-shaped seedpods are composed of 12 to 15 two-beaked, prickly segments, each containing as many as 15 prickly seeds. Blooms July to October.

Life Cycle: Annual, reproducing by seeds.

Prevention and Control: Pulling and hoeing are effective. Flowering occurs in mid-summer and seed sets in late summer to early fall. Do not let seed form on plants in nearby waste places or along fencerows. Seeds can pass through silage unharmed, and can germinate 50 years after being buried in the soil.

Notes: Velvetleaf prefers nutrient-rich, somewhat sandy soils in warm climates. Because the plant is so distinctive and only grows from seed, eliminating it from the garden is not difficult.

Wild Mustard

Brassica kaber

CRUCIFERAE

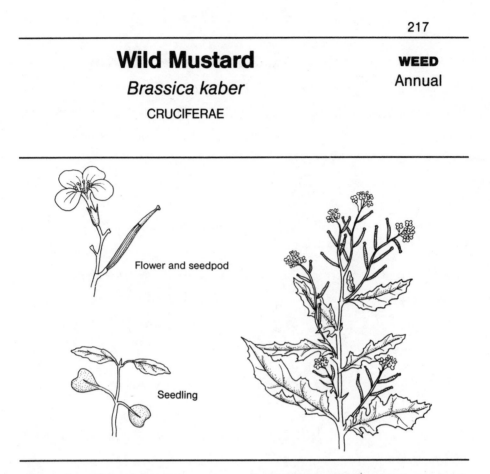

Flower and seedpod

Seedling

Range: Throughout United States and southern Canada.

Description: Plants grow to 3 feet tall. Stems are erect and branched near the top. Leaves toward the bottom of the plant are lobed or deeply toothed. Closer to the top of the plant, they become smaller and more toothed than lobed. A purple-gray cast underlies the light, shiny green of young leaves. Clear yellow, four-petaled flowers are loosely clustered at the ends of branches. Long, cylindrical seedpods form quickly and contain one or more dark seeds. Blooms May to August.

Life Cycle: Annual or winter annual, reproducing by seeds.

Prevention and Control: Hoeing and pulling are effective in the small garden. Because seeds may be viable for a number of years, an old crop of mustard seed will germinate year after year. On fields, mowing prior to flowering is imperative.

Notes: The yellow flowers of wild mustard wave above young field grasses early each summer. Overlooked mustards may also bloom in your garden anytime from early summer to late fall. Mustard has an alkalizing effect on acid soils and should be left in place, although not allowed to bloom, in areas that are undergoing a slow renovation. Liming will decrease prevalence on acid soils. Edible.

WEED
Biennial

Common Burdock

Arctium minus

COMPOSITAE

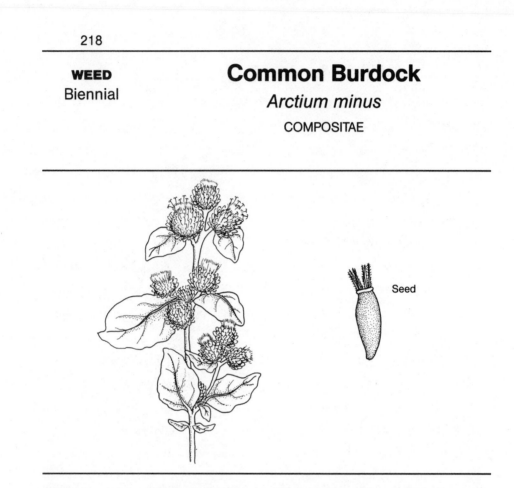

Seed

Range: Roughly northern half of United States, but extending to Florida and through Louisiana in the east; Southern Canada.

Description: Plants grow from 1½ to 5 feet tall. During the first year, hairy stems grow from a crown, forming a dense rosette of large, dull dark green, lightly fuzzy, heart-shaped leaves with noticeable veins. The second year, the plant becomes erect and bushy, branching from a central stem; leaves are alternate. Bottom leaves can be 1⅔ feet long and 1 foot or more in width, but are smaller toward the top. Red-violet to pink-lavender, ⅔- to 1⅕-inch-wide flowers form in racemelike axillary clusters. The ⅔-inch burs are a dark gray-brown. Blooms July to October.

Life Cycle: Biennial, reproducing by seeds.

Prevention and Control: Keep burdock from setting seed by cutting flower stalks or digging plants before they flower.

Notes: Burdock is common in good soil on neglected sites such as roadsides or unused farmland. Burs will stick to whatever they touch, so seed is easily spread by animals.

See photograph, page 293.

Common Mullein
Verbascum thapsus
SCROPHULARIACEAE

WEED
Biennial

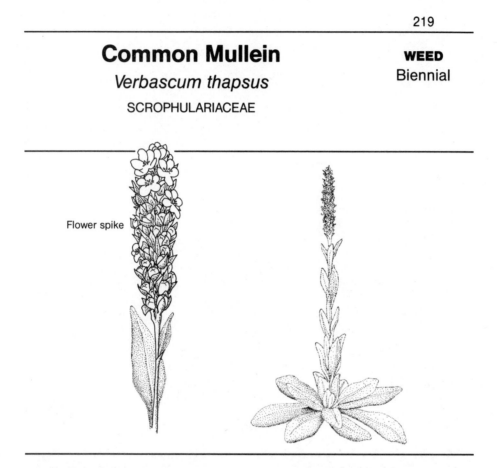

Flower spike

Range: Throughout United States and southern Canada, with the exception of areas in the north central states and Canadian prairies.

Description: Plants grow to 6 feet tall. During its first year, it grows a rosette of large (to 1 foot long), velvety, gray-green leaves. These leaves are oblong, entire, and smooth-margined. Second year's growth is heralded by the emergence of a strong, stout stem which carries smaller and more pointed leaves. The central stem may branch toward the top, where flower spikes form. The flower spikes are dense and nearly cylindrical. Five-lobed, fuzzy calyxes support inch-wide flowers with bright yellow, five-lobed corollas. Downy, two-celled capsules containing many seeds develop at the base of each flower. Blooms June to September.

Life Cycle: Biennial, reproducing by seeds.

Prevention and Control: Mullein is easy to eradicate from garden areas. Hoe it out, cutting below the crown. It cannot reroot, nor can the root resprout. It is rarely a problem in gardens. In unlikely cases of infestation, uproot and leave to dry on the soil surface.

Notes: Mulleins prefer somewhat gravelly and dry soils, and are unlikely to volunteer in well-tended gardens.

See photograph, page 295.

WEED
Biennial

Henbit
Lamium amplexicaule
LABIATAE

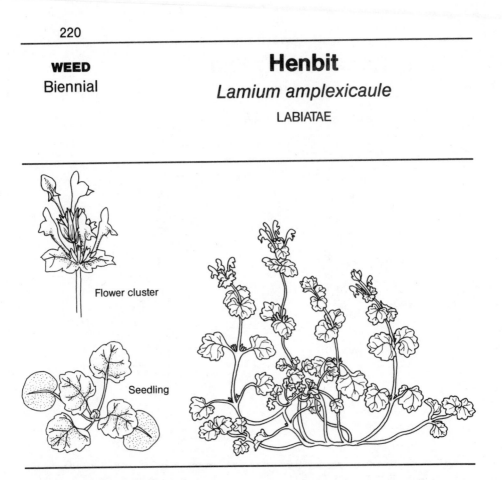

Flower cluster

Seedling

Range: Throughout United States and southern Canada except for areas in the north central states.

Description: Plants are 4 inches to 1⅓ feet tall. Four-sided stems are often decumbent (with ascending tips and branches). They tend to root where the lower nodes are in contact with the soil surface. Internodes are long relative to leaf size, giving the plant a somewhat sparse look. Leaves are opposite, hairy, circular, and palmately veined. Margins are crenate, meaning that the teeth are rounded rather than pointed. Flowers grow in whorls in axils of upper leaves. A visible calyx has five pointed teeth and surrounds the pink or purple tubular corolla. The corolla is two-lipped.

Blooms April to June and again in September.

Life Cycle: Biennial or winter annual, reproducing by seeds and rooting stems.

Prevention and Control: Hoeing and pulling are effective as long as roots are pulled and removed. Look for henbit early in the season and prevent its seeding in the garden or adjacent areas. Remove all pulled plants from the garden to prevent rerooting.

Notes: Henbit prefers good soils and high moisture levels. It prospers in cool, moist weather, and is most troublesome in early spring and fall.

Moth Mullein

Verbascum blattaria

SCROPHULARIACEAE

WEED
Biennial

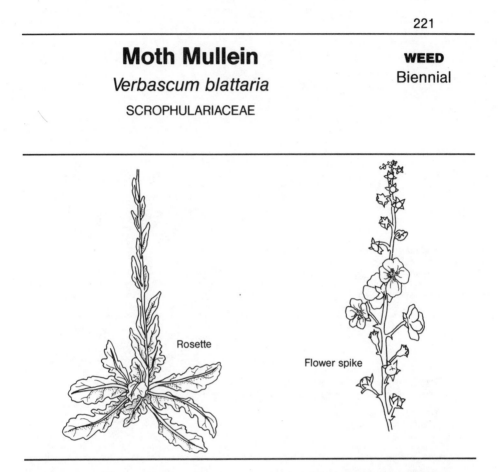

Rosette

Flower spike

Range: Throughout United States and Southern Canada west of the Maritimes.

Description: Plants grow to 6 feet tall. The first year's basal rosette of leaves is dark green. Long, tapering, and only slightly hairy, leaves are irregularly lobed with obvious veins. In late spring of the second year, a tall stem grows from the center of the rosette. The clasping leaves on the stem are alternate, sharply pointed, dentate or toothed rather than lobed, and smaller (to 2½ inches long) and more narrow than those at the base. Leaves become smaller and hug the stem more closely as they approach the top, where flowers form above small bracts. The solitary, inch-wide flowers are usually orange-yellow, although they can be a pinkish-white. The supporting calyx has five green sepals. Flower petals are fused into a corolla at the base and open out into five lobes. Five stamens are bearded with purple hairs. A two-chambered, many-seeded capsule forms at the base of each flower. Blooms June to November.

Life Cycle: Biennial, reproducing by seeds.

Prevention and Control: Moth mullein is impossible to overlook, either in its first or second year. Killing it is as simple as severing the crown from the taproot. It does not often become a serious pest.

Notes: Moth mullein is a beautiful plant.

WEED
Biennial

Poison Hemlock
Conium maculatum
UMBELLIFERAE

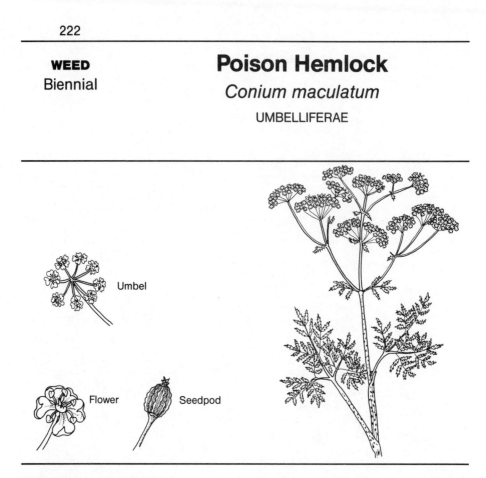

Umbel

Flower   Seedpod

Range: Throughout United States and southern Canada, with the exception of some areas in the north central states.

Description: Plants grow to 9 feet tall. Stems are erect, hairless, ridged, and often spotted with small purple splotches. Leaves are more prevalent at the base than at the top of the stems. Compound and fernlike, with finely cut leaflets arranged along a central stalk, leaves are triangular in overall outline. Terminal, compound umbels are composed of tiny white flowers which soon drop and give way to small, two-chambered, spherical fruits which divide down the center into two mericarps (seed-holding fruits), each containing one seed. Blooms June to September.

Life Cycle: Biennial, reproducing by seeds.

Prevention and Control: Pull or dig the plants early in the season, taking as much of the carrot-shaped root as possible. Infestations on cultivated ground are rare, although it sometimes migrates onto the edges of fields, pastures, and roadways.

Notes: This is the plant which is supposed to have been made into a tea that poisoned Socrates. Whether the story is true or not, all parts of poison hemlock are fatally poisonous. Eliminate this weed.

Queen Anne's Lace

Daucus carota

UMBELLIFERAE

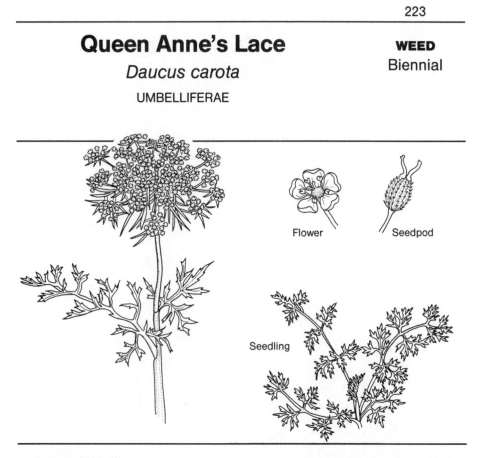

Flower

Seedpod

Seedling

Range: Throughout United States and southern Canada, with the exception of areas in the north central states and Canadian prairies.

Description: Plants grow to 3 feet tall. A rosette of slightly hairy, compound, fernlike leaves with narrow, lobed segments grows from the taproot during the first season. Second year's growth is marked by the emergence of erect, hollow stems that are ridged and hairy. Leaves on the stems are alternate and attached to the stem by sheaths at their bases, whereas those within the rosette have long petioles. Tiny white flowers form in flat, compound umbels at the top of the plant. Very often a single pink or purple bloom sits in the center of the umbel. As fruits carrying seeds mature, the surface of the umbel becomes concave. The light tan mericarps, or seed-holding fruits, are ribbed and prickly. Blooms June to September.

Life Cycle: Biennial, reproducing by seeds.

Prevention and Control: Dig first-year plants as soon as you notice them, taking the large taproot.

Notes: Like many members of this family, Queen Anne's lace provides food for many of the small, parasitic wasps that prey upon aphids, whiteflies, and other insect pests in your garden.

See photograph, page 295.

WEED
Biennial

Tansy Ragwort
Senecio jacobaea
COMPOSITAE

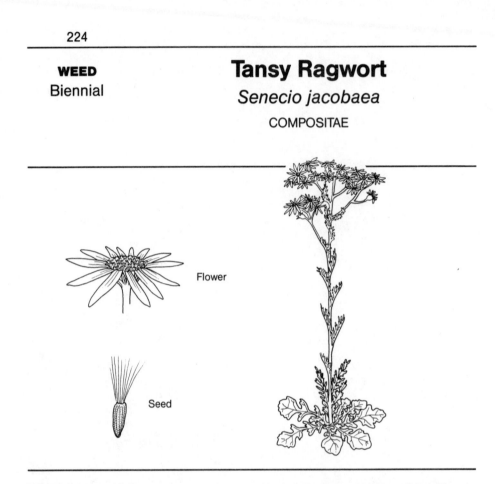

Flower

Seed

Range: Atlantic coast from Maine to Rhode Island. Maritime provinces of Canada. Pacific coast from British Columbia to northern California.

Description: Plants grow to 4 feet tall. Stems are erect and coarse. They are usually solitary until they approach the top, where they may branch below the flowers. Leaves at the base of the plant have petioles and may be hairy on the undersides. They are likely to be oval with toothed margins, and sometimes drop in the fall. Upper leaves are also alternate, but clasp the stem and are lobed or compound with toothed margins. Yellow flower heads grow in wide clusters. Broad centers composed of disk flowers are surrounded by narrow ray flowers. Both ray and disk flowers produce seed. Blooms July to September.

Life Cycle: Biennial or winter annual, but can be a short-lived perennial. Reproduces by seeds.

Prevention and Control: Dig plants in the garden, taking the root. On fields and waste places, mow early and often enough to prevent flowering and setting seed.

Notes: This plant prefers dry soils. Gardeners can help to eliminate it by increasing the humus content of their cultivated land.

Teasel

Dipsacus fullonum

DIPSACACEAE

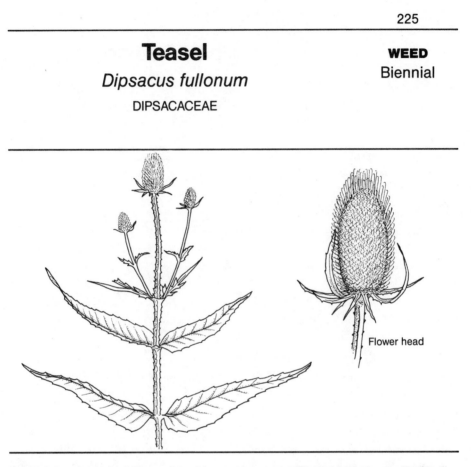

Flower head

Range: Eastern United States, from central Maine to North Carolina and westward in a narrow strip to Utah. Pacific coast to central California.

Description: Plants may grow to 6 feet tall. A rosette of narrow, scallop-margined, prominently veined, and spiny leaves marks the first year of growth. Tall, erect stems grow the second year. They are sturdy, angled, and prickly, and usually branch toward the top of the plant. The opposite leaves growing along the stems often form a bowl-like structure where their bases join around the stem. Stem leaves are narrow, toothed, and prickly at the margins. The underside of the midrib also sports prickles. Flower heads are distinguished by their many dry, brown bracts which extend well beyond the bloom and become stiffly hooked at maturity. Small, elongated, purple, pink, or white four-petaled corollas grow within the heads. Blooms July to October.

Life Cycle: Biennial, reproducing by seeds.

Prevention and Control: Rosettes should be hoed or pulled as soon as they are spotted in the garden. Severing the leaves and stems from the roots kills the plant.

Notes: Dried flower heads of teasel were once used to card wool. Today, they are more likely to be used in arrangements of dried flowers. Pick the heads early in the fall.

See photograph, page 294.

WEED
Biennial

White Cockle
Silene alba
CARYOPHYLLACEAE

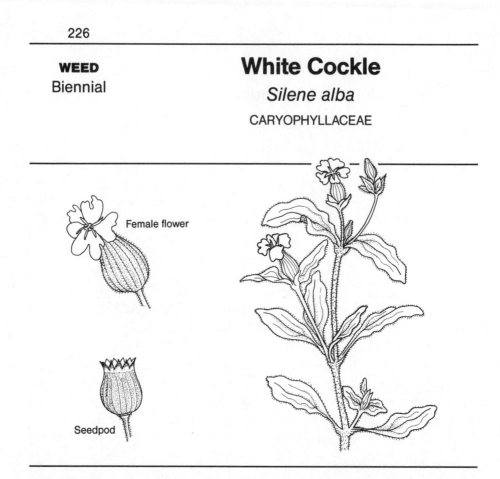

Female flower

Seedpod

Range: Eastern, north central and Pacific Northwest regions of United States to the middle of California. Southern Canada from coast to coast.

Description: Plants grow to 3 feet tall. Stems are hairy, sticky, erect, and somewhat branching with an open habit. Leaves grow directly from the stems in opposite pairs. Simple, hairy, and light green, they are up to 4 inches long and narrow with pointed tips. Flowers are white to pink, have five deeply notched petals, and, topping long stems, are solitary or in three clusters in which the most central flower opens first. Male and female flowers are on separate plants. The bulbous base of the female flower is fatter and more egg-shaped than that of the male

flower. Female flowers are 1 ¼ inches long, males ⅞ inch long. The seed capsule is ten-toothed at the top and holds numerous flat, circular, gray, bumpy seeds. Blooms June to August.

Life Cycle: Biennial or short-lived perennial, reproducing by seeds and rootstocks. The rootstocks do not travel long distances; this plant tends to grow in close groups.

Prevention and Control: Hoe, making sure to dig out the rootstock.

Notes: This plant likes rich, well-drained soils and is often found along roadsides and bordering fields.

Broadleaf Plantain
Plantago major
PLANTAGINACEAE

WEED
Perennial

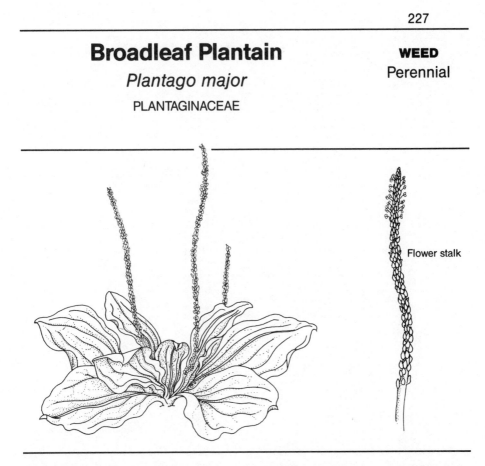

Flower stalk

Range: Throughout United States and southern Canada.

Description: Plants grow to 1 foot tall; flower stalks grow to 1½ feet tall. Forms a basal rosette of alternately placed, 4- to 6-inch-long leaves. The grass-green leaves are thick and rough to the touch. Prominent parallel veins taper to a wide, stiff petiole (also 4 to 6 inches long) which is often slightly hairy at the base. Stems support flower and seed spikes which wave above the leaf rosette. Flowers lack petioles and are quite tiny. Brown or slightly purplish seed capsules containing as many as 15 seeds each soon take the place of the nondescript flowers. Blooms May to September.

Life Cycle: Perennial, reproducing by seeds and, when the plant is stressed, from roots.

Prevention and Control: Dig the roots of broadleaf plantain out of gardens and lawns. Do not let flowers or seeds form. Aerate lawns when plantains begin to intrude, as they are a sign of compacted soil. Increasing organic matter and humus by adding compost or aged manure cuts incidence over a few years. Break up hardpans which may have formed in response to repeated use of a rotary tiller by covercropping with a deep-rooted plant such as alfalfa.

Notes: Broadleaf plantain prefers rich, moist soils that are dense and compacted.

WEED
Perennial

Buckhorn Plantain

Plantago lanceolata

PLANTAGINACEAE

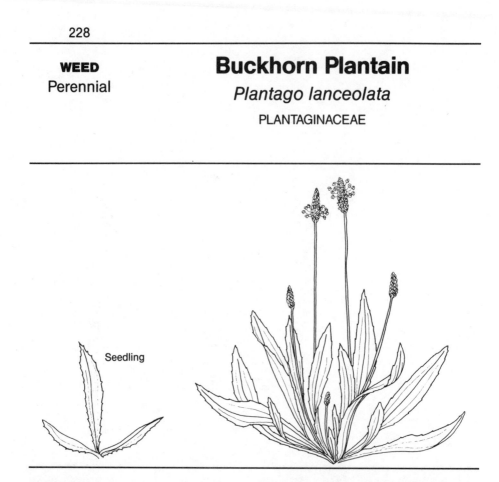

Seedling

Range: Throughout United States and southern Canada.

Description: Flower stalks are 8 inches to 2⅔ feet tall. Stems are erect and leafless, bearing only a flower spike and seeds. Dull green leaves, to 9 inches long and 1½ inches wide, form in a basal rosette and are long and narrow. Leaves may be spreading or somewhat erect and have three to five prominent veins that run laterally and taper toward the stiff, wide petiole. The cylindrical flower spikes are noticeable because they rise above the leaves. Flowers are tiny and numerous. Seed capsules grow in rows along the spike and each contains two smooth seeds. Blooms May to October.

Life Cycle: Perennial, reproducing from seeds and roots.

Prevention and Control: Plantains must be dug to be eliminated. A dandelion weeder is an effective tool for this job. Do not let plantain flower and set seed.

Notes: Buckhorn plantain may plague your lawn and garden paths. Plantains prefer dense, compacted soils, and so were known to the American Indians as the plant that follows the white man's footsteps. Incidence of plantain decreases as a hardpan is broken up and aerated and top layers of the soil develop a friable texture.

See photograph, page 293.

Canada Thistle

Cirsium arvense

COMPOSITAE

WEED
Perennial

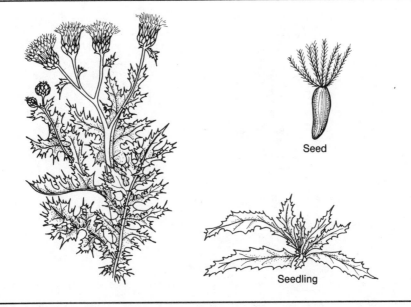

Seed

Seedling

Range: Northern United States and southern Canada from Quebec westward.

Description: Plants grow to 3 feet tall. The stem is erect and branches only at the top. Leaves, to 4¾ inches long, are alternate and deeply lobed with crinkly margins. Inch-wide flower heads are terminal or axillary. Male and female flowers are on different plants. The disk flowers are in shades of mauve, rose, deep lavender, or white. The female flower lacks pollen and has a more pronounced "waist" between petals and receptacle than the rectangular male bloom. Wind carries the light, tufted seed to new locations. Blooms July to October.

Life Cycle: Perennial, reproducing both by seeds and creeping roots. Seeds have a long period of viability, and roots sprout prolifically.

Prevention and Control: Pulling or cutting this plant does not eliminate the sprouting rootstock. Dig as much up as you can find and then, several weeks later, go back and dig again under each new plant. Under no circumstances let this plant flower; hoe it out immediately.

Notes: Rich and somewhat heavy soils are the first choice of Canada thistles, but they will grow in sandy, acid, and nutrient-deficient areas. Good drainage is the thistle's prime requirement.

See photograph, page 292.

WEED
Perennial

Chicory
Cichorium intybus
COMPOSITAE

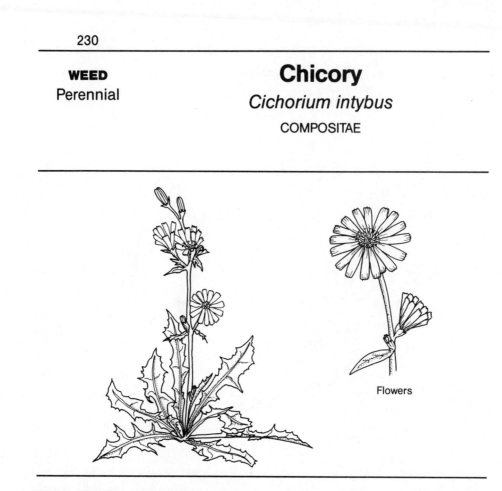

Flowers

Range: Throughout United States except areas south of North Carolina and the Texas panhandle, as well as portions of north central states. Southern Canada from Nova Scotia to British Columbia.

Description: Plants grow from 3 to 5½ feet tall. Erect stems are branched, hollow, and rough-haired with a milky juice inside. Leaves are alternate, lobed to dentate, hairy, and more profuse near the base. Toward the top of the plant, they clasp the stem. Basal lobes may project from either side of the stem attachment. The 1½-inch-wide, many-petaled ray flowers are perfect and are usually colored a clear blue but can be white or pink. Two rows of bracts at the flower base are quite visible and slightly scratchy to the touch. Flow-ers close each evening. Blooms June to October.

Life Cycle: Perennial, reproducing from seeds and roots just below the crown.

Prevention and Control: Hoe plants below the crown early in the spring. Watch waste places for telltale chicory flowers and hoe these plants out before seeds form.

Notes: Chicory prefers neutral to slightly alkaline conditions and is most trouble-some in limestone areas. Most common along roadsides, fences, and unused land. Roots are used as a coffee substitute or additive.

See photograph, page 292.

Coltsfoot

Tussilago farfara

COMPOSITAE

Leaf

Range: Northeastern United States as well as southeastern Canada; eastern areas west to Minnesota, as well as eastern areas in Canadian prairies.

Description: Flower spikes reach 6 inches tall and appear in early spring. They are erect and somewhat woolly when young. Four- to 8-inch-wide leaves appear at the end of the flowering season. They are simple, have long petioles, and are thick with whitish hairs growing on the undersides. In shape, they resemble an ivy-leafed geranium or a valentine, although the margin is broadly toothed. Terminal flower heads contain many yellow disk flowers surrounded by purplish bracts. Flower heads are 1⅜ inches wide. A

pappus spreads the seeds of this plant. Blooms April to May.

Life Cycle: Perennial, reproducing by seeds and rootstocks.

Prevention and Control: Coltsfoot must be dug to be eliminated. Follow the rootstocks, gently lifting them out of the soil. In serious infestations, use the tried-and-true method of obscuring light for a season by mulching heavily with a light-restrictive cover such as black plastic.

Notes: Coltsfoot is an indication that drainage should be improved. It grows best on wet, dense, clay soils. Add organic matter by covercropping, green-manuring, or amending with compost or aged manure.

WEED
Perennial

Common Milkweed
Asclepias syriaca
ASCLEPIADACEAE

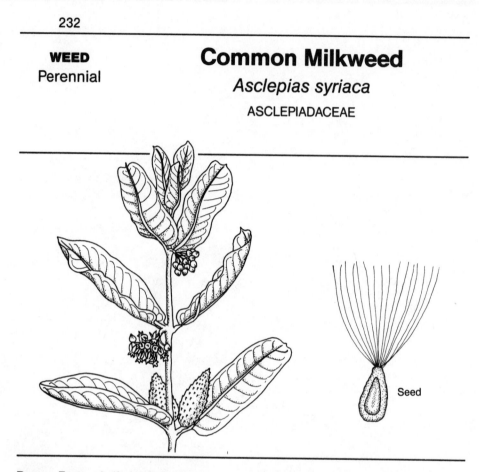

Seed

Range: Eastern half of United States, excluding the Gulf coast. Extends into southern Canada from New Brunswick to Saskatchewan.

Description: Plants are 3 to 6 feet tall. The upright stem is unbranched. Sporting downy hairs, the stem exudes a milky sap when broken or cut. Leaves are 3 inches to 1 foot long, opposite, broadly oblong and rounded, thick and tough, with prominent veins from the midrib; they are smooth on top, downy on the underside. Bell-shaped flower clusters grow from the upper axils and stem tips. The star-shaped blooms are waxy, pinkish-white to darkish pink and smell musky. Pods are initially green and symetrically spiny, ripening into dry, brown husks that open at the lateral midline to release feathery, silky white seeds. Seeds are flat, brown ovals. Blooms June to August.

Life Cycle: Perennial, reproducing by seeds and extensive rhizomes.

Prevention and Control: Pulling is usually sufficient, as long as underground rhizomes are also removed. Do not let pods ripen on plants near your garden.

Notes: Common milkweed is found in old pastures, woods, roadsides, and gardens. Milkweed prefers good drainage and high nutrition. It does not tolerate boggy conditions, but will grow in dry soils.

See photograph, page 295.

Common Woodsorrel

Oxalis stricta

OXALIDACEAE

WEED
Perennial

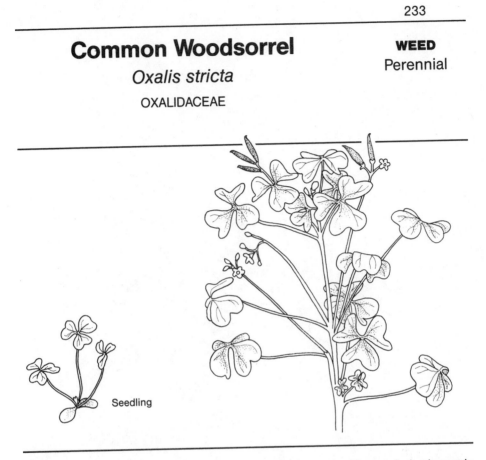

Seedling

Range: Throughout United States and southern Canada.

Description: Plants grow from 4 inches to 1⅔ feet tall. Young stems are often erect, but are thin and weak. As the plant grows, stems are more likely to lie along the ground than stand upright. The plant branches in all directions at the base. Stems are light green and somewhat hairy. Leaves grow on long, thin petioles and are divided into three heart-shaped leaflets with an obvious vein running down the center of each leaflet. Flowers are clear yellow with five petals. Seed-pods are cylindrical, with slightly hairy surfaces and pointed tips. Seeds are tiny and thrown long distances by the pod when it bursts. Blooms May to October.

Life Cycle: Perennial, reproducing by seeds and sometimes rooting from nodes on stems.

Prevention and Control: Hoeing and pulling are effective controls for woodsorrel. Because the plant is perennial and can root from nodes on the stem, do not let large populations grow in your garden. Eliminating woodsorrel is not difficult.

Notes: Woodsorrel is common on acid land and where the soil is gravelly or stony. It grows quite well in shade, and may intrude from the edges of woods or take up residence under perennials. Edible.

See photograph, page 293.

WEED
Perennial

Common Yarrow
Achillea millefolium
COMPOSITAE

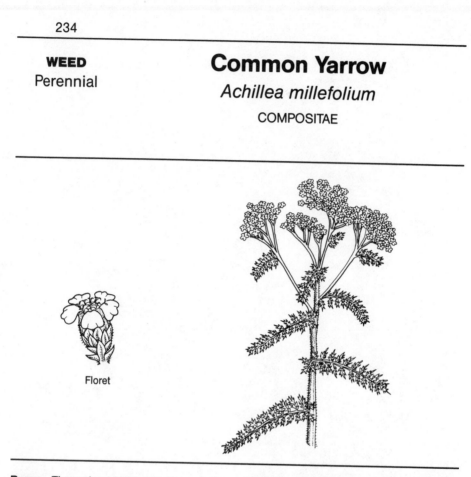

Floret

Range: Throughout United States, except areas in the Southwest, and southern Canada.

Description: Plants reach 3 feet tall. Stems are erect and usually simple, but may fork toward the top. They can be smooth or slightly hairy, depending on environmental conditions. Ferny leaves, to 8 inches long, are alternate and finely dissected. They arise almost directly from the stem. Flat, white flower heads are compound. Numerous small, perfect flowers arise from dense corymbs, meaning that the lower flower stalks in each head are longer than those at the top. Blooms June to October.

Life Cycle: Perennial, reproducing by seeds and rootstocks. Rootstalks do not travel far from the mother plant.

Prevention and Control: Yarrow is rarely a serious pest because it is easy to dig out and destroy. To eradicate, dig rootstocks in the spring and again before plants bloom. Do not let yarrow set seed; reproduction is more often accomplished by the tiny seeds than by a traveling root.

Notes: Yarrow can grow on thin or stony soils. It will also prosper in the good soils of old pastures and neglected fields. Flowers add a nice texture in summer bouquets and dry well for winter arrangements. Plants have a distinctive, almost sour fragrance.

Curly Dock

Rumex crispus

POLYGONACEAE

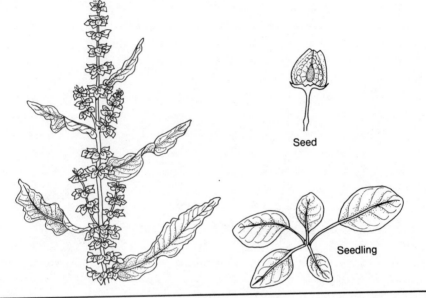

Seed

Seedling

Range: Throughout United States and southern Canada.

Description: Plants grow from 1 to 4 feet tall. Forms a dense rosette of thick, 6-inch- to 1-foot-long leaves and a sturdy, branching taproot during the first year of growth. Stems are hairless and ridged, turning red-brown in fall. Leaf shape is lanceolate, and margins are curly and wavy. Leaves growing on the stems are alternate, with short petioles growing from a papery sheath just above each node. The inflorescence (flower head) has many branches with small, narrow leaves interspersed among the flowers. The small, greenish flowers become red-brown as they age. Green calyxes have six sepals. The innermost three sepals are enlarged and dry out to provide a sail for the fruit, a shiny, brown, triangular achene. Blooms June to September.

Life Cycle: Perennial, reproducing by seeds.

Prevention and Control: Dock cannot be eliminated unless the large, branched taproot is dug out of the soil. Remove this weed when it is young, before the taproot has had a chance to grow long.

Notes: Curly dock is tolerant of poor conditions and often grows along roadsides and ditches, at the edges of fields, and in waste places.

WEED
Perennial

Dandelion

Taraxacum officinale

COMPOSITAE

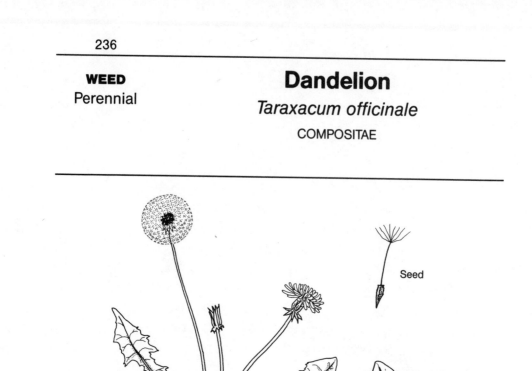

Seed

Seedling

Range: Throughout most of United States and southern Canada.

Description: Flower stalks grow to 1½ feet long. The thick, fleshy taproot can extend several feet into the soil. Stems are underground. The basal rosette of lobed or toothed leaves is dark green. When leaves, which can reach 1 foot long, are broken or cut, milky fluid slowly oozes from the wound. Flower buds are nestled into the leaf rosettes at first, and are green and rounded with two rows of spiky bracts. When the yellow, 2¼-inch-wide heads of ray flowers open, the lower row of bracts hangs down and the upper row stands up. Flower stalks are hollow, smooth on the outside, milky white and almost furry on the inside. The white seed pappuses look like delicate powder puffs. Blooms March to December.

Life Cycle: Perennial, reproducing by seeds and from root crowns. When a plant is cut out or hoed, the root will send up new leaves to take its place.

Prevention and Control: Dandelion must be dug and redug out of lawns and gardens. Each time, get as much of the root as possible. Do not let flower form. Reserved nutrients will be depleted through this treatment and eventually, plants die.

Notes: Dandelion can raise pH on acid soils.

Field Bindweed

Convolvulus arvensis

CONVOLVULACEAE

WEED
Perennial

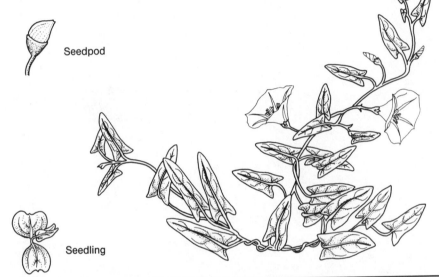

Seedpod

Seedling

Range: Throughout United States, except for Florida and extreme southern areas of Texas and the Southwest, and southern Canada.

Description: Stems are 3 to 10 feet long. Bindweed looks like the domesticated morning-glory, to which it is closely related. Smooth, thin stems climb or lie prostrate on the ground. Leaves are alternate, simple, smooth-margined, and often flare into two lobes at the base. Flowers are perfect and regular, with a white or pink funnel-shaped, inch-wide corolla that flares at the top. The dark seeds have a rough, pebbly texture. Blooms June to September.

Life Cycle: Perennial, reproducing by seeds and creeping roots.

Prevention and Control: Dig roots of this plant to eradicate. Do not let it remain in the garden long enough to gain a foothold. Bindweed can be troublesome because the roots are extensive and can grow 10 feet below the soil surface. If bindweed does take hold and digging does not eliminate it, mulch with a layer of black plastic covered with about a foot of hay or old newspapers. Leave the mulch in place for the entire season. Mow waste areas to prevent new bindweed seeds from being formed.

Notes: Bindweed likes rich soils, good drainage, and bright light conditions.

See photograph, page 293.

WEED
Perennial

Goldenrod
Solidago spp.
COMPOSITAE

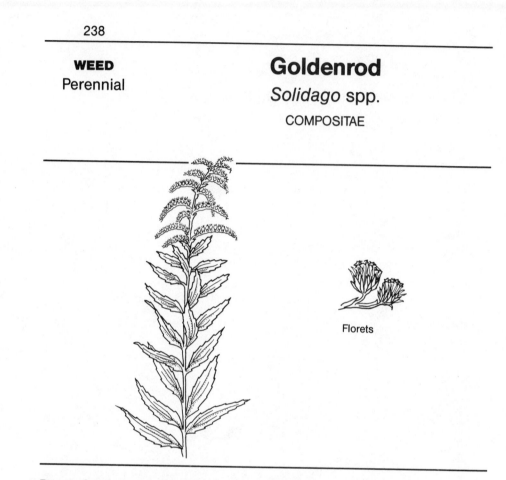

Florets

Range: One or more of the 130 species of goldenrod inhabit most of the United States and southern Canada.

Description: Plants grow from 2 to 6½ feet tall. Stems are often solitary, but may be clustered. Leaves are numerous and crowded, especially toward the middle to the top of the plant. They are 4 inches to 1 foot long, lanceolate, and point upward with three prominent veins and serrated margins. Leaf undersides may be slightly hairy. Basal leaves usually die and drop as the season progresses. The inflorescence (flower head) is terminal and consists of a many-branched panicle. Individual racemes in the panicle droop in graceful arcs. The flowers are yellow to yellow-green and grow in tiny heads along the raceme. Blooms July to October.

Life Cycle: Perennial, reproducing by seeds and creeping rhizomes.

Prevention and Control: Dig out rootstalk and as much rhizome as you can find. Digging may have to be repeated throughout the season whenever new plants sprout from rhizomes missed in the first digging. Mow all plants in waste areas and along fences to prevent their seeding.

Notes: Goldenrod can grow in moist or dry soil and good to poor fertility, but does require good light. Contrary to popular belief, hayfever is not caused by goldenrod.

See photograph, page 294.

Ground Ivy

Glechoma hederacea

LABIATAE

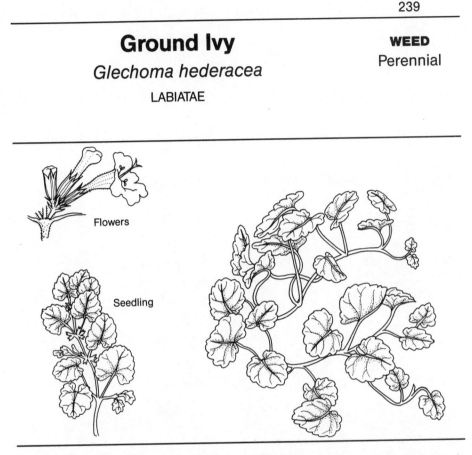

Flowers

Seedling

Range: Throughout eastern half of United States, with the exception of Florida and southernmost areas of Louisiana. Southern Canada.

Description: Stems grow to 1½ feet long. A prostrate, spreading plant. Four-sided stems trail along the ground, branching frequently and rooting at nodes. Leaves, to ½ inch long and ¾ inch wide, are bright green, opposite, palmately veined, smooth, and rounded with scalloped margins. Flowers are formed in axillary clusters on upright branches. The prominent calyx has five teeth, and the corolla is blue-purple. The flower is divided into an erect and somewhat cleft upper lip and a lower lip that is three-lobed. Blooms April to July.

Life Cycle: Perennial, reproducing by seeds and creeping stems.

Prevention and Control: Ground ivy's roots are shallow and easy to dislodge. Pull out crowns growing above the fibrous root system, taking each and every trailing stem. To prevent rerooting, remove all stems from the garden and put them in a compost pile that will reach a temperature of 160°F for three or four days.

Notes: Ground ivy, a mint relative, prefers rich soils that are somewhat moist. It grows well in shade and often tries to form a ground cover under trees.

See photograph, page 292.

WEED
Perennial

Heal-All
Prunella vulgaris
LABIATAE

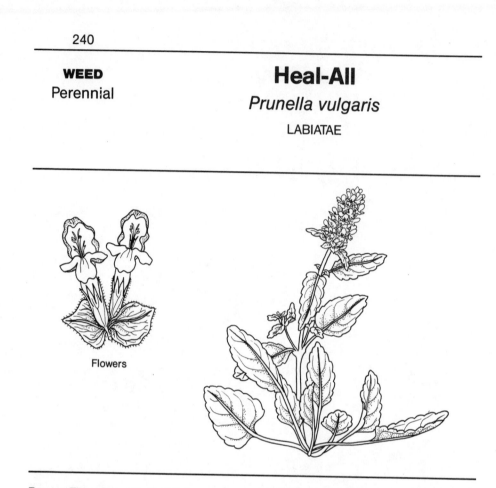

Flowers

Range: Throughout United States, except regions in the north central states. Also in southern Canada.

Description: Stems can reach 1⅔ feet long. Stems are four-sided, and can be erect or prostrate. Leaves are opposite, slightly hairy to hairless, and spaced at relatively long intervals along the stems. Margins are irregularly dentate. Flower spikes, surrounded by visible bracts, grow directly from the stem tops. The spikes are quite thick and dense. Green or purplish toothed calyxes cover half the length or more of the corolla. The corolla may be white, pink, blue, or purple, and is divided into two lips. The upper lip is hood-shaped and the lower one is three-lobed. Blooms May to October.

Life Cycle: Perennial, reproducing by seeds and short, aboveground runners.

Prevention and Control: Even though it reproduces from aboveground runners rather than creeping rootstocks, digging up the central root system is more effective than simply hoeing. Pull up or dig all runners, remembering that they root at the nodes. Take all pulled or dug plants out of the garden to prevent them from rerooting.

Notes: Where heal-all is trampled or frequently mowed, the growth habit changes. It becomes prostrate, and forms a dense mat. A member of the mint family.

Hedge Bindweed

Calystegia sepium

CONVOLVULACEAE

WEED
Perennial

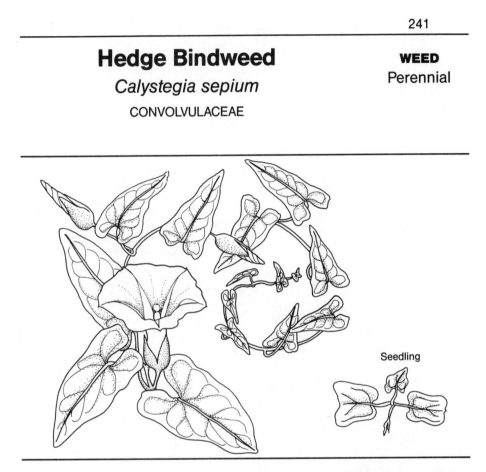

Seedling

Range: Eastern half and Northwestern areas of United States, and southern Canada.

Description: Stems are 3 to 10 feet long. Stems are often smooth, but may be covered with small hairs. Leaves, to 3 inches long, are alternate, arrow- or heart-shaped with pointed tips, hairless, entire, and smooth-margined. Flaring white, pink or rose-colored flowers, to 2½ inches long and 1 to 3 inches wide, are carried on long, four-sided stalks and look like slightly smaller morning-glory blooms. Blooms June to August.

Life Cycle: Perennial, reproducing by seeds and creeping rootstocks.

Prevention and Control: Hedge bindweed has a shallower root system than the closely related field bindweed, and is thus somewhat easier to eradicate. Dig every time you see a shoot. Mulch heavily for the entire season if digging does not eliminate a bindweed patch. Do not let wild plants in the area go to seed.

Notes: Hedge bindweed can climb nearby plants or fences, but without a support will trail along the ground. It likes rich, moist soils and good light. It is quite invasive, and will quickly cover the edges of roadways or fields, choking out less vigorous plants.

WEED
Perennial

Hoary Vervain

Verbena stricta

VERBENACEAE

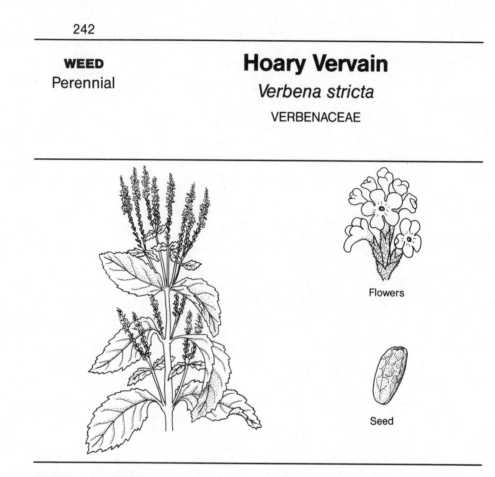

Flowers

Seed

Range: Northeastern and Mid-Atlantic United States, west to Idaho and Texas with the exception of areas in the north central states, and along the Pacific coast.

Description: Plants grow to 1½ feet tall. Stems are erect, simple or branched toward the top and covered with soft, white hairs. Leaves, to 4 inches long, are opposite, simple, oval, and toothed. They lack petioles and their coating of soft, white hairs makes them look almost downy. Flowers grow in erect, terminal spikes. Small purple, pink, or white corollas open successively along the spike. Hairy bracts and white calyxes are apparent. Dark brown nutlets form along the spike. Blooms June to September.

Life Cycle: Perennial, reproducing by seeds.

Prevention and Control: Dig out scattered plants in the garden. On fields, mow before the plant flowers. If the infestation is severe, the land should be plowed or tilled and planted to a cleanly cultivated crop for a year or two.

Notes: Hoary vervain likes dry, gravelly soils and grows well where fertility is low. It is unlikely to infest garden areas that are well tended and have high levels of humus.

Horse Nettle

Solanum carolinense

SOLANACEAE

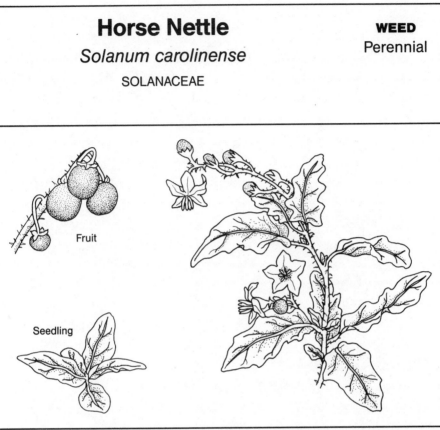

Fruit

Seedling

Range: In eastern half of the United States, and in the West from Idaho and Arizona to California, except Washington state; also southern Canada.

Description: Plants grow to 3 feet tall. Stem is stout, simple or branched, with yellowish spines along its length. Leaves, to 5 inches long, are alternate, forest green, elliptic to oval with toothed lobes, and often hairy. Prickly yellow spines grow from petioles, veins, and both upper and lower surfaces of midribs. This plant flowers in racemes, prickly along their stalk length, which become one-sided in that flowers tend to bend and open in only one direction on each raceme. The five-lobed violet, blue, or white, 3/4-inch corolla is surrounded at the base by a green, five-sepaled calyx. Numerous seeds develop within a round, yellow-orange, 5/8-inch-wide berry that becomes wrinkled as it matures. Blooms June to September.

Life Cycle: Perennial, reproducing by seeds and creeping underground rhizomes.

Prevention and Control: Dig out plants, including the rootstock and rhizomes. On areas where horse nettle has infested, dig plants and then mulch heavily with an organic substance such as old hay and cover with a layer of black plastic.

Notes: Horse nettle prefers good nutrition, full sun, and good drainage. Poisonous.

WEED
Perennial

Joe-Pye Weed
Eupatorium maculatum
COMPOSITAE

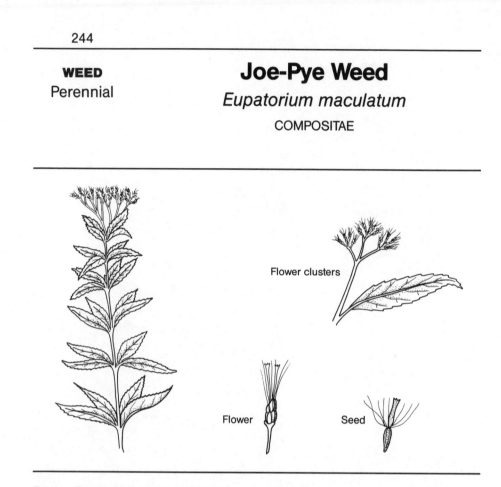

Flower clusters

Flower

Seed

Range: Eastern half of United States to North Carolina and west to New Mexico. Also in Washington state and southern Canada.

Description: Plants are 2 to 6 feet tall. Stems are unbranched, erect, and thick with ridges and sprinklings of purplish spots. Leaves grow in whorls of three to six. They are 2½ to 8 inches long, simple, narrowly oval or lanceolate, slightly hairy on the undersides, and have coarsely toothed margins. Flowers grow in dense, flat, compound corymbs. The cylindrical blooms have purple corollas. Seeds have bristly pappuses to carry them to new ground. Blooms July to September.

Life Cycle: Perennial, reproducing by seeds.

Prevention and Control: Dig Joe-pye weed, taking the roots to prevent resprouting. This weed does not easily survive being disturbed. Several successive years of cultivated row crops and winter cover crops generally eliminate it from a field, particularly if humus levels are also being increased.

Notes: Joe-pye weed grows well where drainage is poor. Very often, populations decrease as soil aeration is improved with the addition of organic matter and compost or aged manure.

Oxeye Daisy

Chrysanthemum leucanthemum

COMPOSITAE

WEED
Perennial

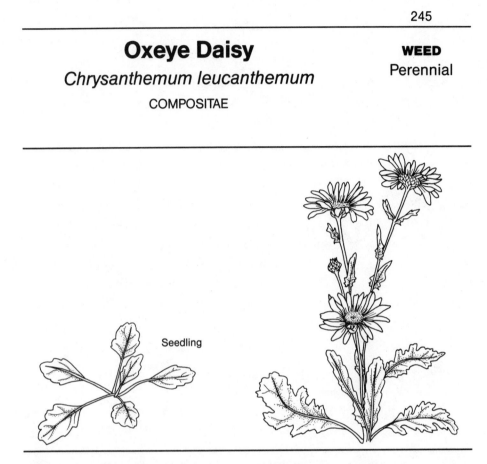

Seedling

Range: Throughout United States and southern Canada except for areas in the north central states and Canadian prairies.

Description: Plants grow to 3 feet tall. Stems are erect and spreading, and often fork toward the top. Leaves along the stem are sparsely placed, to 6 inches long, alternate, simple, and toothed at the margins. A basal rosette of leaves is pennatifid, meaning that leaves are divided to almost the central vein. The 1- to 2-inch-wide blooms are composed of white ray flowers, containing only pistils, encircling the bright yellow center of perfect disk flowers. Blooms June to August.

Life Cycle: Perennial, reproducing by seeds and creeping rhizomes.

Prevention and Control: Dig out as much rootstock as you can find under each leaf rosette early in the spring. Cut and enjoy all flowers that appear later in the season before repeating your digging operation. Dig again in the fall and in the following spring.

Notes: Oxeye daisies take up residence in old fields, pastures, and waste areas. They tolerate a wide range of environmental conditions, but are particularly adapted to grow in areas which lack good drainage and/or are becoming too acid.

WEED
Perennial

Pokeweed
Phytolacca americana
PHYTOLACCACEAE

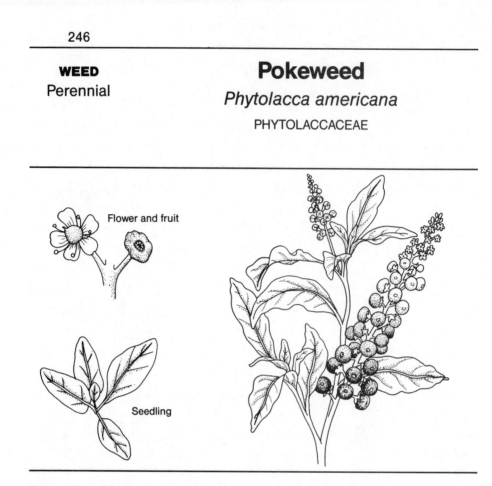

Flower and fruit

Seedling

Range: Throughout United States from Maine to Minnesota, and southward including the area between Florida and the eastern two-thirds of Texas.

Description: Plants reach 5 to 12 feet tall. Stems are thick and sometimes slightly reddish. They may be simple toward the base, but are as likely to be branched. At a foot or two above the soil surface, they are always branched unless they are growing in a very shady area. Leaves are 6 inches to 1⅙ feet long, alternate, oval, and smooth, with alternate veins from the central midrib. The inflorescence forms 6-inch-long racemes arising from stalks opposite upper leaves. Small, white flowers have five petals. They drop quickly and a dark purple, ten-sided berry containing ten seeds forms. Blooms June to September.

Life Cycle: Perennial, reproducing by seeds or, less frequently, roots.

Prevention and Control: Young plants are easy to hoe or pull, but large plants must be cut below the crown with a sharp spade. On ground that is being renovated, cut off and remove each group of stems before mowing the area.

Notes: Pokeweed likes deep, rich, well-drained soils and is not averse to some acidity. Except for young shoots, entire plant is poisonous.

See photograph, page 292.

Purple Loosestrife

Lythrum salicaria

LYTHRACEAE

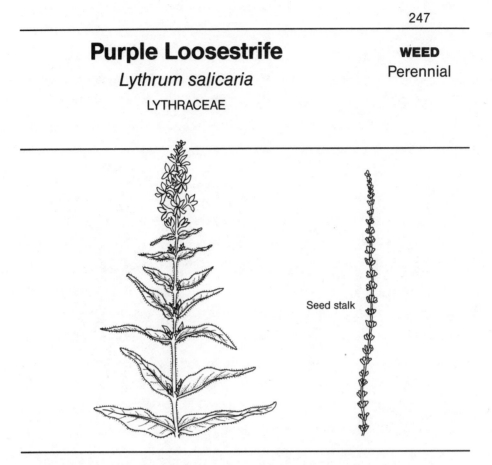

Seed stalk

Range: Northeastern United States to Virginia and Missouri. Also western Washington state and southern Canada.

Description: Plants grow to 6 feet tall. Stems are stout and erect. Like the leaves, they may be smooth or have small, downy hairs. Leaves, to 4 inches long, are opposite or arise in three-leafed whorls that clasp the stem. Many of them are lanceolate in shape with a smooth margin, although those at the base are broader and cordate, or shaped like the top of a valentine, close to their attachment. Flowers are a clear purple color and very showy. They grow in terminal spike-like panicles and are interspersed with large, green, leafy bracts. Blooms June to September.

Life Cycle: Perennial, reproducing by seeds.

Prevention and Control: Loosestrife must be dug to be eliminated. Roots are not extensive. Do not let the plant flower. On fields, mow before buds form, and dig individual clumps. Improving drainage may help eliminate the problem.

Notes: Loosestrife is a weed where it has escaped, but in the flower garden it can be a valuable addition. It likes high moisture, good friability, and high humus levels. Good light is also appreciated. Once established, it spreads slowly but surely, so bear this quality in mind when planting it.

WEED
Perennial

St.-John's-Wort
Hypericum perforatum
GUTTIFERAE

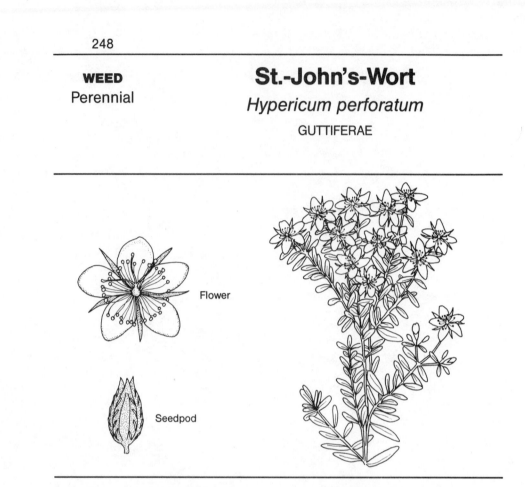

Flower

Seedpod

Range: Throughout eastern half of United States, Pacific Northwest states south to central California; also southern Quebec and Ontario.

Description: Plants grow to 2 feet tall. Stems are smooth, erect and multi-branched. The numerous inch-long leaves are opposite, elliptical, and extend vertically from the stem. Small, almost transparent spots dot the leaves. Stems carrying the terminal flower cymes are quite leafy. The five-petaled flowers, to 1 inch wide, are orange to yellow and have black dots close to the petal margins. The stamens are quite noticeable because they are numerous, long, and grow in three distinct groups. The central pistil has three long styles. The three-chambered seedpod contains numerous seeds. Blooms June to September.

Life Cycle: Perennial, reproducing by seeds and short rootstocks.

Prevention and Control: Dig this plant out of the garden. If an area becomes infested, water heavily and cover with a deep hay mulch. If the plant grows through the mulch, dig, water, and mulch heavily again, adding a layer of black plastic.

Notes: St.-John's-wort prefers dry, gravelly or sandy soils, and will not grow in damp areas.

Sheep Sorrel
Rumex acetosella
POLYGONACEAE

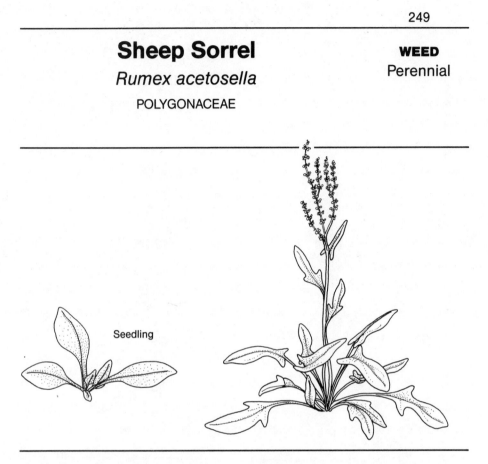

Seedling

Range: Throughout Unites States and southern Canada.

Description: Plants are 1 foot tall. A basal rosette of inch-long, arrow-shaped leaves appears first. Stems grow from the center of the rosette within a few weeks and branch toward the top of the plant. Leaves growing from stems are more narrow than those in the rosette and have two distinct basal lobes. A reddish cast may be apparent under the dull green leaf color. The inflorescence is composed of terminal, erect panicles. Male and female flowers grow on different plants. Sepals of both genders are red or, less often, yellowish. The fruit, which forms from the pistillate flowers, is longer than the sepals and a shiny red-brown color. Blooms May to October.

Life Cycle: Perennial, reproducing by seeds and extensive creeping rhizomes.

Prevention and Control: Pull this plant by hand, making sure to lift roots and rhizomes as well as leaves. Do not throw the roots or rhizomes into bed areas or paths because they reroot quite easily. They will also root in the compost pile, unless they are placed in the center where temperatures are high and darkness prevails.

Notes: Sheep sorrel often indicates poor fertility. It grows on acid, shallow, dry, or gravelly ground.

WEED
Perennial

Stinging Nettle
Urtica dioica
URTICACEAE

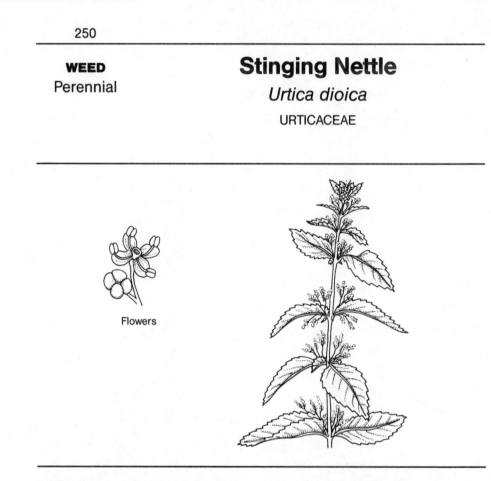

Flowers

Range: Eastern half of United States, except Florida; eastern Washington state, Idaho, Colorado, and into northern Texas. Southern Canada.

Description: Plants grow from 2 to 6 feet tall. Stems are erect, ridged, and bristled. Leaves, to 6 inches long, are usually hairy as well. The hairs contain a compound, made chiefly of formic acid, which stings and burns bare skin. Leaves are opposite and oval to slightly heart-shaped, with coarsely toothed margins. Stipules at the leaf axils are quite large. Tiny green flowers grow in panicled spikes originating from axils. Flowers are dioecious, meaning that male and female flowers form on different plants. Tiny, grayish-brown fruits containing one seed develop from the female flowers. Blooms June to September.

Life Cycle: Perennial, reproducing by seeds and creeping rootstocks.

Prevention and Control: Stinging nettle must be dug to be eliminated. Wear good boots, thick pants, and tough gloves, and use a sharp spade. Follow the traveling rootstocks through the soil, lifting them. Let the plant wilt on the soil surface before touching it, and even then, continue to protect yourself with thick gloves.

Notes: Stinging nettle is no friend to bare skin.

Tall Ironweed

Vernonia altissima

COMPOSITAE

WEED
Perennial

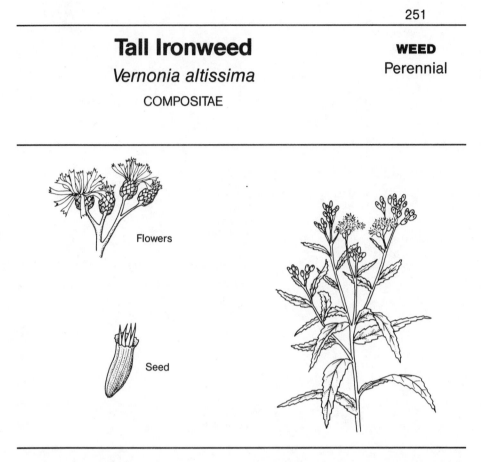

Flowers

Seed

Range: Eastern half of United States south of Vermont and New Hampshire.

Description: Plants may reach 10 feet tall. The smooth stem is simple at the base, branching widely toward the top. Leaves, to 10 inches long, are alternate, widely lanceolate with pointed tips and small pointed teeth at the margins. They have very short petioles and usually point upward rather than spread horizontally from the stem. Flower heads grow in open cymes. Each ½-inch-wide head is composed of 15 to 30 reddish-purple flowers. Green, sharply toothed involucres, leaf-like structures that protect the reproductive system of a flower, enclose the base of the flower heads. Blooms August to October.

Life Cycle: Perennial, reproducing by seeds and rhizomes.

Prevention and Control: Dig tall ironweed, making sure to remove underground rhizomes. If all else fails, employ a deep mulch for the entire season. On waste areas near the garden, mow or scythe plants in the late summer, just before they bloom and set seeds.

Notes: Tall ironweed prefers very moist, rich soils, such as those you may be developing in your garden. Keep your eyes open for volunteers of this weed and eradicate them.

WEED
Perennial

Wild Garlic

Allium vineale

LILIACEAE

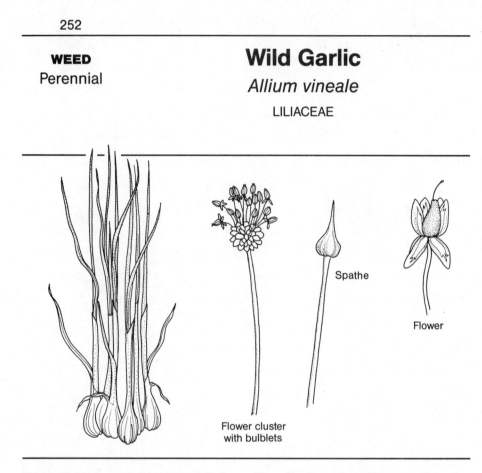

Spathe

Flower

Flower cluster
with bulblets

Range: Eastern and central United States except northern areas, and Pacific Northwest into northern California.

Description: Plants grow to 3 feet tall. Stems are stiff and erect, with leaves growing only from the lower half. Hollow leaves have a basal sheath that encircles the stem. In some areas, wild garlic flowers and sets seed. The flower head is an umbel of whitish-green flowers, and sets seeds in the early spring. Aerial bulblets as tiny as grains of wheat form on these flowering plants. Nonflowering plants have fewer leaves and are less conspicuous. Underground, both plants form hard-shell bulbs that overwinter in all but the coldest areas. Central bulbs are formed around the main axis of the plant on nonflowering plants toward the end of summer. Flowering plants form soft offset bulbs in the axils of the underground portions of the innermost leaves from midsummer to fall. Blooms May to June.

Life Cycle: Perennial, reproducing from seeds, aerial bulblets, and bulbs.

Prevention and Control: Dig every plant, removing as many underground bulbs as you can find. If it is becoming a serious weed, mulch heavily infested areas for an entire season.

Notes: Wild garlic tolerates almost any environment. Leaves smell garlicky.

Yellow Rocket, Winter Cress

Barbarea vulgaris

CRUCIFERAE

WEED
Perennial

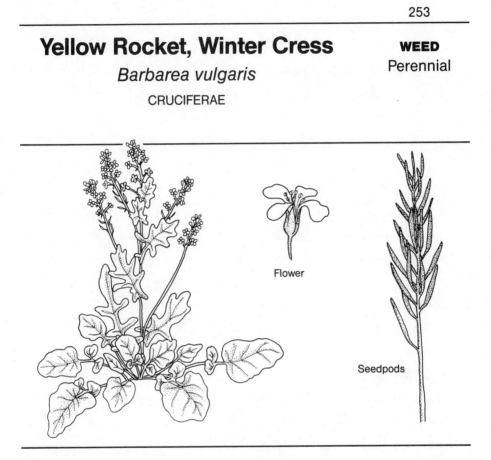

Flower

Seedpods

Range: Northeastern United States south to Arkansas, areas in the north central states and Pacific Northwest. Southeastern provinces of Canada.

Description: Plants grow to 3 feet tall. During the first year, a rosette forms close to the ground. Leaves are lobed, but the rounded terminal lobe is so large that lower lobes look more like smaller individual leaves than portions of the same leaf. These leaves are glossy green and may persist even under light winter snows. In the spring of the second season, groups of stems arise from crowns just at the soil level. The stems are hairless and feel ridged. Leaves coming off the erect stems are alternate and lobed at the base. Bright yellow flowers grow in loosely grouped racemes and are followed by inch-long seedpods. Blooms April to August.

Life Cycle: Perennial, reproducing by seeds and from crowns, but in many areas, behaves more like a winter annual.

Prevention and Control: Hoeing and pulling will eradicate this plant. In cases of serious invasion in a cover-cropped area, mow frequently enough to prevent the plant from flowering and setting new seed.

Notes: Rocket likes rich soils with good moisture levels, and is particularly happy to take up residence in newly planted areas. Edible.

WEED
Woody
Perennial

Japanese Honeysuckle
Lonicera japonica
CAPRIFOLIACEAE

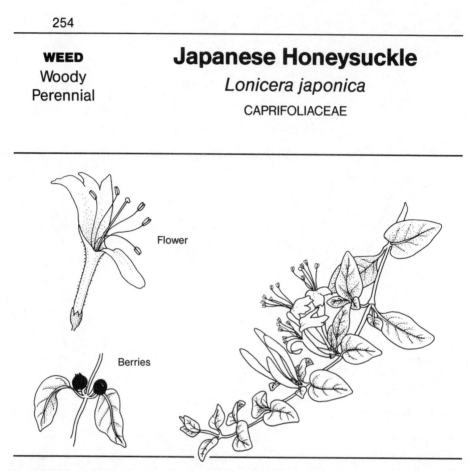

Flower

Berries

Range: Eastern half of United States from Massachusetts south; southern Michigan and Kansas to Texas.

Description: Plants are 25 to 45 feet long. Stems are woody and green to brown. Those that grow on the soil surface strike roots at nodes. Leaves, to 3 inches long, are slightly hairy, opposite, simple, ovate, and short-petioled. Paired, highly fragrant flowers arise from each side of nodes just above the leaf. The five petals form a 1½-inch-long corolla with two uneven lips. Five prominent stamens and one pistil emerge from the white, pink, or yellow blooms. Berries are purplish-black and shiny. Two or three seeds are enclosed in each berry. Blooms June and July.

Life Cycle: Perennial, reproducing from seeds, trailing stems and underground rhizomes.

Prevention and Control: Dig up rootstock, rhizomes and rooting stems. This job takes several seasons; honeysuckle spreads rapidly.

Notes: Honeysuckle will twine up fences or nearby trees or, without support, will trail along the ground. Berries are a favorite food of many seed-spreading birds. In the Deep South, leaves remain on the plant all winter.

Kudzu

Pueraria lobata

LEGUMINOSAE

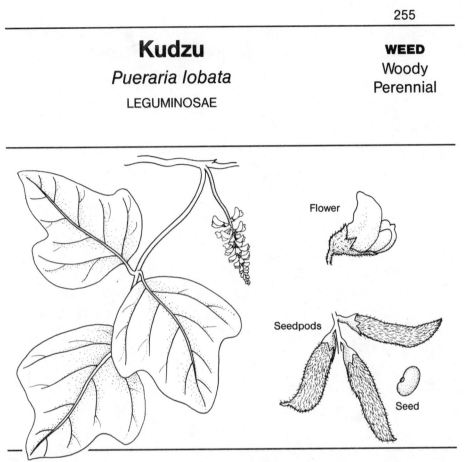

Flower

Seedpods

Seed

Range: Southeastern half of United States below Pennsylvania and extending into eastern Texas.

Description: Plants grow to 60 feet long. When young, stems are herbaceous and slightly hairy, but as they age, they become more woody and smooth. Leaves, to 6 inches long, are divided into three leaflets and are usually lobed. Flowers are borne on racemes and look like a long cluster of fancy pea flowers. The corolla is a red-purple color and smells something like red grapes and the standard (the large petal that stands up at the back of the bloom) is bright yellow at the base. Seedpods, to 4 inches long, look like very hairy pea pods. Blooms late August to September.

Life Cycle: Perennial, reproducing by seeds and from roots.

Prevention and Control: Cut vines and dig out each root you find. After digging roots, mulch the area with layers of news-papers and/or mulch hay covered with black plastic weighted down with rocks. Regard elimination as a two- to three-year job.

Notes: The branching stems of kudzu twine around upright supports or trail long distances across the ground.

Multiflora Rose
Rosa multiflora
ROSACEAE

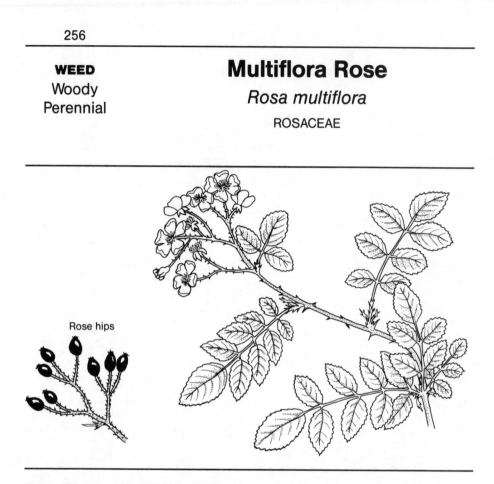

Rose hips

Range: Throughout most of the United States except the far North, the Rocky Mountain area, deserts and southeastern coastal plain areas.

Description: Plants grow to 10 feet tall. Stiff thorns protect the stems. The deciduous leaves are compound, divided into seven to nine 1¼-inch-long leaflets arranged along a central stalk with a centrally placed leaflet at the tip. Leaflets are oval and have serrate margins. Their pale undersides are covered with short hairs. Roses grow in terminal clusters. Most blooms are white, although some are slightly pink. Pea-sized hips which develop from the ¾-inch-wide flowers are initially bright red, but darken as they age.

If not picked, they can persist on the canes until spring. Blooms May to June.

Life Cycle: Perennial, reproducing by seeds and from cane tips that touch the soil surface.

Prevention and Control: Dig this plant, roots included. Eliminating it may take several seasons of concerted digging. If a patch is stubbornly persistent, mulch the soil for a season with a thick, tough, light-restrictive mulch.

Notes: A full-grown multiflora rose is a huge shrub, with long stems that stand erect for 4 or 5 feet, then arch back to the ground.

Poison Ivy

Rhus radicans

ANACARDIACEAE

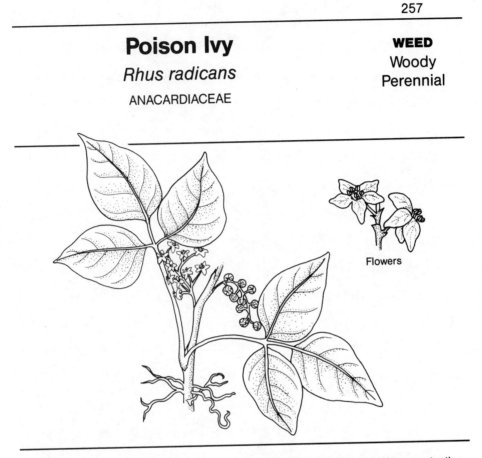

Flowers

Range: Throughout United States and southern Canada.

Description: Running rootstocks extend to 12 feet from the parent plant, sending up new plants from nodes along their length. This woody plant can grow as a shrub or as a climbing or creeping vine. Leaves bear three leaflets on long, oppositely placed petioles. The leaves, to 10 inches long, can be glossy or dull green, hairy, smooth, evenly margined, slightly toothed, or lobed. Tiny yellow-green flowers grow in panicles. The fruit is a dry, grayish-white drupe, or stone fruit. Blooms late May to July.

Life Cycle: Perennial, reproducing by seeds and creeping rootstocks that grow from the bottom stem nodes.

Prevention and Control: Wear protective clothing. Dig out roots as soon as you notice the characteristic three leaflets. In the fall, about a week after the first bad frost, check all areas for vibrant red-orange leaflets. Load poison ivy into plastic bags and put them out for the trash. Never burn this plant. Some people's lungs are extremely allergic to poison ivy fumes.

Notes: Poison ivy likes good light, rich soil, and rail fences, but will grow in dense clay or sand, heavy shade, or up an old creosoted telephone pole. Birds landing in your garden are responsible for the new plants you find there. See poison oak (page 258) for more information.

WEED
Woody
Perennial

Poison Oak

Rhus toxicodendron

ANACARDIACEAE

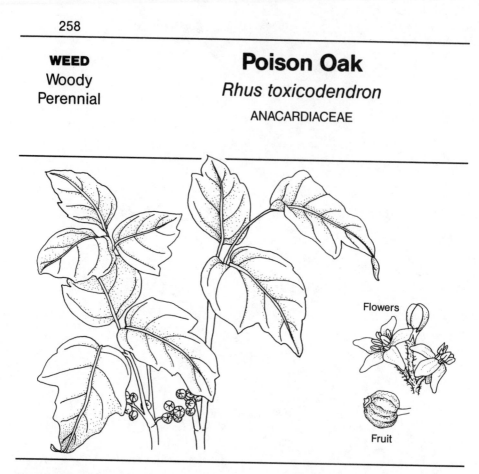

Flowers

Fruit

Range: Southeastern United States from New Jersey to Florida, west to Missouri, Oklahoma, and Texas.

Description: Plants grow to 6½ feet tall. Stems are slender and woody. Unlike poison ivy, poison oak does not grow aerial roots, nor does it climb supports. Leaves grow on long petioles with soft hairs and are divided into three leaflets. Leaflets are also hairy and are variously shaped. They often have deep teeth or lobes and can resemble a maple or oak leaf in shape. Flowers grow in clusters and are small and whitish with five petals. Green to light tan berries form in the fall. Blooms May to June.

Life Cycle: Perennial, reproducing by seeds and underground stolons.

Prevention and Control: Dig this plant, taking care to follow and lift the woody stolons. Wear good boots, thick clothes, and strong gloves because every portion of this plant is poisonous.

Notes: If you touch poison oak or ivy, wash immediately with a half and half mixture of alcohol and water mixed with 5% chlorine. Do not wash with an oil-based soap, because the toxin is soluble in oil and will spread. Instead, use an alkaline soap to wash away the chlorine mixture.

Bermuda Grass
Cynodon dactylon
GRAMINEAE

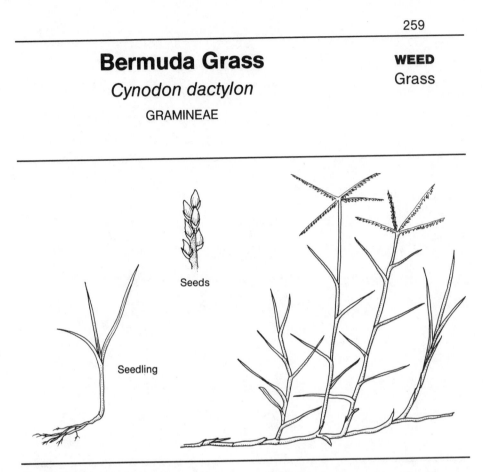

Seeds

Seedling

Range: Southern two-thirds of United States. Serious only in southeastern and south central states; hardy only south of Pennsylvania.

Description: Stalks grow to 1⅓ feet tall. A prostrate, creeping plant that forms a dense sod. Stolons lie along the soil surface, branching, rooting, and carrying the culms, or stems, of the plant. Leaves are gray-green, with a fringe of hair just above the sheathed stem attachments. The inflorescence is divided into three to seven 1- to 2-inch-long spikes that radiate from the ends of the culms. The spikes are held erect on stalks that are much taller than the main body of the plant. Two rows of deep orange, prickly seeds develop along each spike. Blooms June to August.

Life Cycle: Perennial, reproducing by scaly rhizomes, stolons, and occasionally by seeds.

Prevention and Control: Dig out rootstocks and stolons to eliminate Bermuda grass. In gardens with heavy infestations, mulch with a 6-inch layer of hay and then a light-restrictive cover such as black plastic. On northern fields, fall plowing to expose roots to heavy frosts kills the plant.

Notes: This grass can be used as a lawn or pasture grass in dry, sandy soils.

WEED
Grass

Johnson Grass
Sorghum halepense
GRAMINEAE

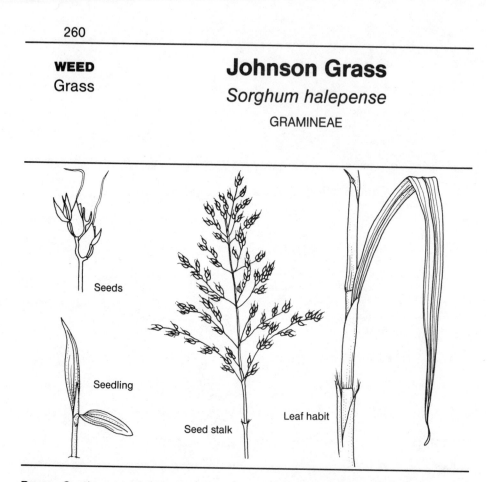

Seeds

Seedling

Seed stalk

Leaf habit

Range: Southern two-thirds of United States and areas in Washington state and Oregon.

Description: Plants grow to 5 feet tall and have strong, erect stems. Long, smooth, alternate leaves are connected to stems by sheaths. Flower panicles, to 1½ feet long, are large, hairy, and purplish. The caryopses, or seeds, are red-brown. Blooms June to October.

Life Cycle: Perennial, reproducing by seeds and three different kinds of rootstock.

Prevention and Control: Dig Johnson grass out of the garden, paying particular attention to lift all rootstocks. If this fails, mulch the area deeply and cover with a light-restrictive layer such as black plastic. The mulch may have to stay in place for two seasons. In cases of serious infestation on fields, very frequent mowing or close grazing is necessary to decrease the vigor and extensiveness of the tertiary rootstocks, those that are the most likely to be so deep that digging or plowing does not uproot them. After two years of close mowing, the rootstock should be close enough to the soil surface so that it can be dug out or plowed.

Notes: Make sure that innocuous-looking clumps of Johnson grass do not go unweeded through the season. The longer they are allowed to sit and the better the soil in which they grow, the wider and deeper the rootstock burrows.

Quackgrass, Witchgrass, Couchgrass

Agropyron repens

GRAMINEAE

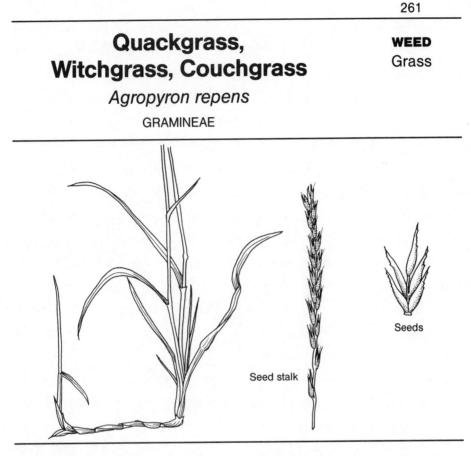

Seed stalk

Seeds

Range: Throughout southern Canada and all of United States except the Deep South.

Description: Plants grow to 3 feet tall. Stems are smooth with three to six joints. Upper nodes are circled with a cartilaginous band. Leaves have sheaths and are narrow and rough to the touch on the upper surface. Terminal spikes, 2 to 6 inches long, have two opposite rows of tiny flowers arising from sharp and tiny bracts. The seeds are tiny, yellow-brown, and grain-shaped. Roots are fibrous, but the succulent-looking white rhizomes from which they grow are more apparent. Blooms late May to September.

Life Cycle: Perennial, reproducing by seeds and the rapidly growing, extensive under-ground rhizomes that root and send up a shoot at every node.

Prevention and Control: Dig out the roots under all shoots and mulch grassy areas very deeply. Weed areas around large, underground rocks; roots snuggle up to these protected sites. Mulch heavily for several feet around all garden areas to prevent the invasion of this pest from nearby hay, pasture, or waste places.

Notes: Quackgrass can be abundant in almost any soil, although it prefers the high fertility, good drainage, and slightly acid pH which it can find in your garden.

WEED
Grass

Smooth Crabgrass
Digitaria ischaemum
GRAMINEAE

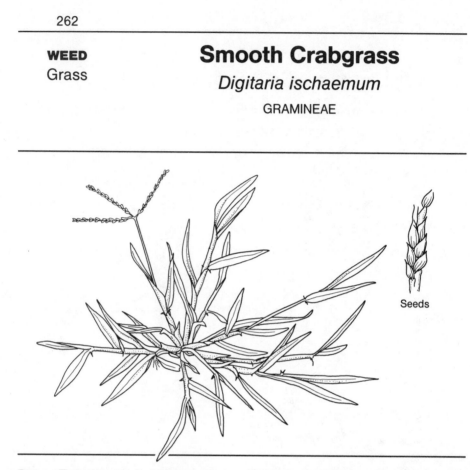

Seeds

Range: Throughout United States, with the exception of southern Florida and areas in the Southwest; southern Canada.

Description: Plants range from ⅘ inch to 1⅓ feet tall. Culms, or stems, are both erect and prostrate. The plant can root from stem nodes lying on the soil surface and because of this, often forms a dense mat. Leaves are alternate and smooth with a blue to purple cast. Florets grow in terminal racemes on upright stems and are often quite purple. Tiny hairs grow both from the areas where leaves arise from their sheaths and on the bracts below the florets. Blooms July to September.

Life Cycle: Annual, reproducing by seeds or from roots growing from stem nodes.

Prevention and Control: Dig out the crown of this plant and remove all stems from the lawn or garden. Because seeds germinate only when the soil is warm, fertilize lawns early in the spring to promote the growth of desired grasses and decrease the area open to crabgrass growth. If prostrate stems form unsightly brown patches in the late summer lawn, dig out the crabgrass, fertilize the area, and reseed with a desired grass, making sure to keep the area moist.

Notes: Crabgrass is most common in dry and sandy soils, but will grow in other conditions.

Yellow Foxtail
Setaria glauca
GRAMINEAE

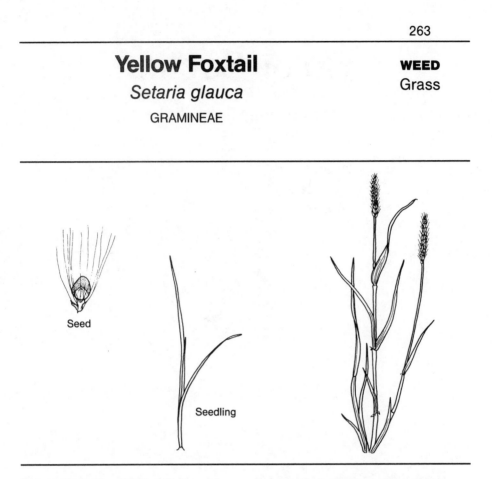

Seed

Seedling

Range: Throughout United States and southern Canada.

Description: Stalks are 1⅔ to 4 feet tall. Erect or ascending stems branch close to the base. Leaves are smooth and flat. Flower spikes are hairy. The spikelets, or individual flowers growing on the spike, are one-flowered, but sometimes have a staminate or male flower below the terminal perfect flower that contains both genders. After the flowers drop, shiny yellow grains develop. Blooms June to September.

Life Cycle: Annual, reproducing by seeds.

Prevention and Control: Pull out small plants that appear in the spring garden and, later in the season, dig out larger plants with a trowel. If renovating a field, mow before midseason, when the plant flowers and sets seed. The next spring, plow and harrow or till several times before planting a cultivated, late-season crop. Several years of clean cultivation will rid the area of viable seeds.

Notes: Yellow foxtail likes bare spots in rich soils and is likely to take up residence in newly plowed land, stubble, or open areas in your garden. It will not germinate in the fall, but sits dormant until spring. Because it does not reproduce by underground stolons or rhizomes, digging up scattered clumps is relatively easy.

See photograph, page 295.

Color Section

Bean aphid, adult, *page 28*

Pea aphid, wingless adult, *page 30*

Ant, adults herding aphids, *page 22*

Bumblebee, adult, *page 23*

Honeybee, adult, *page 24*

Braconid wasp, adult, *page 26*

Yellow jacket, adult, *page 27*

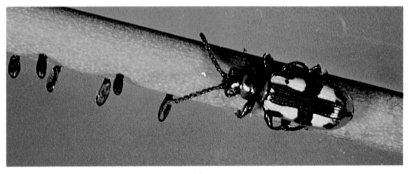

Colorado potato beetle, adults, *page 34*

Colorado potato beetle, larva, *page 34*

Asparagus beetle, adult with eggs, *page 32*

Bean leaf beetle, adult, *page 33*

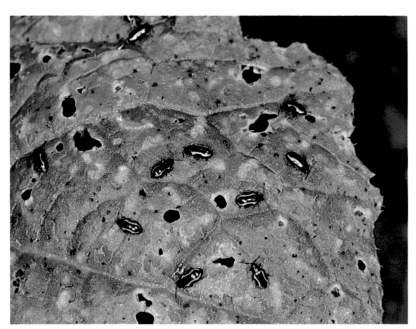

Striped flea beetle, adults, *page 36*

Ground beetle, adult, *page 37*

Fiery searcher, adult, *page 38*

Japanese beetle, adults, *page 39*

Mealybug destroyer, adult, *page 44*

Lady beetle, adult feeding on aphid, *page 41*

Mexican bean beetle, adult, *page 45*

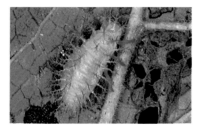

Mexican bean beetle, larva, *page 45*

Spotted cucumber beetle, adult, *page 49*

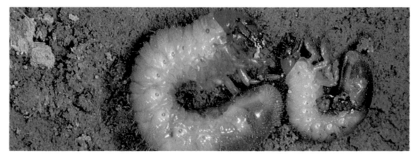

June beetle, grubs, *page 40*

European corn borer, larva, *page 52*

European corn borer, adult, *page 52*

Striped cucumber beetle, adult, *page 51*

Squash vine borer, larva, *page 56*

Squash bug, adult, *page 62*

Harlequin bug, adult, *page 60*

Tarnished plant bug, adult, *page 63*

Cabbage looper, adult, *page 65*

Cabbage looper, larva, *page 65*

Codling moth, adult, *page 66*

Codling moth, larva, *page 66*

Imported cabbageworm, larva, *page 75*

Cutworm, larva, *page 68*

Imported cabbageworm, adult,
page 75

Corn earworm, larva, *page 67*

Parsleyworm, adult, *page 77*

Parsleyworm, larva, *page 77*

Tomato hornworm, larva, *page 78*

Praying mantid, adult, *page 83*

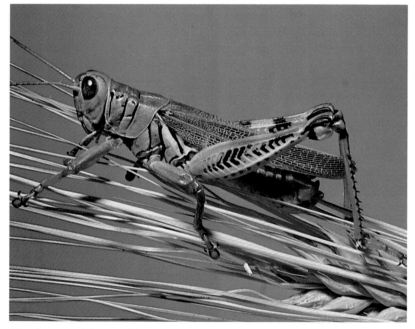

Grasshopper, adult, *page 81*

Hover fly, adult, *page 89*

Tachinid fly, adult, *page 95*

Katydid, adult, *page 82*

Antlion, larva, *page 96*

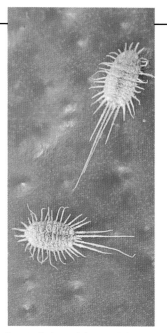

Longtailed mealybug, adults, *page 104*

Cottonycushion scale, colony, *page 107*

Plum curculio, adults, *page 114*

Greenhouse whitefly, adults, *page 116*

Slug, immature gray garden, *page 122*

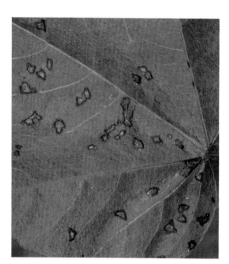

Angular leaf spot on red maple, *page 140*

Bacterial bean blight on kidney bean, *page 140*

Bacterial blight of pea, *page 141*

Bacterial leaf spot on soybean, *page 143*

Bacterial blight of tomato on tomato, *page 142*

Brown rot on plum, *page 147*

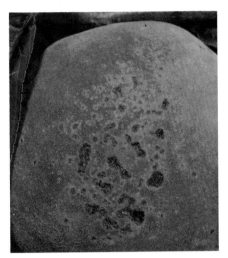

Bacterial spot on peach, *page 143*

Bacterial wilt of cucurbits on cucumber, *page 144*

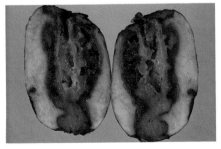

Blackleg of potato on tuber, *page 145*

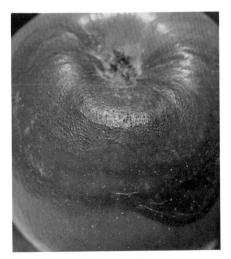

Black rot on apple, *page 146*

Soft rot on sweet potato, *page 150*

Crown gall on rose, *page 148*

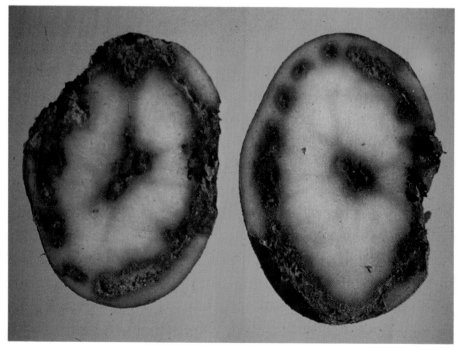

Potato ring rot on potato, *page 148*

Ascochyta blight on cotton, *page 153*

Botrytis on tulip, *page 154*

Alternaria blight of cucurbits on muskmelon, *page 151*

Anthracnose on dogwood, *page 152*

Cabbage yellows on cabbage, *page 154*

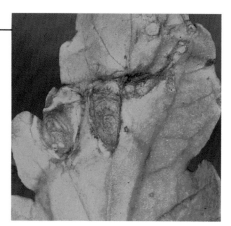

Early blight, *page 159*

Clubroot on cauliflower, *page 155*

Damping-off on seedlings, *page 157*

Fusarium wilt on tomatoes, *page 160*

Southern leaf blight on corn, *page 156*

Northern leaf blight on corn, *page 156*

Early blight of celery, *page 160*

Late blight on potato, *page 161*

Downy mildew on cantaloupe, *page 158*

Powdery mildew on forget-me-not, *page 163*

Root rot on peach, *page 164*

Red stele on strawberry, *page 164*

Soil rot on tomato, *page 165*

Scab on potato, *page 149*

Cedar-apple rust on crabapple, *page 166*

Corn smut on corn, *page 167*

Verticillium wilt on eggplant, *page 169*

Nematode on roots, *page 170*

Bean mosaic on green beans, *page 172*

Aster yellows on marigold, *page 171*

Beet curly top on beet, *page 172*

Cucumber mosaic on muskmelon, *page 173*

Potato leaf roll on potato, *page 174*

Tobacco mosaic on tomato, *page 175*

Tobacco ring spot on tobacco, *page 176*

Ground ivy,
page 239

Chicory,
page 230

Canada thistle,
page 229

Pokeweed,
page 246

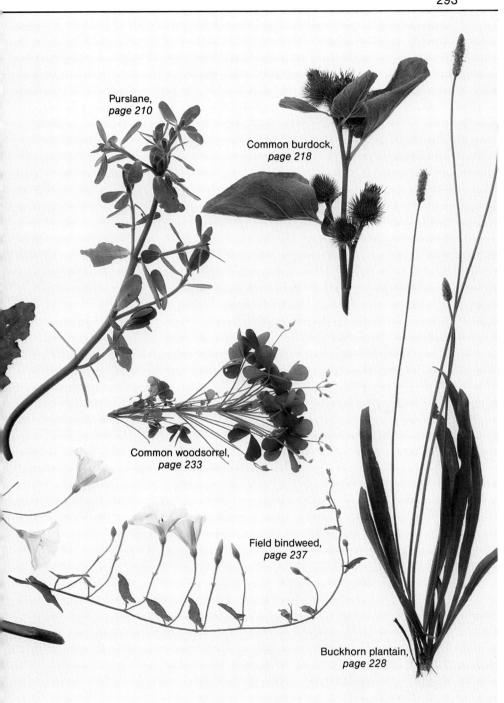

Purslane,
page 210

Common burdock,
page 218

Common woodsorrel,
page 233

Field bindweed,
page 237

Buckhorn plantain,
page 228

Teasel,
page 225

Goldenrod,
page 238

Common ragwee
page 196

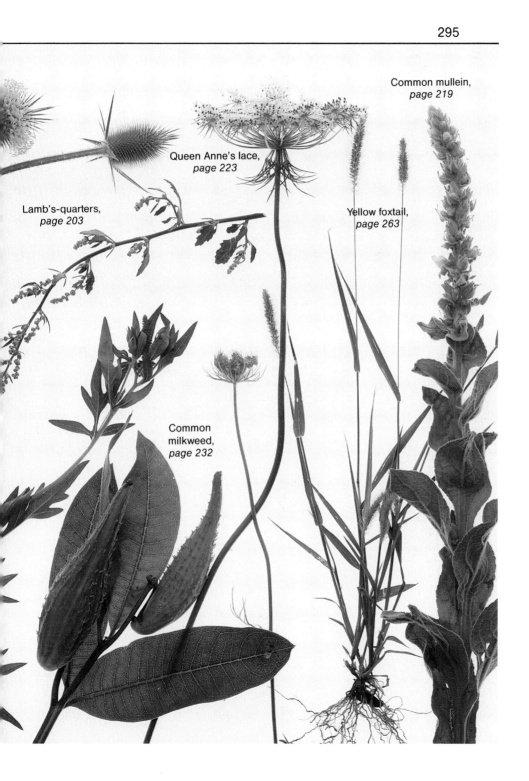

Common mullein,
page 219

Queen Anne's lace,
page 223

Lamb's-quarters,
page 203

Yellow foxtail,
page 263

Common
milkweed,
page 232

PHOTOGRAPH CREDITS

Max E. Badgley: bean aphid, p. 265; pea aphid, p. 265; lady beetle, p. 271; mealybug destroyer, p. 271; European corn borer larva, p. 273; cabbage looper adult, p. 275; cabbage looper larva, p. 275; codling moth larva, p. 275; tachinid fly, p. 279; longtailed mealybug, p. 280; cottonycushion scale, p. 280

Cornell University: bacterial blight, p. 282; bacterial blight of tomato, p. 282; blackleg, p. 283; potato ring rot, p. 284; cabbage yellows, p. 285; early blight of celery, p. 287; verticillium wilt, p. 289; tobacco mosaic, p. 291

Lee Jenkins: bean leaf beetle, p. 268; Colorado potato beetle adults, p. 268; Colorado potato beetle larva, p. 268; striped flea beetle, p. 269; June beetle grubs, p. 272; Mexican bean beetle adult, p. 272; Mexican bean beetle larva, p. 272; European corn borer adult, p. 273; tarnished plant bug, p. 274; imported cabbageworm larva, p. 276; cutworm, p. 276; antlion, p. 280; plum curculio, p. 281

Ray R. Kriner: asparagus beetle, p. 268; striped cucumber beetle, p. 273; squash vine borer, p. 273; codling moth adult, p. 275; corn earworm, p. 276

Sturgis McKeever: parsleyworm adult, p. 277

Alison Miksch, Rodale Press Photography Department: weed photos, pp. 292–95

Wayne S. Moore: powdery mildew, p. 288

Oregon State University: ground beetle, p. 269

Ann F. Rhoads, Morris Arboretum of the University of Pennsylvania: bacterial wilt of cucurbits, p. 283; brown rot, p. 283; crown gall, p. 284; cedar-apple rust, p. 289; aster yellows, p. 290; bean mosaic, p. 290; tobacco ring spot, p. 291

Rodale Press Photography Department: tomato hornworm, p. 277; praying mantis, p. 278; potato leaf roll, p. 291

Edward S. Ross: ants, p. 265; bumblebee, p. 266; braconid wasp, p. 267; yellow jacket, p. 267; fiery searcher, p. 270; Japanese beetles, p. 270; spotted cucumber beetle, p. 272; harlequin bug, p. 274; squash bug, p. 274; imported cabbageworm adult, p. 276; parsleyworm larva, p. 277; grasshopper, p. 278; katydid, p. 279; hoverfly, p. 279

Patricia Seip, Rodale Press Photography Department: honeybee, p. 266

University of Illinois: bacterial bean blight, p. 282; alternaria blight, p. 285; clubroot, p. 286; late blight, p. 287; red stele, p. 288; cucumber mosaic, p. 291

USDA: angular leaf spot, p. 282; bacterial leaf spot, p. 282; bacterial spot, p. 283; black rot, p. 283; soft rot, p. 284; anthracnose, p. 285; ascochyta blight, p. 285; botrytis, p. 285; damping-off, p. 286; early blight, p. 286; fusarium wilt, p. 286; southern corn leaf blight, p. 286; northern corn leaf blight, p. 286; downy mildew, p. 287; root rot, p. 288; soil rot, p. 288; scab, p. 288; corn smut, p. 289; nematode damage, p. 290

Ron West: greenhouse whiteflies, p. 281; slug, p. 281; beet curly top, p. 290

Resources

Mail-order sources of natural controls include:

Beneficial Insects Co.
P.O. Box 323
Brownsville, CA 95919

Beneficial Insects Ltd.
P.O. Box 154
Banta, CA 95304

Bio-Control Co.
P.O. Box 247
Cedar Ridge, CA 95924

Bio Insect Control
1710 S. Broadway
Plainview, TX 79072

Bio-Resources
1210 Birch St.
Santa Paula, CA 93060

W. Atlee Burpee Co.
Warminster, PA 18974

California Green Lacewings
P.O. Box 2495
Merced, CA 95340

Foothill Agricultural Research Inc.
510 W. Chase Dr.
Corona, CA 91720

Gardener's Supply Co.
128 Intervale Rd.
Burlington, VT 05401

Integrated Pest Management
305 Agostino Rd.
San Gabriel, CA 91776

King's Natural Pest Control
224 Yost Ave.
Spring City, PA 19475

Mellinger's Nursery
2310 W. South Range Rd.
North Lima, OH 44452

Natural Pest Controls
9397 Premier Way
Sacramento, CA 95826

The Necessary Trading Co.
New Castle, VA 24127

The Nematode Farm
2617 San Pablo Ave.
Berkeley, CA 94702

Peaceful Valley Farm Supply
11173 Peaceful Valley Rd.
Nevada City, CA 95959

Progressive Agri-Systems, Inc.
201 Center Street
Stockertown, PA 18083

Rincon-Vitova Insectaries, Inc.
P.O. Box 95
Oak View, CA 93022

Unique Insect Control
P.O. Box 15376
Sacramento, CA 95852

For more complete listings, write:

Rodale's Organic Gardening
Readers' Service
33 E. Minor St.
Emmaus, PA 18098

(Request their pamphlet, "Resources for Organic Pest Control"; enclose a business-size SASE and two first-class stamps.)

Glossaries

INSECTS

Abdomen The last section of an insect's body, following the head and thorax. Digestive and reproductive organs are found in the abdomen.

Antenna Paired, segmented structures, also called feelers. One on each side of the head. Aids sensory perception. Plural antennae.

Beak Long, styluslike mouthpart used by sucking insects to pierce the surface of a plant or animal. Hollow and jointed. One or more tiny needles in the beak pierce the tissue.

Brood All the insects that hatch from eggs laid by a given mother, or those that hatch and mature at the same time. Commonly applied to bees.

Caterpillar Larval stage of a butterfly or moth. Segmented or wormlike, with a distinct head, 12 simple eyes, a pair of very short antennae, and usually 6 well-developed legs, as well as 2 to 5 pairs of prolegs.

Chitin A hornlike substance that forms a layer of the exoskeleton.

Chrysalis The tubular, hard pupal shell of a butterfly.

Class The largest subgroup of a phylum. Insects belong to the class Insecta or Hexapoda (meaning six-legged).

Cocoon The silken pupal case of a butterfly or moth.

Compound Eye The eye of an insect, composed of many separate hexagonal lenses fitted closely together. Sensitive to movement and color. Larvae lack compound eyes.

Crawler The first active instar of a scale.

Cuticle The outer layer of the exoskeleton.

Dormant Inactive; in suspended animation; hibernating. Dormancy occurs in winter.

Elytra The hard, opaque wing covers of beetles, which meet in a straight line down the insect's back and cover most of the thorax and abdomen, giving an armored appearance.

Exoskeleton The hard outer covering or skeleton that protects an insect's body like armor. Forms a jointed frame.

Family The largest subdivision of an order. Each family contains a group of related genera (see Genus). Family names end in "-idae."

Frass The sawdustlike excrement of borers such as the peachtree borer and squash vine borer.

Genus The largest subdivision of a family. Each genus is made up of a small group of closely related members. Plural is genera.

Gregarious Living in groups, as in ants, aphids, and honeybees.

Glossaries
INSECTS

Grub The larva of a beetle. Grubs are plump, flat, or wormlike, with well-developed heads and 3 pairs of legs. They pupate in the soil or other protected sites.

Hibernation A winter period of suspended animation passed by many insects that live more than one season. Usually spent in soil or garden debris.

Honeydew Excess sap; a sweet substance secreted by feeding aphids that is relished by ants. Also produced by mealybugs, scales, and whiteflies.

Host Plant That on which an insect feeds, lives, or lays eggs.

Instar The form of an insect between each molt. Most insects pass through 3 to 6 instars.

Larva Immature form of an insect which is more or less wormlike and may be legged or legless and smooth or covered with spines or tufts of hair. They have chewing mouthparts. Plural is larvae.

Maggot The larva of a fly, usually a small, white, legless worm without an obvious head. Mouthparts are hooked. Maggots tend to feed inside the host plant or animal.

Mandibles The strong chewing jaws of arthropods.

Maxillae Second pair of jaws just behind the mandibles.

Metamorphosis A form change during which an insect molts and passes through nymph to adult stages (incomplete metamorphosis) or through larval to pupal and adult stages (complete metamorphosis).

Molt A shedding of the exoskeleton so that an insect can grow. The old skin splits after a new one has formed beneath it.

Nymph An immature adult with undeveloped wings and, in some cases, different markings from the adult.

Ocellus The simple, single-lensed eye of an insect. It perceives light but produces no image. Insects usually have them as well as compound eyes. Found at the base of the antennae or on top of the head. Larvae rely on them entirely. Plural is ocelli.

Order The largest subgroup of a class. Insects are divided into 26 orders. Each order contains a large group of insects that share similar wing structures.

Oviparous Egg-laying.

Ovipositor The egg-laying organ in female insects.

Parasite An insect that lives and feeds in or on another insect or animal for at least part of its life cycle.

Pheromone A chemical substance, such as a sexual attractant, secreted by an

Glossaries
INSECTS

insect to create a response in others of its species.

Phylum A major division of the Animal Kingdom. Insects belong to the phylum Arthropoda (meaning joint-legged).

Predator An insect that feeds on another live insect or animal.

Proboscis Long, retractable sucking tube through which nectar is syphoned by insects such as butterflies and moths.

Proleg A plump, fleshy, false leg that enables larvae to move more easily. Caterpillars have hooked prolegs that enable them to hang from a host plant. Caterpillars and sawflies bear up to 5 pairs of prolegs.

Pubescent Downy; covered with short, fine hairs.

Pupa An inactive stage between larva and adult in which adult features develop. The pupa may be encased in a chrysalis or cocoon, or may roll itself in a leaf. Plural is pupae.

Pupate To turn into a pupa.

Scavenger An insect that feeds on dead plants, animals, or decaying matter.

Sessile Incapable of movement; immobile. Some female scales are sessile.

Species The fundamental unit in classi-fication. The species refers to a single insect that may be distinguished from others in its genus by a particular feature or habit. Plural is species.

Spiracle One of many tiny holes in the thorax and abdomen of an insect which serve as breathing pores.

Thorax The center section of an insect's body, between the head and the abdomen. Wings and legs are attached to the thorax.

Vector A disease-carrier.

Viviparous Bearing live young. Aphids can be viviparous.

DISEASES

Acervulus A shallow, saucer-shaped mass of hyphae with a depression in the center that bears conidiophores, stalklike filaments with conidia, nonsexual spores, at the tips. Spores are released when the acervulus grows and ruptures cells of the host plant.

Alternate Host One of two plants upon which a parasitic fungus must live.

Anthracnose A disease characterized by lesions that show on the epidermis. Caused by fungi that produce nonsexual spores in acervuli.

Ascomycetes A fungal group characterized by a membranous sac, or ascus, in which the cells divide to form ascospores. Yeasts, molds, and mildews are ascomycetes. Ascospores are sexual.

Bacteria One-celled microorganisms that reproduce by division. Plants that lack chlorophyll, bacteria are dependent on either dead or living organic matter for food.

Bacteriophage A virus-like organism that destroys bacteria.

Basidiomycetes A group of fungi characterized by mycelium with cross-walls and the production of sexual spores on club-shaped filaments called basidia. Rusts, smuts, and mushrooms are basidiomycetes.

Blasting Failure to produce fruit or seeds.

Blight General description of diseases that cause sudden leaf, flower, or stem death.

Blotch A superficial spot or necrotic area.

Canker A diseased or dying area on a stem. Most commonly applied to woody plants.

Carrier A plant or animal bearing an infectious disease agent without showing symptoms. Carriers can transmit the disease to other organisms. Most bear the disease agent internally, although the term can be used when the agent is carried externally.

Causal Organism The organism responsible for causing a disease.

Certified Seed Seed monitored to ensure varietal purity and freedom from disease organisms.

Chlamydospore A nonsexual spore formed by a mycelial cell. Thick-walled, chlamydospores are resting spores and can remain dormant until conditions are correct for development.

Chlorosis Yellowing caused by partial failure of chlorophyll development. Symptomatic of many diseases.

Coalesce Grow together to form one spot or splotch.

Conidiophore Hyphae on which conidia are produced.

Conidia Asexual spores formed at the tips of conidiophores. Produced most numerously during the height of the growing season, conidia are wind- or rain-borne.

Glossaries
DISEASES

Damping-Off Used to describe the death of seedlings, emerged or not, caused by a number of organisms.

Defoliate To cause most leaves on a plant to die and drop.

Dieback Progressive death of branches or stems from the tip backwards toward the main stem or trunk.

Enzyme A chemical produced by cells which brings about changes in processes such as ripening or digestion. Some pathogenic bacteria produce enzymes that damage host plants.

Epidermis The outermost layer of cells of a plant part.

Epinasty An abnormal growth pattern of leaves caused by rapid growth of cells on the upper surface, resulting in a downward cupping of the leaf.

Escape Applied to plants that do not have resistance to a particular pathogen but do not acquire it.

Exudate Any substance produced within a plant which is then released or discharged through natural openings or injuries.

Facultative Parasite An organism that can grow on either living or dead organic matter.

Fasciation Plant distortion caused by injury or infection resulting in flattened or curved shoots. Stems may look fused.

Flagellum A whiplike filament of a cell enabling it to swim through liquids.

Fruiting Body The fungal structure containing or bearing spores.

Fungus A plant that lacks chlorophyll and is dependent upon either dead or living organic matter for food supplies. Fungi reproduce by both sexual and asexual spores, and are composed of a body of filaments called hyphae that form branched systems called mycelia.

Gall A localized swelling composed of unorganized cells. Caused by bacteria, fungi, or insects.

Gamete A mature sex cell.

Girdle A lesion that encircles the stem or root, causing death.

Haustorium A specialized fungal hypha that penetrates the cells of a host plant and absorbs food from them.

Host A plant infected or parasitized by a pathogen.

Hyperplasia Abnormal increase in cells, resulting in formation of galls and tumors.

Hyphae Threads or filaments of a fungal mycelium or body.

Lesion A spot or area of diseased tissue.

Mildew A fungus that grows on the surface of plant parts.

Mold A fungus that produces a woolly growth on the surface of plant parts.

Mosaic A disease caused by a virus and characterized by mottled patterns of yellow and green on the leaves.

Mycelium The vegetative body of a fungus, composed of many hyphae.

Necrotic Dead. Necrosis is death.

Nematode Nonsegmented, microscopic roundworms that live in soil, water, plants, animals, and dead organic matter. Some nematodes are plant parasites.

Nodule A lump or knot.

Obligate Parasite An obligate parasite can live only on living matter.

Parasite An organism that obtains its nutrients from a secondary organism.

Pathogen An organism capable of causing disease in other organisms.

Perfect Stage The period of a fungal life cycle when spores are produced sexually.

Penetration Peg A strong hypha anchored to the host surface with a sticky substance. Produced in order to bore into a host.

Phycomycetes One group of fungi. Characterized by sexual reproduction and few cross walls in the hyphae.

Primary Infection The first infection by a fungus after a resting period.

Pustule A blisterlike structure.

Pycnidium A flask-shaped, fruiting body of a fungus that contains nonsexual spores. Usually located near the surface of the host.

Pycnium The flask-shaped, fruiting body of a rust fungus which contains pycniospores. These spores are unisexual, and are usually fertilized by insects feeding on the nectar produced in the pycnium.

Resistance Ability of a plant to remain relatively healthy despite infection by a pathogen. Resistance is an inborn quality and is not caused by environmental factors.

Resting Spore A spore that can remain dormant for long periods of time before germinating. Most resting spores are very thick-walled.

Ring Spot Symptomatic of some diseases. Ring spots are brownish-yellow on the margin and green in the center.

Rogue To remove a plant. Plants infected with some diseases are normally rogued to prevent the spread of the disease.

Rosette Formation of short-stalked leaves that radiate from a central stem. Some diseases produce an unnatural rosette in their hosts.

Russet A corky, roughened area on the skin surface. Russeting can be caused by pathogens, insects, or cultural techniques.

Glossaries
DISEASES

Rust The disease caused by a rust fungus or the fungus itself. Rusts may have one or more hosts through their life cycles and, in some cases, have as many as five types of spores.

Saprophyte An organism that feeds on dead organic matter.

Scab A disease that is characterized by rough, scaly tissue on the skin surface.

Sclerotium A resting mass of fungal hyphae which does not contain spores, but which is capable of becoming dormant and remaining so for many years before resuming growth.

Scorch A burning of tissue caused by a pathogen or environmental conditions.

Secondary Infection A disease caused by infectious material produced following a primary infection or by reproductive material that has not undergone a resting period.

Shothole A disease symptom in which small round holes die and drop out of leaves.

Sign Any visible portion of a pathogen. Signs can include mycelia, spores, fruiting bodies, or even a mass of bacteria.

Smut A disease caused by a smut fungus, or the fungus itself. Smuts are characterized by the formation of dark masses of resting spores.

Sporangium A fungal fruiting body that produces nonsexual spores.

Spore A single or multi-celled reproductive unit. Fungi produce sexual and asexual spores. The resting structures of some bacteria are also called spores.

Strain Synonym for race when describing plant pathogens. A strain, or race, is a subgroup within a species which differs in host range or affect from other members of the species.

Summer Spore A spore that proliferates during the best growing conditions and that does not rest between release and germination.

Susceptibility Without inherent resistance to a pathogen.

Systemic Applied to a pathogen or chemical that travels throughout the plant body. Many systemics travel through the vascular system.

Thallus The vegetative body of a thallophyte, a simple plant, including fungi, algae, bacteria, slime molds, and lichens.

Tolerant Capable of sustaining an infection by a pathogen, or of enduring environmental stress or injury without much damage.

Toxin A poison.

Vascular Applied to the vessels in the plant which carry water or nutrients.

WEEDS

Respectively, these are the xylem and phloem vessels.

Vector An organism or agent that transmits diseases. Many insects are vectors of plant diseases.

Vein-banding A symptom of some viral diseases in which regions along the veins are a darker green color than regions between veins.

Virulent Strongly capable of producing disease.

Virus An obligate parasite composed of genetic materials and protein which is capable of reproducing within living materials.

Wilt Drooping plant tissue as a consequence of insufficient water supply. Some diseases cause wilt by plugging the vascular system.

Xylem The vessels that carry water in the plant.

Yellows Diseases that cause abnormal yellowing of leaves and stems.

Zoospore A spore that swims.

Achine A dry, one-seeded fruit that does not open readily. The seed is distinct from the fruit. Common among members of the composite family.

Acute Sharply pointed.

Alternate An arrangement of leaves, branches, or flowers in which each is placed singly at different heights along the stem.

Annuals Plants that live from seed to maturity, reproduction, and death in only one growing season.

Anther The part of the stamen which bears pollen.

Apex The uppermost point; tip.

Awn A bristlelike appendage. Found most commonly on grass flowers.

Axil Upper angle where a leaf or branch joins the stem.

Axillary Situated in an axil.

Barb A rigid bristle or point, usually reflexed.

Beak A long, prominent point.

Berry A fleshy fruit containing two or more seeds, such as tomatoes and grapes.

Biennial Living two growing seasons, usually flowering during the second.

Bipinnate Twice pinnately compound.

Glossaries
WEEDS

Blade The flat, expanded part of the leaf.

Bract A small rudimentary or underdeveloped leaf. Often found in flower clusters.

Bristle A stiff, hairlike growth.

Bulb An underground bud with fleshy scales or bracts.

Bulbet A small bulb borne on the inflorescence or stem.

Calyx All the sepals of a flower cluster considered collectively, the outer perianth whorl.

Capsule The dry, dehiscent fruit of two or more carpels.

Carpel One of the ovarian portions of a compound pistil.

Chlorophyll The green pigment necessary for photosynthesis, developed in the chloroplasts of plant cells.

Clasping Applied to leaves, partly or completely surrounding a stem, as seen in grasses.

Compound Leaf Leaf in which the blade is divided into two or more sections, or leaflets.

Cordate Heart-shaped, with the point away from the base.

Corolla The inner set of floral leaves, or petals. Sometimes fused, as in morning-glories.

Corymb A raceme with the lower flower stalks longer than those at the tip so that the head gives a flattened appearance. Outer flowers open first.

Culm The stem of a grass. Usually hollow except at the nodes.

Decumbent Lying flat, with the tip pointing upward.

Decurrent An organ extending along the sides of another, as in leaves where the blade extends as wings along the petiole or stem.

Dehiscent Opening by valves or slits, as in a seed capsule. Poppy capsules are dehiscent.

Dentate Toothed, with outward-pointing teeth.

Dioecious A plant bearing only one sex on a plant; male and female flowers are on separate plants.

Disk Flower The tubular flowers in the center of the head of many composites. The yellow center of the daisy is composed of disk flowers.

Divided Separated to the base.

Drupe A single-seeded fruit with a fleshy outer part. Stone fruits such as peaches and cherries are drupes.

Elliptic Oval in shape.

Glossaries
WEEDS

Entire Describes a smooth leaf margin. Not toothed, lobed, or serrated.

Fibrous Fine adventitious roots, usually in a mass.

Floret An individual flower of a cluster, head, or spike.

Fruit The ripened ovary or ovaries with attached parts.

Grain Fruit of grasses particularly; seed coat and ovary walls fused into one body.

Habit The general growth pattern of a plant or its mode of growth, such as shrubby, trailing, or erect.

Habitat The environmental conditions of a specific place in which a plant grows.

Head A short, compact flower cluster of sessile or nearly sessile florets.

Herbaceous Not woody.

Imperfect Describing flower lacking either stamens or carpels. It is "imperfect" because it has only one sex.

Indehiscent Applied to a seedpod or capsule that does not readily open at maturity.

Internode The part of a stem between two nodes.

Involucre A whorl of small leaves or bracts just under a flower or flower cluster. Generally protects reproductive structures.

Lanceolate Lance-shaped, several times longer than wide and tapering to a pointed apex.

Leaflet One part of a compound leaf.

Legume A member of the family leguminosae. Characterized by a fruit that splits readily along two sides at maturity, such as a pea pod.

Lobed Divided to about mid-point.

Mericarp One of the two carpels of a fruit of the parsley family.

Midrib The central rib or vein of a leaf or other organ.

Monoecious Having both male and female flowers on the same plant, such as many kinds of squashes.

Netted Applied to veins, meaning they form a network pattern.

Node The part of a stem where leaves or branches emerge.

Nut A hard, indehiscent, one-seeded fruit.

Obovate Ovate, with the narrower end at the bottom.

Opposite Two leaves or buds at a node.

Ovary The part of the pistil bearing the ovules.

Ovate Egg-shaped, with the broader end at the bottom.

Glossaries
WEEDS

Ovule An undeveloped or immature seed.

Palmate Radiating from a central point like a fan or the fingers of a hand.

Palmately Compound Leaflets radiating from a central point.

Panicle An inflorescence. A branched raceme with each branch bearing a cluster of flowers. Overall, a panicle is shaped like a pyramid.

Pappus A ring of fine hairs developed from the calyx. A pappus often acts as a dispersal mechanism, as in dandelion seeds.

Peduncle Stem of a solitary flower or flower cluster.

Perennial Growing three or more seasons.

Perfect Applied to flowers having both stamens and carpels.

Perianth The floral envelope, the calyx and corolla together. Most often used to describe flowers without clear divisions between calyx and corolla, such as lilies.

Petal One of the leaves of the corolla, usually colorful.

Petiole The stalk of a leaf.

Phloem The vessels in the plant which carry dissolved sugars from leaves to the rest of the plant. One of the two vessels in the vascular bundle.

Pinnate Similar in appearance to a feather, having leaflets along each side of a common axis.

Pinnately Compound Leaflets arranged on each side of a common axis.

Pinnatifid Leaflets cleft to the middle or beyond.

Pistil The seed-bearing organ with style (a tube bearing the stigma at its apex), stigma (part of the pistil which receives the pollen grains), and ovule.

Pistillate Having pistils and no stamens. Female.

Pod Usually describes a dry, dehiscent fruit.

Pollen The spores or grains borne by the anther which contain the male element.

Prickle A stiff, pointed outgrowth from the epidermis or bark.

Procumbent Trailing on the ground without rooting.

Prostrate Lying flat on the ground. Some prostrate stems can root.

Pubescent Covered with short, soft hairs.

Raceme An inflorescence composed of pedicled florets growing from a common axis. Flowers open from the base upward.

Ray Flower A flower growing on the margin of the disk flowers, strap-shaped. The white petals of the daisy are ray flowers.

Rhizome Underground or barely superficial reproductive stem.

Rhombic Shaped like an equilateral parallelogram, usually having oblique angles.

Rib A primary vein in a leaf or flower.

Rootstock Roots that can develop adventitious buds. Often used to mean underground reproductive stems as well.

Rosette A cluster of leaves, usually basal, and shaped like a rose, or radiating from a center.

Runner A slender, trailing stem that takes root at the nodes.

Sepal One of the divisions of a calyx.

Serrate Having sharp teeth that point forward.

Sessile Without a petiole or stalk.

Sheath A long structure surrounding an organ or part.

Simple Leaves Leaves in which the blade is in one piece, not divided.

Spike A flower spike with sessile or nearly sessile flowers.

Stamen The pollen-bearing, or male organ, of a flower.

Staminate Having stamens and no pistils. Male.

Stipule A basal appendage of a petiole.

Stolon A stem that bends to the ground and takes root at the tip or nodes.

Succulent Fleshy tissues storing much water.

Taproot A central, tapering, main root with smaller lateral roots. A carrot is a taproot.

Tendril A slender organ, leaf, or stem, with which a plant clings to a support.

Terminal At the end of a stem or branch.

Thorn A stiff, sharply pointed, and somewhat degenerate branch.

Toothed Dentate. Having pointed edges along the margins.

Trifoliate A compound leaf with three leaflets, such as poison ivy.

Tuber A modified underground stem that usually stores food. Reproductive. A potato is a tuber.

Umbel A flower cluster that is shaped like an umbrella, such as dill flower heads.

Glossaries
WEEDS

Utricle A small, one-seeded fruit.

Valve The separate parts of a pod or capsule.

Vascular Bundle The term applied to describe phloem and xylem vessels, or veins, in plants. Nutrients and water are carried through these vessels to each part of the plant.

Veins The vascular bundles of leaves, containing phloem and xylem vessels.

Whorled An arrangement of three or more structures at a node.

Xylem Vessels in which water is carried from roots to the rest of the plant. One of the two vessels in vascular bundles.

Bibliography

GENERAL

Brooks, Audrey, and Andrew Halstead. *Garden Pests and Diseases.* New York: Simon and Schuster, 1980.

Cravens, Richard H., and the editors of Time-Life Books. *Pests and Diseases.* Alexandria, Va.: Time-Life Books, 1977.

Smith, Michael D., ed. *The Ortho Problem Solver.* 2d ed. San Francisco: Ortho Information Services, 1986.

USDA Forest Service, Southern Region. *Insects and Diseases of Trees in the South.* Atlanta: USDA Forest Service, 1985.

Yepsen, Roger B., Jr., ed. *The Encyclopedia of Natural Insect and Disease Control.* Emmaus, Pa.: Rodale Press, 1984.

INSECTS

Borror, D. J., and D. M. DeLong. *Introduction to the Study of Insects.* 3d ed. New York: Holt, Rinehart and Winston, 1970.

DeBach, P. *Biological Control of Insect Pests and Weeds.* New York: Reinhold, 1964.

Fabre, J. H. *Social Life in the Insect World.* Detroit: Gale Research, 1974.

Forbes, A. W. *Our Garden Friends the Bugs.* New York: Exposition Press, 1962.

Goldstein, J., ed. *The Least is Best Pesticide Strategy.* Emmaus, Pa.: JG Press, 1978.

O'Toole, Christopher, ed. *The Encyclopedia of Insects.* New York: Facts on File Publications, 1986.

Parenti, U. *Insects: World of Miniature Beauty.* New York: New Dimensions Library, 1972.

Swan, L., and C. S. Papp. *The Common Insects of North America.* New York: Harper and Row, 1972.

Teale, E. W. *The Strange Lives of Familiar Insects.* New York: Dodd, Mead and Co., 1962.

Westcott, Cynthia. *The Gardener's Bug Book.* 4th ed. New York: Facts on File Publications, 1986.

Bibliography

DISEASES

Lucas, G. B., C. L. Campbell, and L. T. Lucas. *Introduction to Plant Diseases: Identification and Management.* Westport, Conn.: AVI Publications Co., Inc., 1985.

MacNab, A. A., A. F. Sherf, and J. K. Springer. *Identifying Diseases of Vegetables.* University Park, Pa.: The Pennsylvania State University, 1983.

Roberts, Daniel A., and Carl W. Boothroyd. *Fundamentals of Plant Pathology.* 2d ed. New York: W. H. Freeman and Co., 1984.

Shurtleff, Malcolm C. *How to Control Plant Diseases in Home and Garden.* Ames, Iowa: Iowa State University Press, 1962.

Staples, Richard C., and Gary H. Toenniessen. *Plant Disease Control, Resistance and Susceptibility.* New York: John Wiley and Sons, 1951.

Strobel, Gary A., and Done El Mathre. *Outlines of Plant Pathology.* New York: Van Nostrand Reinhold Co., 1970.

USDA. *Plant Diseases: The Yearbook of Agriculture 1953.* Washington, D.C.: U.S. Government Printing Office, 1953.

Walker, John C. *Plant Pathology.* 2d ed. New York: McGraw-Hill Book Co., Inc., 1957.

Westcott, Cynthia. *Plant Disease Handbook.* 4th ed. New York: Van Nostrand Reinhold Co., 1979.

WEEDS

Agricultural Research Service, USDA. *Common Weeds of the United States.* New York: Dover Publications, Inc., 1971.

Aldrich, R. J. *Weed-Crop Ecology: Principles in Weed Management.* Belmont, Ca.: Breton Publishers, 1984.

Allan, Mea. *Weeds: The Unbidden Guests in Our Gardens.* New York: The Viking Press, 1978.

Cocannouer, Joseph. *Weeds, Guardians of the Soil.* New York: Devin-Adair Co., 1964.

Crockett, Lawrence J. *Wildly Successful Plants.* New York: Collier Books, 1977.

Embertson, Jane. *Pods: Wildflowers and Weeds in Their Final Beauty.* New York: Charles Scribner's Sons, 1979.

Isely, Duane. *Weed Identification and Control in the Northern Central States.* Ames, Iowa: Iowa State University Press, 1960.

Lampe, Dr. Kenneth F., and Mary A. McCann. *AMA Handbook of Poisonous and Injurious Plants.* Chicago, Ill.: American Medical Association, 1985.

Martin, Alexander C. *Weeds.* New York: Golden Press, 1972.

Muenscher, Walter Conrad. *Weeds.* 2d ed. Ithaca, N.Y.: Comstock Publishing, Cornell University Press, 1980.

Bibliography

Schmutz, Ervin M., and Lucretia B. Hamilton. *Plants That Poison.* Flagstaff, Ariz.: Northland Press, 1987.

Spencer, Edwin R. *All About Weeds.* New York: Dover Publications, Inc., 1974.

Stucky, Jon M. *Identifying Seedling and Mature Weeds Common in the Southeastern United States.* Raleigh, N.C.: North Carolina State University Press, 1981.

Weed Science Society of America. *Common Weed Seedlings of the U.S. and Canada.* Champlain, Ill.: Weed Science Society of America, 1979.

Index

Page references in *italics* indicate photographs.

Index

Index

Index

Index

Index

Index

Index

Index

Index

Index

Index

Index

Index

Index

Rodale Press, Inc., publishes RODALE'S ORGANIC GARDENING®,
the all-time favorite gardening magazine.
For information on how to order your subscription,
write to RODALE'S ORGANIC GARDENING®, Emmaus, PA 18098.